Gender Equality, HIV, and AIDS

A Challenge for the Education Sector

Oxfam GB

Oxfam GB, founded in 1942, is a development, humanitarian, and campaigning agency dedicated to finding lasting solutions to poverty and suffering around the world. Oxfam believes that every human being is entitled to a life of dignity and opportunity, and it works with others worldwide to make this become a reality.

From its base in Oxford in the United Kingdom, Oxfam GB publishes and distributes a wide range of resource materials for development and relief workers, researchers and campaigners, schools and colleges, and the general public, as part of its programme of advocacy, education, and communications.

Oxfam GB is a member of Oxfam International, a confederation of 13 agencies of diverse cultures and languages, which share a commitment to working for an end to injustice and poverty – both in long-term development work and at times of crisis.

For further information about Oxfam's publishing, and online ordering, visit www.oxfam.org.uk/publications

For information about Oxfam's development, advocacy, and humanitarian relief work around the world, visit www.oxfam.org.uk

Gender Equality, HIV, and AIDS

A Challenge for the Education Sector

Edited by
Sheila Aikman, Elaine Unterhalter, and Tania Boler

Oxfam

Practical Action Publishing Ltd
25 Albert Street, Rugby, CV21 2SD, Warwickshire, UK
www.practicalactionpublishing.com

First published by Oxfam GB 2008
Reprinted by Practical Action Publishing

Paperback ISBN: 9780855985868
PDF ISBN: 9780855987480

A catalogue record for this publication is available from the British Library.

Front cover: *Children at play on their way home from school in Kitwe, Zambia. (Annie Bungeroth/Oxfam)*

The manufacturer's authorised representative in the EU for product safety is Lightning Source France, 1 Av. Johannes Gutenberg, 78310 Maurepas, France.
compliance@lightningsource.fr

Contents

Acknowledgements

An edited collection is always more than the sum of its parts, and this book is no exception. Many teachers, learners, writers, readers, administrators, and activists have contributed to the ideas we have brought together. Unfortunately we cannot list them all, but we want to highlight some particular contributions without which the book would never have gone beyond the sketchy outline the three of us discussed one day in a snatched coffee break between meetings.

First and foremost our thanks go to all the authors. They have worked with us over many months, often to tight time schedules, and we very much appreciate their involvement with this project and commitment to our approach.

The Beyond Access team are a second group to whom we owe special thanks. The Beyond Access project aims to develop and circulate knowledge about gender equality and education for policy makers, researchers, and practitioners. Sheila and Elaine have co-ordinated the project since 2003, and a number of chapters in this collection were first presented as papers at Beyond Access seminars. We are grateful to all those who helped make Beyond Access happen, and we particularly want to record our thanks to the UK government's Department for International Development (DFID) for the first phase of our funding and to Chloe Challender, Rajee Rajagopalan, and Amy North, who were so central to the achievements of the project.

We owe thanks to all those in Oxfam GB, ActionAid, and the Institute of Education who supported our work on this book through general encouragement, responses to queries, and critical commentaries, particularly our close colleagues Tom Noel, David Archer, Akanksha Marphatia, Debbie Gaitskell, and Jenny Parkes.

The book would never have been brought to completion without the support and dedication of the Oxfam Publishing Team, especially Claire Harvey and Katie Allan, Kevan Ray who guided the process, and Jackie Smith for her excellent copy editing. We are enormously grateful for this help, for the insights of the anonymous readers, for the meticulous work done by Amy North and Helen Poulsen as editorial assistants on a number of chapters, and for the attention to detail given by Sophie Crawford in preparing several chapters for publication. Lastly, our families saw each of us through another book project with kindness and good humour. Their warm support sustained our collaboration, and we are enormously grateful for their care and consideration.

Sheila Aikman, Elaine Unterhalter, and Tania Boler

List of contributors

Sheila Aikman is Senior Lecturer in Education and Development at the School of Development Studies, University of East Anglia. Prior to this she was Oxfam GB Global Education Adviser, working with Oxfam education programmes across sub-Saharan Africa and Asia. She has researched and written extensively on indigenous education and gender equality in education and co-directed the 'Beyond Access: Gender, Education and Development' project with Elaine Unterhalter.

Deevia Bhana is an Associate Professor at the University of KwaZulu-Natal. She works in the areas of gender, sexuality, HIV, and AIDS.

Tania Boler is Head of Research at Marie Stopes International, an international NGO specialising in sexual and reproductive health. Prior to this, she was at UNESCO and ActionAid where she researched and published extensively on the education sector response to HIV and AIDS. Her books include The Politics of Prevention: A Global Crisis in AIDS and Education (with David Archer, 2008, Pluto Press).

David Clarke is a freelance consultant currently based in Bangkok, Thailand. He was Senior Education Adviser in the DFID AIDS Team in London before deciding to work independently. He has worked in more than 50 countries and has recently undertaken consultancies on the education response to HIV in India, Indonesia, and Cambodia.

Usa Duongsaa is Lecturer at the Faculty of Education, Chiangmai University, Thailand. She is also co-founder of the AIDS Education Programme in Thailand, the Asia-Pacific-based Positive Learning Working Group, and the international non-profit non-government organisation Constellation for AIDS Competence.

Debbie Epstein is a Professor at Cardiff University's School of Social Sciences and is currently training as a psychotherapist. She has published widely in the fields of sexuality, gender, race, and education in the UK and in South Africa. Her books include *Silenced Sexualities in Schools and Universities* (with Sarah O'Flynn and David Telford, Trentham 2003) and *Schooling Sexualities* (with Richard Johnson, Open University Press 1998). She also works on issues to do with globalisation and higher education and edited the *World Year Book of Education 2008* (with Rebecca Boden, Rosemary Deem, Fazal Rizvi, and Susan Wright).

Gill Gordon is a Senior Technical Advisor in sexual and reproductive health and prevention of mother-to-child transmission at the International HIV/AIDS Alliance. She has been providing technical support to a programme in rural Eastern Province of Zambia to increase the capacity of teachers in basic primary schools to teach pupils aged 10 to 15 sexuality and life-skills. She has also supported a programme in Zambia, Malawi, and Zimbabwe, working on young people's sexual, reproductive, and psychosocial health and rights.

James Hargreaves is an epidemiologist conducting research into social influences on people's health. He has recently published papers on socio-economic influences on the spread of HIV and TB. He was a key member of the research team running the Intervention with Microfinance for AIDS and Gender Equity study. IMAGE was a prospective matched and randomised community-intervention trial that sought to explicitly examine the role of a community-based poverty alleviation and gender-empowerment programme in changing sexual behaviour and preventing intimate-partner violence and HIV infection.

Omokhudu Idogho is the International HIV and AIDS Coordinator (Programmes) with ActionAid International, based in Johannesburg. In this position he leads on ActionAid's women's-rights-centred community-mobilisation approach to achieve HIV and AIDS universal access. Prior to this position, Dr Idogho was the Head of Programmes in ActionAid Nigeria, where he provided a strategic leadership steer to the Education, HIV, and AIDS themes, and supported cross-cutting elements of Women's Rights and Governance Programmes.

Doris Kakuru is a Researcher and Lecturer at Makerere University, Uganda. Her research on gender, education, HIV, and AIDS began in the early 2000s, and she has published widely on the subject. Her current research focuses on the educational challenges of orphans living in child-headed households.

Sujata Khandekar is a founder member and Director of a non-governmental organisation called 'CORO (Committee of Resource Organisation) for Literacy' in Mumbai, India. A gender activist and a researcher, Sujata has worked extensively with both men and women on promoting gender equality, especially in grassroots communities. Currently she is pursuing her doctoral research on the construction of masculinities among Dalit young men in low-income communities in Mumbai, India.

Fiona Leach is Professor of International Education at the University of Sussex, UK. She has worked in the field of education and development for many years, and before becoming an academic was a teacher and adviser in Africa. She has published widely in the field of gender and education, and has carried out several studies on gender violence in African schools. She is author of *Practising Gender Analysis in Education* (Oxfam, 2003) and co-editor of *Combating Gender Violence in and around Schools* (Trentham, 2006).

Vaishali Sharma Mahendra is a Senior Programme Officer in the HIV and AIDS Programme at the Population Council in New Delhi. She has 15 years of work experience in the field of sexual health, HIV, and AIDS. Her main areas of research and programme development include HIV prevention with vulnerable populations including youth; promotion of gender equity and sexual health with young men and women; HIV-stigma reduction; and integration of sexual health and HIV.

Relebohile (Lebo) Moletsane is Director of the Gender and Development Unit at the Human Sciences Research Council (HSRC), South Africa. She has extensive experience in teaching and research in the areas of curriculum studies and gender and education, including gender-based violence and its links to HIV and AIDS and AIDS-related stigma, as well as a focus on girlhood in the era of AIDS in Southern African contexts.

Robert Morrell is Professor of Education at the University of KwaZulu-Natal. He works in the area of men and masculinity studies and has edited *Changing Men in Southern Africa* (University of Natal Press/Zed Books, Pietermaritzburg/London, 2001) and co-edited (with Lahoucine Ouzgane) *African Masculinities* (Palgrave/University of KwaZulu-Natal Press, New York/Pietermaritzburg, 2005) and (with Linda Richter) *Baba: Men and Fatherhood in South Africa* (Cape Town, HSRC, 2006).

Amy North is a researcher based at the Institute of Education, University of London. She is currently working with Elaine Unterhalter on a project looking at the way in which global declarations concerning gender equality, education, and poverty are interpreted and acted on in different sites at local, national, and global levels. Previously she was the Policy Officer for the 'Beyond Access: Gender, Education and Development Project', and has worked with education advocacy networks in Kenya, Bangladesh, and Tanzania. She also has wide experience of working on gender issues and with civil-society organisations in Latin America.

Julie Pulerwitz is Director of the HIV/AIDS & TB Global Program at PATH. Prior to this, she was Research Director of the Horizons Program/Population Council, a 10-year global HIV and AIDS operations research programme funded by USAID. Her main areas of research and programme development include HIV/STI prevention, behaviour-change communication, gender and male engagement, and HIV-related stigma. Dr Pulerwitz and colleagues developed the Gender Equitable Men (GEM) Scale, and she has led evaluations of male engagement, gender equity, and HIV/violence-prevention projects in Brazil, Ethiopia, Namibia, and Tanzania.

Mahendra Rokade is currently working as Project Director of 'CORO (Committee of Resource Organisation) for Literacy', a Mumbai-based NGO. Mahendra co-ordinated the operations research on addressing unequal gender norms as a strategy to reduce sexual risk behaviour among young men and violence against women in low-income communities of Mumbai, done by CORO in collaboration with Population Council New Delhi and Institute of Promundo, Brazil.

Vilas Sarmalkar is a founder member of 'CORO (Committee of Resource Organisation) for Literacy', a Mumbai-based NGO. Vilas led the community-based campaign for the programme 'Yari Dosti', to promote gender equality among young men as a strategy to reduce sexual risk behaviour among young men and violence against women in low-income communities of Mumbai.

Elaine Unterhalter is a reader in Education and International Development at the Institute of Education, University of London. Together with Sheila Aikman she co-ordinates the 'Beyond Access: Gender, Education and Development' project. Her books include *Gender, Schooling and Global Social Justice* (Routledge, 2006), *Beyond Access* (with Sheila Aikman, Oxfam, 2005) and *Amartya Sen's Capability Approach and Social Justice in Education* (with Melanie Walker, Palgrave, 2007).

Ravi Verma is Regional Director of the International Center for Research on Women (ICRW), Asia Regional Office (ARO) based in New Delhi. He has worked extensively on promoting gender equity; working with men and boys; and reducing HIV vulnerabilities and gender-based violence.

Introduction

Sheila Aikman, Elaine Unterhalter, and Tania Boler

This book examines the challenges of working for gender equality in the education sector as it engages with HIV and AIDS. Applying a gender-equality lens highlights a range of responses on which those who work in education systems – policy makers, planners, teachers, and learners – need to reflect and act if they are to reduce girls' and boys' vulnerability, change behaviour, and challenge some of the unequal gender relations that are driving the AIDS epidemic. The book provides a comprehensive approach to thinking about gender and gender equality in education, from an appreciation of the way in which girls and women are becoming disproportionately infected with the HIV virus, to an analysis of the assumptions about gender and women that underpin much writing on the epidemic and the educational responses.

While gender inequalities in society generally, and particularly within the education sector, are driving aspects of the AIDS epidemic, and can limit prevention and care, the book argues that there are actions that have been taken in every sector – be it government, community, or school initiatives – to confront and transform gender inequalities. These actions enhance work in combating the spread of HIV and caring for people who are infected and affected. The challenges of working on gender inequality in education in the context of the epidemic need to be acknowledged, but once some of their dimensions are known, the assumptions, fear, and stigma can be discussed and begin to be addressed.

In the short span of 25 years, the HIV virus has spread to all regions of the world, infecting over 65 million people globally (UNAIDS 2006). The epidemic has been fuelled by gender inequalities. It has hit hardest in sub-Saharan Africa: although the region is home to only ten per cent of the world's population, 61 per cent of all people with HIV are from this region and 57 per cent of all infected people are women (UNAIDS 2007). Despite the number of new HIV cases (incidence) per year having peaked in the late 1990s, there are still over 22.5 million people living with HIV in sub-Saharan Africa and over 11 million orphans (*ibid.*). In sub-Saharan Africa the major means of transmission is through heterosexual sex, and in many African countries the epidemic is categorised as a generalised AIDS epidemic – meaning that over one per cent of the general adult population is HIV-positive. However, there is diversity in the severity of the epidemic in Africa, with the worst-affected countries located in the southern region, including South Africa, Botswana, Namibia, Swaziland, Zambia, Zimbabwe, and Malawi, where prevalence rates are in excess of ten per cent of the adult population. Although the prevalence rate has levelled off in some countries, this simply means that the number of AIDS-related deaths equals the number of new infections – disguising the thousands of people who are becoming infected or dying every day. UNAIDS estimate that only one in six people in need of treatment in the region is currently receiving it (*ibid.*).

After sub-Saharan Africa, Asia has the largest number of people living with HIV: latest estimates suggest that in 2007 over 4.9 million adults in Asia were living with HIV. Despite relatively low prevalence rates and concentrated epidemics (defined as below one per cent of the adult general population), the sheer size of many Asian countries has resulted in a large number of HIV infections. For example, India has a prevalence rate of 0.36 per cent (defined as a concentrated epidemic), which equates to about 2.5 million adults living with HIV.

Although, overall, the actual number of people living with HIV in Eastern Europe is small, concentrated epidemics are growing at alarming rates. Of particular concern are Ukraine and the Russian Federation, where HIV is spreading fast through injecting drug use, especially among young people: over 75 per cent of new infections in Russia are in people under the age of 30 years (UNAIDS 2006).

The number of people living with HIV in Latin America has risen to an estimated 1.6 million, and although across the region the majority of countries have prevalence rates of less than one per cent, the prevalence among specific groups, such as men who have sex with men, and sex workers, is often very high (UNAIDS 2007; www.avert.org/aidslatinamerica.htm).

Generally, worldwide, those people who are already living marginalised vulnerable lives are less likely to be able to protect themselves from HIV infection. Poor people are the least powerful, and often the least able to effect change, to receive appropriate treatment, or to have their voices heard about how the epidemic is affecting their lives (Hargreaves and Boler 2006). Stark gender inequalities often compound this. Women are increasingly more likely to become infected with HIV than men.

How has this epidemic – which is preventable – been able to spread uncontrolled across the globe, already claiming the lives of 25 million people? The answer lies in the fact that HIV is a sexually transmitted disease or is associated with injecting drug users, and sex and drugs remain taboo issues, which reflect deep divisions between people and expose gendered relations in particularly destructive forms. HIV shines a light on the contradictions between societal expectations in many countries not to have sex, and the reality that many people have many sexual partners over their lifetime. HIV also disproportionately affects groups in society who are already highly stigmatised and viewed as immoral: injecting drug users, sex workers, and men who have sex with men. It exposes some of the gendered power which often characterises interactions concerning sex, drug use, and stigma.

HIV destroys the body's immune system, and after several years the body is too weak to fight off infection and succumbs to an onslaught of opportunist infections and tumours collectively known as AIDS. The gradual debilitation and eventual death (in the absence of treatment) of AIDS sufferers further stigmatises the virus, sexual activity, and people who are associated with those who have been infected.

Transmission of the virus can be prevented through a variety of different behavioural strategies including use of condoms, reduction in number of sexual partners, abstinence from sexual intercourse, and use of sterilised needles when injecting drugs. The education sector is considered key to developing these protective strategies, and education is sometimes referred to as a 'social vaccine' (Global Campaign for Education 2004). The term is extremely useful, in that it captures the way in which education is an important site for developing knowledge, understanding, and social relations that are important both for prevention of the virus and for assisting people to care for those who are infected and affected. But the term also carries assumptions that schooling is a place where relationships are problem-free, and behavioural change is easily injected into people, like a vaccination. Schools are complex places. Pupils and teachers may be divided by class, race, ethnicity, or gender. They are certainly divided by age. There are differences between managers, planners, and policy makers, and diverging and converging networks of relationships with parents, communities, employers, non-government organisations (NGOs), and a wider citizenship. School may offer the protection of a vaccine, but this is not achieved only by a simple act of injecting training, materials, or monitoring into schools. These may be a necessary part of addressing the epidemic, but on their own they are insufficient.

Despite the dissemination of knowledge on the causes and nature of the epidemic, behaviour change has not occurred at the scale needed to curb its spread. Shifts towards more equal gender relations are associated with preventing the disease, but changes in gender relations and gendered power relations are difficult to effect, and education is one sector where these difficulties are writ large.

The starting point for producing this book comes from the work of 'Beyond Access: Gender, Education and Development', a joint project of the Institute of Education, University of London and Oxfam GB, with three years of funding from the Department for International Development (DFID) (www.ioe.ac.uk/efps/beyondaccess; Aikman and Unterhalter 2005; Aikman and Unterhalter 2007). This project examined policy, practice, and research with a wide network of people around the globe to identify new knowledge and document good practice. HIV and AIDS was a theme which cut across all the work on gender and education and was a particular focus in each of the five international seminars hosted by the project between 2002 and 2005. This volume brings together some of the papers commissioned by the project as well as contributions from key researchers, policy makers, and practitioners in the field of HIV and AIDS and education.

The book draws on research and experience from many different levels and parts of the education system. It brings together an international group of writers from different disciplinary and methodological backgrounds, experiences, and practices. Their work ranges from small-scale qualitative studies which elicit rich description of the gendered lives of students and teachers in the context of HIV and AIDS, to discussions of the literature in the field, and analysis of the policies of international agencies, national and local governments, and NGOs. The chapters provide many points for discussion from multiple perspectives. The book is intended for audiences who wish to contribute to policy, develop new knowledge through research, and change practice.

In bringing this work together we have tried to be alert to the varied characteristics of the HIV and AIDS epidemic as it has developed in different settings around the globe. However, a majority of chapters are concerned with contexts within sub-Saharan Africa, and Southern Africa in particular. This is because sub-Saharan Africa has the largest number of people living with HIV – in some countries, over ten per cent of the adult population. Hence this has been the setting for some of the most extensive research and documentation of educational challenges and responses. Here heterosexual transmission has been the main mode of spreading the virus for some time, and a number of the chapters in the book deal with issues concerning sexualities, family relationships, and the cultural delineation of gender inequalities, which have a bearing on the way schooling can address the epidemic. In Asia, on the other hand, research has focused on specific groups at risk of HIV such as injecting drug users, sex workers, and men who have sex with men; it has not looked extensively at schooling. Our book reflects this, as the chapters providing case studies of Thailand and India deal with adult education initiatives, rather than schooling.

While the book maintains a strong focus on the formal education system and schools in particular, it also recognises the importance of non-formal education and education for adults, and the need for comprehensive strategies and practices that engage the wider community in which education and schooling take place. Some of the chapters investigate the ways in which policy and programme interventions that serve to promote gender equality at school and in other educational contexts can contribute to reducing the vulnerability of young people (girls and women in particular) to HIV infection. Reducing vulnerability entails understanding different dimensions and frames of vulnerability, such as that of the impact of HIV and AIDS on children and especially orphans (see Boler, this volume), the way in which schooling can expose vulnerable young people to violence and increased risk of contracting HIV (see Leach this volume), and looking to change the behaviour of dominant groups (see Khandekhar *et al.*, this volume, which discusses young men and their concepts of masculinity).

The UNAIDS Inter-Agency Task Team on Education (UNESCO 2006) calls for an examination of current practices to ensure relevant, effective, inclusive, and qualitative learning about HIV and AIDS. There is an urgent need for fine-grained studies of what good teaching and learning about HIV and AIDS looks like in classrooms and schools. Research in schools in Durban and Gauteng in South Africa, in Maputo, Mozambique, and in Uganda shows how teachers' attitudes sometimes undermine the equality and respect which are needed to support forms of empowerment of both girls and boys in relation to negotiating sex (Morrell and Ouzgane 2005; Thorpe 2005; Kakuru 2006). Nonetheless a number of initiatives also point to the ways in which teachers are contributing to change, as this book documents (see Unterhalter *et al.*, this volume). There is a growing need for the insights gained from these local initiatives to be used in policy making and planning at national and international levels.

The book is divided into two sections. The first outlines some of the ways in which gender inequalities in schools and in the social relations that surround school have exacerbated the epidemic. Chapter 1 sets the scene for the chapters which follow by providing a brief overview of the AIDS epidemic and the gender dynamics embedded in it. It considers some of the assumptions about gender often associated with the epidemic, and draws on debates in feminist theory to elucidate the different concepts under discussion. It then considers ways in which schooling, education, and learning themselves are not socially neutral places but highly gendered social spaces, and what this can mean for the educational experience of young people. The chapter poses questions about how and why the education sector has responded to the HIV epidemic in terms of particular orientations with regard to policy and planning, and maps some of the challenges to ensuring greater responsiveness and a more transformative agenda.

In Chapter 2 James Hargreaves and Tania Boler undertake a systematic review of literature on young people, risk, and HIV, and consider what the research evidence indicates about whether school does provide a form of protection against HIV infection. Doris Kakuru (Chapter 3) looks at the extensive national-level response by the government of Uganda and examines what success there has been in taking energetic policy commitments down to the level of the school. In Chapter 4 Fiona Leach alerts us to emerging research on forms of violence that girls and boys encounter in school, and the gender dynamics embedded in these. She considers some of the links between these studies, illuminating the hierarchical and often violent school environment and the need for HIV and AIDS education to address these broad contexts of gender differentiation and power in sexual relationships for it to be effective. In the last chapter of this section, Chapter 5, Tania Boler presents data from a study of orphans in South Africa, drawing out gender differences in terms of educational outcomes for orphaned boys and girls, and providing new evidence to link gendered patterns of parental death with increased sexual vulnerability. All the chapters in this first section warn that too optimistic an approach involving turning to schools to protect against HIV and AIDS must be tempered by an acknowledgement of the forms of gender, class, and race inequalities that are associated with the provision of education.

The second section of the book addresses some initiatives that have attempted to change the marked gender inequalities in schooling that either exacerbate or fail to ameliorate the effects of the epidemic. David Clarke (Chapter 6) reviews the international response by multilateral and bilateral organisations, showing how money can be linked to addressing gender equality in policy, planning, and practice. In Chapter 7 Gill Gordon looks at work in eastern Zambia, where schools have become the hub for a participatory approach that engages community groups, teachers, and students in analysing and understanding the complex and specific social factors that put them at risk of unsafe sex. The programme supports participants in developing actions to overcome factors that prevent them from leading enabling and healthy lives. In Chapter 8 Elaine Unterhalter, Amy North, Rob Morrell, and their co-authors chart how teachers in South Africa have responded with care and concern to the ravages of the epidemic on their schools, and how this suggests the emergence of new gendered identities. The chapter looks at the opportunities that the school itself provides for proactively engaging with the epidemic, even though old hierarchies are slow to change.

Chapters 9 and 10 by Usa Duongsaa and Sujata Khandekar and colleagues look at adult education and the non-formal sector. Duongsaa, drawing on her work in Thailand, takes the case of a young woman – Pimjai – to illustrate the way in which HIV and AIDS, poverty, and lack of education are putting women at risk of infection. Pimjai provides an inspiring example of determination to overcome stigma and inequality through counselling others and becoming an advocate for women's rights. Khandekar examines a research and community-mobilisation programme for young men in Mumbai. Through participatory research with community youths, the programme sets about changing concepts of masculinity and ways of understanding gender, power, and identity in order to address violent gendered behaviour by young men which puts them and their partners at risk of HIV and AIDS. Omokhudu Idogho in Chapter 11 charts the development of HIV and AIDS-education projects and programmes in Nigeria through an examination of different partnerships that have been driving change. This chapter outlines the importance of, as well as the tensions and challenges involved in, bringing together the health and education sectors to form multi-sectoral partnerships. It warns that until women's-rights organisations join the partnership, the unequal gendered power relations which underpin the HIV and AIDS epidemic will continue.

In our conclusion we assess what can be expected of the education sector with regard to gender equality, HIV, and AIDS. We contrast the 'optimistic' approach which assumes that behaviour change can be taught in school or educational settings as if it were immune to the gender relations of the wider society, and the 'pessimistic' approach whereby the inequalities within schools place young people at severe risk, unable to challenge or counter these forces. We consider some of the research, policy, and practice challenges of persistent gender inequalities, and the indications that steps can be taken to make gender equality a reality in the face of the ravages of the epidemic.

References

Aikman, S. and E. Unterhalter (2005) *Beyond Access: Transforming Policy and Practice for Gender Equality in Education*, Oxford: Oxfam GB.

Aikman, S. and E. Unterhalter (2007) *Practising Gender Equality in Education*, Oxford: Oxfam GB.

Global Campaign for Education (2004) 'Learning to Survive: How Education For All would Save Hundreds of Young People from AIDS', Brussels: Global Campaign for Education, available at: www.campaignforeducation.org/resources/Apr2004/Learning%20to%20Survive%20final%20 2604.pdf (last accessed February 2008).

Hargreaves, J. and T. Boler (2006) 'Girl Power: The Impact of Girls' Education on HIV and Sexual Behaviour', Johannesburg: ActionAid.

Kakuru, D. (2006) *The Combat for Gender Equality in Education: Rural Livelihood Pathways in the Context of HIV/AIDS*, Wageningen: Wageningen Academic Publishers.

Morrell, R. and L. Ouzgane (2005) *African Masculinities: Men in Africa from the Late Nineteenth Century to the Present*, New York and Basingstoke: Palgrave Macmillan.

Thorpe, M. (2005) 'Learning about HIV/AIDS in schools: does a gender equality approach make a difference?', in S. Aikman and E. Unterhalter (eds.) *Beyond Access: Transforming Policy and Practice for Gender Equality in Education*, Oxford: Oxfam GB.

UNAIDS (2006) 'Report on the Global HIV/AIDS Epidemic', Geneva: UNAIDS.

UNAIDS (2007) 'HIV and AIDS in Latin America', www.avert.org/aidslatinamerica.htm.

UNESCO (2006) 'Quality Education and HIV and AIDS', Paris: Inter-Agency Task Team (IATT) on Education, UNESCO.

Part 1

Gender, Education, and HIV –
Mapping the Challenges

1 Essentialism, equality, and empowerment: concepts of gender and schooling in the HIV and AIDS epidemic

Elaine Unterhalter, Tania Boler, and Sheila Aikman

The HIV and AIDS epidemic is often described as 'a feminised epidemic'. The term refers to some features of the epidemiology, in that in many countries which are experiencing generalised epidemics,[1] the numbers of women infected are significantly higher than the numbers of men. During the early years of an HIV epidemic, the virus is contained within certain key populations such as men who have sex with men, sex workers, and injecting drug users. This type of epidemic is known as a concentrated epidemic and is typical of the epidemics found in most parts of Europe, North America, South America, and Asia. In these regions, the greatest burden of infection is among men. However, in sub-Saharan African countries experiencing generalised HIV epidemics, women now make up 57 per cent of infections, with some 17 million women living with HIV at the end of 2003 (UNAIDS 2007). The situation is particularly acute among young people in Southern Africa, with studies suggesting that young women are two to seven times more likely to be infected with HIV than young men are (Glynn *et al.* 2001; Gregson and Garnett 2000; Macphail *et al.* 2002).

The term 'feminised epidemic' is also sometimes used as shorthand to signal that unequal gender relations are associated with HIV infections, as either cause or consequence. The reports of UNESCO, the UNAIDS Inter-Agency Task Team on Education, and the Global Campaign for Education urge us with generalisations to 'recognise that gender issues are key to the problem of HIV and AIDS' (UNAIDS IATT on Education 2006c; Global Campaign for Education 2005a). What these reports point to is that many women cannot act to protect themselves by requesting men to use condoms or requiring men to reduce their numbers of sexual partners. Such forms of female vulnerability are seen as a manifestation of the gender issues at the heart of the epidemic. In addition, the term 'gender issues' often signals that many women who are infected or affected take on extra burdens of care within households, without shifts in gender relations within the family, community, or society (Voluntary Service Overseas 2006).

However, the term 'feminised epidemic', despite its usefulness in directing attention to some aspects of women's needs, is also immensely problematic, in that it associates the actions of women, not men, with the epidemic, and suggests that all women are similarly vulnerable, ill, or burdened with responsibility. While in many countries these terms apply to a large number of women, it is important to scrutinise these over-generalised and one-dimensional characterisations. In this chapter we place the 'feminised epidemic' within the context of a broader examination of concepts of women and gender associated with research and policy on education, HIV, and AIDS. But before turning to an exploration of these important distinctions, some background on the education-sector response to the epidemic is necessary.

The education-sector response to the epidemic

One of the most frustrating dimensions of the current HIV and AIDS crisis is that it is fairly well acknowledged that enough is known about how to prevent the further spread of the virus and yet, globally, some 6,800 new infections continue to occur daily (UNAIDS 2007). Despite increasing amounts of money being spent on school-based HIV and AIDS education, the results have been disappointing for a number of possible reasons, including:

- lack of understanding of the social factors which affect sexual behaviour – especially in different cultural contexts;

- structural barriers, such as poverty and gender inequality, which may hamper behaviour change;

- low-quality and under-resourced educational institutions, hindering the quality of provision of HIV and AIDS education;

- insufficient funding spent on equipping and supporting AIDS educators with the skills and resources they need;

- insufficient attention to international evidence on the characteristics of effective HIV education programmes.

As the epidemic first began to spread around the globe in the 1980s, HIV and AIDS were considered to be a problem demanding a response first and foremost from the health sector. But as it became clearer through the 1990s that there was not – and not likely to be – a medical vaccine to protect against the HIV virus, the education sector needed to find ways to respond. As students and teachers died from the disease, the viability of education systems came under threat. Education came to be seen as having an urgent role to play in reaching young people and children with messages about the epidemic (Shaeffer 1994). The response was a sporadic implementation of different programmes such as life-skills, reproductive-health programmes, and other health interventions. These were introduced with little knowledge of their impact and a growing awareness of acute problems of lack of teacher knowledge, understanding, and commitment.

Many programmes lacked connection with the real choices and social pressures that young people experienced (Coombe and Kelly 2002). Sometimes gender was considered in these initiatives. Often it was not.

AIDS has drastically changed the demands on educators, schools, and students, posing formidable challenges to education systems that are already over-stretched and under-resourced. These new challenges – like the epidemic – are complex and require new ways of thinking and responding. Research and thinking about the role of the education sector in the epidemic are fairly nascent, controversial, and ambiguous. There are divergent understandings and positions taken on questions such as:

- the extent to which AIDS is undermining the provision of education in high-prevalence countries;

- the role of education in protecting young people from HIV;

- what messages should be taught, how, and to which age groups.

Often the pressure to align education appropriately with an assessment of the nature of the epidemic and the response means that gender issues are ignored.

Actions being taken by ministries of education indicate different degrees of progress in developing overarching HIV and AIDS strategies to guide policy and practice change (Global Campaign for Education 2005b; UNAIDS IATT on Education 2008). Zambia, for example, has carried out an assessment of the needs of the education sector and developed a comprehensive national response for HIV and AIDS education. Other countries, such as Brazil, Senegal, and Thailand, have illustrated what can be done with political leadership and commitment to confront HIV through a dual policy of HIV-prevention programmes and free access to anti-retroviral medication (UNAIDS 2006). By 2004, 72 per cent of ministries of education reported having established HIV and AIDS management structures with senior staff represented (UNESCO 2006b). But planning still suffers from a lack of reliable national data and a lack of linking and collaboration between key government departments such as health, social welfare, and finance. This situation impacts on the conceptualisation of approaches, the operationalisation of plans at sub-national levels, and the availability of funding for plans. The International Institute for Educational Planning (IIEP) in Paris now offers courses for education ministry staff in how to confront HIV and AIDS in their work, and how to make the management of HIV and AIDS a routine function within the education system. But structural and historical barriers to good communication between and across government still persist, despite examples of goodwill and specific initiatives. The extent to which gender is a major concern in approaches to planning often depends on how seriously gender policies are being promoted elsewhere in a ministry of education.

There has been considerable focus on planning for and managing a stable and strong education system that can respond to the ravages of the disease in terms of its impact on student and teacher numbers. But there is considerable debate about the extent to which HIV and AIDS are affecting teachers. HIV and AIDS have, unequivocally, led to increased levels of morbidity and mortality among young adults in many parts of the world. Although all sectors of society have been affected, one sector in particular has been the focus for attention and controversy: teachers (Bennell 2005; Kelly 2000b). Sub-Saharan Africa is already facing a serious teacher shortage, and AIDS-related sickness and mortality is exacerbating this problem. Long before an HIV-positive teacher dies, she or he is likely to be ill, and therefore absent from school, for substantial periods, leading to teacher shortages or classes being taught jointly. A lack of HIV-related workplace policies compounds the problem, as there is often no sick pay, no access to treatment, and inadequate teacher-replacement policies. AIDS mortality also substantially increases the education wage bill, as attrition costs are high and death benefits soar. During early phases of the epidemic, it was reported that in sub-Saharan Africa, teachers were actually more at risk of HIV than the general population. This trend now appears to be changing; indeed, teachers may be changing their behaviour faster than the general population. The problem is that there simply are not enough data on HIV rates among teachers, or about the associated gender dynamics, to estimate accurately the impact of the epidemic on the provision of education. It is clear that the impact will be felt differently in different contexts.

Excellent planning is needed to manage teacher absence and to increase recruitment and support. Similar skills are needed to assess and support children. UNAIDS estimated in 2007 that every day over 1,000 children under the age of 15 become infected with HIV (UNAIDS 2007). Some of the negative effects of this on children's education relate to observations that without anti-retroviral treatment, children with HIV have weaker language skills and poorer visual-motor functioning than their peers, as well as particular socio-emotional developmental needs, and sometimes erratic attendance patterns (Jukes 2006). Barnett and Whiteside documented falling enrolment ratios in KwaZulu-Natal where infection rates were high, suggesting that children were not attending school in significant numbers because they were ill (Barnett and Whiteside 2002). Unfortunately we know little about the gender dimensions of these effects.

Adequately supporting children who have been orphaned through AIDS is a matter for cross-ministry planning and co-operation, so that orphans can be fully integrated into national education systems in a way which overcomes stigma, poverty, the need for counselling, and the needs of other family members. As Doris Kakuru shows in this volume, girls are particularly likely to take on extra work burdens when parents and other carers are sick, obliging them to drop out of school. Research into understanding the educational needs of orphans and vulnerable children has mainly focused on the impact which orphanhood has on enrolment in school, with less attention given to other dimensions of their vulnerability (Boler and Carroll 2003). However, it is necessary to understand some of the dynamics that result when there are considerable numbers of orphans in classrooms. Very particular professional practice and insight is required from teachers, which schools do not always support. Kathryn Wiggins, in a study of men and women teachers and their interactions with orphans attending a school in South Africa, analysed the ways they used 'loving' and 'lecturing' as styles to perform gender identities and encourage learning among orphans, and the tensions these generated with other school practices relating to punishment and examination success (Wiggins 2007). Clearly there is much to be gained from detailed attention to some of the gender issues involved in the support of orphan children.

There is also considerable debate over the role of education in protecting young people from HIV. The evidence varies from country to country, over time, and across regions. There has been increasing evidence which seems to suggest that formal education helps individuals protect themselves against HIV infection, although exactly why or how is not clear, as levels of infection seem to be lower even where schooling includes no specific programmes aimed at preventing HIV (Coombe and Kelly 2001). This may be because most schools offer opportunities for learning about AIDS, even if not necessarily from teachers or through the official curriculum. They also offer non-HIV and AIDS-related skills and knowledge about information-handling and changes in affective and socio-cultural routines which can boost girls' and boys' self-confidence and status. The notion of education as a 'social vaccine' has given impetus to school-based efforts to change behaviours that put people at risk, and to ensuring that all girls and boys attend school. Studies of changes in legislation have shown that one of the most important ways of ensuring attendance is to abolish school fees and other hidden costs that prevent girls and those from the poorest families going to school (UNESCO 2006b, 71). The need to pay for schooling puts girls at increased risk of infection as they may rely on getting the necessary funds through exploitative relationships with older men, such as 'sugar daddies', or selling sex to pay for school books (Hunter 2002; Leach 2006).

While there is little understanding about how simply going to school might reduce HIV vulnerability, there are also divergent views on how much schooling is needed: is primary schooling enough, or is it secondary education that really matters? Girls, it is suggested, get the greatest payoff from secondary schooling, which makes a difference to their confidence and ability to try out different approaches to sexuality and negotiate safer sex (Burns 2002; Hargreaves and Boler 2006; Grown *et al.* 2005). For boys, it seems that schooling needs to be combined with promoting alternative visions of masculinity (i.e. not characterised by risk-taking and domineering sexuality), and that out-of-school actions are as important for building such cultures as those in school (Morrell 2006; Walker 2005).

By far the greatest efforts from the education sector have been in terms of developing and delivering education programmes to teach about HIV and AIDS in the expectation of changing behaviours and the spread of HIV (Kelly 2006). With strong support from UNICEF, many ministries of education have developed life-skills courses which include material on HIV and AIDS. NGOs and non-state education providers have been implementing formal and non-formal HIV and AIDS programmes for children and young people, often in innovative ways that deal with questions of gender and power. However, this work is largely small-scale and un-co-ordinated, and many of the experiences and learning undocumented.

Curriculum design and delivery of HIV and AIDS education remains contested terrain, with debates on whether to 'mainstream' HIV and AIDS across the curriculum, or have it as a 'stand alone' topic. The position of gender in these different approaches is not clear-cut. In the majority of classrooms, the emphasis continues to be on learning facts from a medical perspective rather than tackling the more problematic area of acquiring new attitudes, discussing sexual relationships, and adopting safer behaviours. In high-incidence countries such as Botswana and South Africa, life skills are a compulsory part of the school curriculum, and wider issues about gender and rights are on the syllabus, although unevenly addressed in lessons (Magnani *et al.* 2005; Rooth 2005; Langley Smith 2002; Phaladze and Tlou 2006). But in many countries, even where HIV and AIDS programmes or life-skills programmes exist, young people are not receiving them because of a combination of factors such as lack of training and capacity of teachers and school heads, teachers' unwillingness to engage with what they feel are sensitive topics, and already overcrowded curricula which mean that teachers are under pressure to teach other subjects (UNESCO 2006b).

It can be seen that the education-sector response to the epidemic has been marked by sporadic action, lack of systematic research, and generally inadequate attention to gender. In this context a number of 'common sense' assumptions circulate about what the term 'gender' means. In the next section we examine three different ways in which the term is used, draw out some of the benefits and difficulties associated with these meanings, and then examine what some of the consequences are for developing strategies for the education sector.

Contrasting approaches to gender in writing on HIV and AIDS and education

There are three widely circulating, but generally undefined meanings associated with the term 'gender' in the context of discussions of HIV and AIDS and education. We have defined these as *essentialism,* which stresses that concern with women's vulnerability must lie at the heart of education responses; *equality,* the view that schools need to be concerned with addressing unequal gender power relations; and *empowerment,* the view that existing gender relations and identities need to be transformed, entailing changes not only within schools but also in the wider society.

Essentialism

The underlying idea in work that draws on an essentialist view is that all women are vulnerable and all men are sexually predatory and domineering in relation to household decision-making. Thus, for example, the Inter-Agency Task Team (IATT) on education viewed gender in its 'Toolkit for mainstreaming HIV and AIDS in the education sector' in the following terms:

> *[Higher infection rates for women are]...in part because of the greater biological vulnerability of women, to a large extent it is also due to traditional gender roles that reinforce the subordinate role for women in all matters – including sexual relations – and to the lower social and economic status of women, which increases their dependence on men. In many cultures, men are expected to demonstrate masculine behaviours such as having frequent and multiple sexual relations and engaging in violence. Such behaviour not only makes women vulnerable, but also puts men at a greater risk of HIV infection.*
> (UNAIDS IATT on Education 2008, 53)

It can be seen from this passage that the document refers to women only in terms of vulnerability and subordination, and to men in terms of sexual promiscuity and violence. It is implied that this is age-old behaviour – 'traditional gender roles' – and that it is sanctioned by 'culture'. What this wording fails to make clear is that not all men and women conform to these stereotypes, that it is not tradition, but history and social relations at work in forming relationships with these characteristics, and that many women and men question and contest identities of vulnerability or violence.

To some extent, statistics about HIV transmission support the assumptions of essentialism. Biologically, young women are at a double disadvantage in terms of becoming infected with HIV. During sex, women are at least one and a half to four times more likely to become infected than men; it also appears that the younger the woman, the more likely she is to contract the virus, as her reproductive system may not be fully mature (Glynn *et al.* 2001). In addition, the likelihood of becoming infected during sex increases if somebody has untreated sexually transmitted infections (STIs), which affects women particularly as these infections are more likely to go undiagnosed. Young women are also vulnerable to HIV during violent sex because of possible damage to the female genital tract.

But a counter to the essentialist argument is that sexual behaviours are themselves influenced by a wide array of cultural, community, economic, and social factors. One of the biggest problems with discussing why women are vulnerable to HIV is the level of complexity involved in human sexual relations (Aggleton 2004). Sexual behaviour also changes within relationships. For example, people might use condoms at the beginning of a relationship but over time – as trust grows – stop using them.

The general criticism that all girls and women are not the same in their sexual behaviours can be extended to other areas of social life. Essentialism is not helpful in understanding the ways in which different groups of girls access and progress through school, their responses to the teaching and the curriculum, or their lives as adults. There are clearly significant differences for girls with regard to a family's wealth, the extent of education provision, social relations concerning marriage, women's work, and involvement in decision-making. Wide variations in these dimensions mean that the explanatory value of essentialist arguments is not very wide-ranging.

A further critique of the essentialist argument, which depicts only women's vulnerability, is that it suggests women are passive, that their actions are characterised by weakness, and that they are properly located in feminised realms – the family, the household, the women's organisation, and in some accounts primary schooling. To stray beyond these into public spaces – the workplace, political contests, secondary and higher education – is to invite danger and attack. It is clear that these assumptions are inaccurate and serve to further subordinate women. But these problems notwithstanding, essentialist arguments circulate widely.

Equality

A second approach to discussing gender in the context of HIV and AIDS is to stress the importance of equality. In this group of writings, gender equality may mean equal levels of provision of schooling or training. Thus gender describes girls and boys, and their different biological and social characteristics. This is sometimes analysed as viewing gender as a noun, an external descriptive category. Gender is given by biology or social norms, and observing this is merely about describing and noting differences (Unterhalter 2007). The objective of gender policy from this perspective is that whatever is planned for one group should be provided equally to the other. Thus for example, the IATT Toolkit quoted above suggests that work on sexual and reproductive health and AIDS should include:

- Encouraging both men and women to discuss and address issues related to sex and sexuality and other factors that enhance vulnerability, such as drug misuse

- Improving access to information, counseling and support for girls and boys and men and women (UNAIDS IATT on Education 2008, 54).

It is evident that there is concern that the toolkit should be disseminated to both men and women, girls and boys. This is an important aim, but there is little concern with the gendered power relations that might make it difficult for the two groups to discuss or address sex and sexuality honestly; or the barriers, for example of time or official sanction, that mean girls or boys do not gain access to the same amounts or form of counselling and support. The concern with gender equality in provision, understood simply as the same amounts given to boys and to girls, thus masks the deep structures of inequality that make dissemination or interventions so difficult.

A second approach to gender within the equality frame is to assert that gender equality is about addressing unequal power relations; hence gender is not just a description of girls and boys, but signals particular structures of exclusion, discrimination, or subordination. An assessment of gender that is alert to forms of power relations associated with income, wealth, political and social power, and the cultural forms through which these are addressed, generally cannot be made without taking account of other forms of social division linked to class, race, ethnicity, or location. An example is the document 'Building a gender friendly school environment: a toolkit for educators and their unions' prepared in 2007 for Education International. This discussed gender in the following terms:

> *Learning institutions play an important part in teaching modeling and reinforcing gender roles. The environment within a learning institution is an important factor in the development, sanctioning and reinforcement of gender roles and identities. The opportunities given to learners, the ways learners treat one another, and how educators treat learners and their colleagues are all elements of the learning environment all of which are influenced by the prevailing gender roles in the society. Reinforcement of unequal gender roles and disrespect for girls and women experienced constantly over time in*

> *learning institutions can lead to dominance of males over females. This can lead to men taking advantage of the power differences between men and women and result in gender-based physical, sexual and verbal violence.*
> (Pulizzi and Rosenblum 2007)

It can be seen that in this definition social norms have particular consequences in which women are subordinated.

Unequal power relations lie behind what often appear as essentialist features of women's vulnerability. These power relations are not only inscribed in public institutions where they are open to discussion and amenable to collaborative struggles for change, but they are also part of everyday actions and intimacies that are private and difficult to disentangle from emotional expression, and thus much harder to name and transform. At an epidemiological level, there are three broad factors that influence vulnerability to HIV infection in epidemics where heterosexual transmission is the main mode of infection: level of sexual activity, the HIV status of a sexual partner, and the likelihood that HIV is transmitted during sex. These factors are only the immediate risk factors for infection. They are also associated with a wide range of social, political, economic, and cultural processes, often coloured by gender power relations. Gendered power relations between women and men which are sanctioned, taken for granted, and very difficult to contest are the context out of which risks emerge and make it difficult for change to occur.

Gendered power relations are clearly at work when we analyse which women become infected with HIV. Women who are more sexually active are more vulnerable to HIV infection. A number of important behavioural traits are related to this, notably the age at which young women first start to have sex, their overall number of sexual partners, the frequency with which they have sex with these partners, and the type of relationships they have (for example serial monogamy or concurrent sexual partnerships).

Generally engaging in sex at an early age, or having multiple sexual partners, are not simply a matter of choice and desire. In some societies economic and social relations mean that young girls are married to much older men. Social requirements for a transfer in money or goods to a bride's family generally mean that younger men do not have enough income accumulated to marry, and families look to older men as appropriate husbands. Women may have little capacity to ensure that they can delay the age of their first sexual relationship, that men have few sexual partners, or that their access to status or wealth is not linked to sexuality. These constraints are particularly acute when the position of women is generally low, when women are prohibited from owning land, or when they have few opportunities for employment or decent work conditions. Sex workers are a group who are extremely vulnerable to HIV infection throughout the world. Women working in the sex industry, which is generally unregulated, may have very little control over whether they can insist on condom use or on limits to the number of clients they work with.

One serious risk factor for young women in Africa is having sexual partners who are much older than themselves: older men have had a longer time to become infected, and age-mixing is an important but neglected dimension of the AIDS epidemic in Africa (Gregson *et al.* 2002; Kelly *et al.* 2003). If new generations of young men and women were to have sex only with individuals of their own age group, HIV would not spread to this group and they would remain free of HIV infection. In practice, young women in most sub-Saharan African settings form partnerships with older men as well as with young men from their own peer group, and this is key in propagating infection from one generation to the next.

Evidence from epidemiological studies shows that inequalities between older men and younger women affect how often a woman has sex, the type and frequency of sex, and whether condoms are used or not (Luke 2005). Gendered power relations mean that a woman often cannot request the use of a condom without inviting the comment that either she is accusing her partner of unfaithfulness or she is unfaithful. Secondary school and teacher training courses are generally not free in most countries in Africa, and a number of studies document how young women begin sexual relationships with older men or 'sugar daddies' in return for fees (Hunter 2002; Leach 2006). In a number of societies in Africa and Asia when a man dies, it is required that his wife is married to his brother. The inequalities inherent in these relationships make it difficult to negotiate about sex.

Analyses which focus on gendered power relations generally view school as a site which reproduces the power relations of the wider society. The assumption is that schools mirror unequal gender relations, privileging the learning needs of boys, who progress through primary school in larger numbers. Boys have access to more school space and more teacher encouragement (Page 2004; Raynor 2008; UNESCO 2007). Schools also reproduce the sexual hierarchies which drive the HIV epidemic, being sites where gender-based violence has been noted, as Leach reports in this volume. Teachers often encourage a 'hard' masculinity linked to sexual conquest and multiple partners (Morrell 2003; Duffett 2006; Martino and Kehler 2006).

However, the depiction of schools simply as mirrors of unequal gender relations in the wider society is one-sided. The stress on structures of gender inequality leads to a denial of the forms of agency and action that women and men take, or the relational ways in which structure and agency intermesh. Schools do not only reproduce unequal gender relations, but provide a context in which girls and boys may, under different conditions, act to continue these inequalities, or learn and act to change them. Thus, viewing schools only as places where gender inequalities are not questioned, and abuse and violence is condoned, overlooks the complicated ways in which children and adults make sense of gender and violence, negotiate meanings around sexuality and power, and attempt to take action for change. For example, Jenny Parkes, in a detailed study of children's gendered negotiations with experiences of violence and crime in a South African township, noted how girls and boys were both attracted and repelled by these processes and how school could offer languages and practices to support resistance (Parkes 2005; 2007). Charlotte Watts and colleagues, in a randomised control trial looking at the effects of different interventions protecting women from sexual violence in South Africa, concluded that attending adult education classes with other women was the most significant effect (Pronyk *et al.* 2006). These works suggest that analysing unequal power relations and working on structures of inequality may be necessary, but not sufficient in understanding gender and processes of change.

Empowerment

Studies which focus on empowerment consider gender to be formed by relationships that are neither reducible to gender roles and structures of inequality, nor simply the outcomes of the actions of men and women. As formulated in the work of Nelly Stromquist, for example, empowerment is concerned with a personal dimension which stresses self-confidence and self-expression, a cognitive dimension which focuses on the development of emancipatory knowledge, an economic dimension which ensures access to resources, and a political dimension which ensures participation in relations of power (Stromquist 1995). Naila Kabeer's discussion of empowerment stresses the importance of concern with women's access to resources, agency and action, and valued outcomes. In adapting these ideas of empowerment to develop a research project with ActionAid, working with NGOs on girls' education and protection against HIV and AIDS in Tanzania and Nigeria, the following gender empowerment framework was developed:

> *We understand girls as active agents, who think about their lives, articulate their views and act. These girls are engaged in social relations with boys, parents (mothers and fathers), teachers, education officials, men and women in their communities, the implementing partners to bring about change. Thus although we see each girl as important, we acknowledge the networks of social relations in which they live. At present a range of forces constrain the opportunities for education and empowerment of these girls. They live in societies that are stratified by gender, class, ethnicity, religion etc. These social*

divisions, which each have complex histories and dynamics, currently entail forms of discrimination, inequality, and poverty. We see the girls' lives as being constrained by a range of forces which 'press down' through the exercise of various forms of power… but girls have some spaces and opportunities and act back in a range of ways, with different outcomes. In conducting the research we wish to document how girls work with others to bring about change, and what changes in the power dynamics they can make, through expanding opportunities for action at the individual and community level, through taking particular actions and engaging in forms of discussion.
(ActionAid 2007)

HIV is one feature of the environment in which girls live, as are gendered structures of inequality. But this framework is seeking to look at the ways in which social relations are formed and girls and boys, women and men act both to contest the harmful effects of inequalities (which might include vulnerability to HIV), and to work to make a decent life, even in conditions where AIDS is prevalent.

The critiques of this approach argue that it is not easy to sustain the mobilisation of women and girls, or to develop work with government that is structured around long-term programmes of political accountability for girls' education (Chapman and Miske 2007); that a celebration of empowerment without a realistic assessment of its consequences may invite a backlash (Odora-Hoppers 2004); and that evaluations of empowerment often do not keep all the features of the framework in play (Kabeer 1999). Unfortunately, very few projects which focus on empowerment have been fully researched, but Jo Manchester has drawn out some of the implications of women's activism to demand attention to gender issues in the epidemic, showing how empowering this has been, even for women who are HIV-positive (Manchester 2004); and Chinouya (2007) has shown some of the empowerment effects of women's local organisations. What these studies of adult women show is that empowerment might be effected among school children, even in societies marked by gender inequalities, but that it cannot be effected only through seeking to transform schools. Connections need to be made for example with the health sector, women's organisations, and church groups; and changes need to be effected not just in education but in wider political, economic, and social relations.

Essentialism, equality, and empowerment are found to different degrees in policy writings and the work of researchers in analysing gender, HIV and AIDS, and education. Essentialism, because of the congruence between these ideas and certain 'common sense' views about men and women, is a widespread view, as is the notion that interventions for girls and boys must be equal. Concerns with changing unequal gendered power relations and nurturing empowerment are both less researched and less evident in the policy literature. We now turn to an assessment of how these different approaches to viewing the problem of gender shape our understanding of the education sector's response to the HIV and AIDS epidemic.

Essentialism, equality, and empowerment in the assessment of the education-sector response to the HIV and AIDS epidemic

Gender has only sporadically been a feature of the education sector's response to HIV and AIDS. Many aspirations in policy and practice about the ways in which education might help control or ameliorate the epidemic have been based on assumptions about schooling, education, and learning that offer only partial accounts of this complex relationship. For example it is assumed in many policy documents developed in response to the epidemic that schools are neutral spaces in which learning and teaching takes place as intended by those who develop curricula or train teachers. Thus, although successive issues of UNESCO's 'EFA Global Monitoring Report' have commented on how conditions in schools affect the quality of learning, the general assumption is that improving pupil–teacher ratios, deepening understanding of children's learning needs, and effective monitoring will yield considerable improvements (UNESCO 2005; UNESCO 2006b).

However, much sociological work on schools highlights how they are marked by race, class, and gender division (Chisholm 2004; Doggett 2005, Mirembe and Davies 2001). These social divisions intersect, so that individuals are located within systems of discrimination and subordination which constrain the ways in which they can act to bring about change for themselves and their societies. Thus girls and boys trying to negotiate and articulate their aspirations to complete school are working within histories and gendered relations of poverty, schooling, and sexuality that place enormous constraints on what they can achieve, even were they to receive outstanding teaching and support. This is not to say that schools cannot provide young people with some of the knowledge and confidence to overcome these constraints, but they generally cannot do this in isolation from other organisations and other forms of social relations located in families, friendship networks, and religious, cultural, or political groups .

There are two ways in which gender, HIV, and education have been linked in policy documents and the work of commentators. The first, the optimistic view, sees gender relations as outside of school, constraining who does and does not attend, the kinds of negotiations about sex that take place between young people and adults, and the form of care and support in families. School is a neutral space. It can support work to combat the epidemic in relatively straightforward ways. School can give pupils key knowledge to combat HIV and AIDS and to help develop appropriate relationships in order to use that knowledge. For example, schools can instill openness to information, confidence to speak up to claim rights, and status in a society. In this view school can help change some of the unequal gender relations that drive the epidemic. This idea, with its emphasis on school as *cause* for optimism and HIV protection as *effect,* often assumes that gender is a descriptive term denoting girls and boys, but not signalling further dimensions of social relationships. This approach is associated with the view that behaviour change can be taught in schools or other education settings. From this perspective, HIV-prevention messages focus solely on reducing the number of sexual partners, delaying the age at which young people first have sex, and encouraging condom use. It is often overly simplistic and based on the assumption that individuals have control over their behaviour, and that sexual behaviour is rationally determined (Coleman *et al.* 1966).

The second view is more pessimistic. It sees unequal gender relations as deeply entrenched within schools, undermining even the most well-conceptualised HIV prevention. Gendered attitudes diminish teachers' capacity to teach the relevant lessons with equality and respect, either because teachers find it difficult to talk about sex, or because their actions contradict the lessons they give. There are different kinds of gender dynamics at work within schools. For example there are a number of studies that highlight how teachers talk to pupils and what they say. Sometimes teachers' off-the-cuff comments regarding what is desirable in sexual relations undermine safe-sex messages (Kent 2004; Chege 2006; Pattman and Chege 2003).

Relationships between teenage pupils also point to a gender dynamic in how boys talk about girls who do and do not have sex, placing girls in an impossible situation where they are the object of scorn if they have sex with fellow pupils and also if they do not (Makoni 2006; Mirembe and Davies 2001). The hidden curriculum, which confers particular status on certain spaces in the school, and certain activities, like sport or beauty contests, undermines straightforward academic messages about sex or HIV (Kent 2004; Thorpe 2005; Bhana and Epstein 2007; Casely-Hayford 2008; Vavrus 2003). Assumptions within a school about girls' capacity to learn and progress in high-status subjects might contribute to boys' ideas as to whether girls can negotiate sexual relations or express their views. Cultures of masculinity associated with sport, music, or particular areas of academic prowess that do not challenge some of the gendered relations in which these are located risk perpetuating the kinds of unequal sexual relations which are contributing to the spread of the epidemic (Duffet 2006; Reddock 2006).

In addition to the different views on what the effects of teaching about gender and HIV in schools are, ideological and religious agendas are being advanced under the banner of HIV prevention. This has come to the fore with the explicit funding from the USA of abstinence-only HIV and AIDS education. On the one side there are those who stress that sexual abstinence is the only 100 per cent safe prevention method against HIV infection, while, on the other side, there are those who argue that abstinence-only education not only does not work, but is unrealistic, as well as constituting an abuse of human rights. At a simple level, the term 'abstinence' can be (and often is) used in two different ways: sexual delay among children and young people; and delayed sex until marriage. Very few educators or practitioners would argue against encouraging sexual delay, in many circumstances, for children. From a medical point of view, there are good physical and psychological health reasons for encouraging and/or enabling some young people to delay sexual debut, but there exist no parallel health-related reasons for delaying until marriage (despite the US government's claim to the contrary). There is nearly universal consensus that children should not be having sex until they are physically and emotionally mature. With regard to 'young people', however, the situation is not so clear. There is abundant evidence that some early sex is coercive, resulting from peer and/or partner pressure (often highly gendered), financial necessity, and other demeaning forces. In these cases, delay until individuals are empowered to make fully informed and mutually respectful choices is welcomed from many points of view.

Conflict still exists between public-health concerns and those that are driven by particular ideological positions. The two major constituencies advocating abstinence-only education (the Catholic church and the US government) are referring explicitly to a second interpretation of delay – complete sexual abstinence until marriage – that is clearly ideologically motivated. Panic about HIV has – unfortunately – allowed such viewpoints to gain scientific legitimacy through the use of slogans such as 'risk elimination versus risk reduction', in which it becomes impossible to argue that abstinence does not eliminate risk of HIV (Boler and Ingham, forthcoming). Certainly, if people abstain from sex, then risk of HIV is eliminated, but the bigger question is: can and should people be told to abstain and provided with little else, or should they be fully informed and empowered to make choices (one of which may be to abstain)? It can be seen that these different positions on abstinence invoke different ideas about gender. The 'simple' injunction to abstain sees gender largely in biological terms, while the approach of considering empowerment and negotiations about sexuality emerges from notions of gender as socially powerful but contestable.

Deeply entrenched features of the hidden curriculum, youth culture, or adult prejudice shape gendered languages which make it difficult to change ideas or actions. In this view gender inequality within schools is contributing to the HIV epidemic, and educational opportunities paradoxically place young people at severe risk. The policy implications here are much more difficult to prescribe at a national level. It requires leadership and management of gender-equality initiatives at school level, drawing in teachers, pupils, support services, and communities to change the social relations of learning and attend to gendered school cultures and out-of-school social relations. This is not a quick-fix approach.

The argument this book is advancing is that neither the optimistic nor the pessimistic view is complete on its own. We do believe schools are significant spaces for empowerment and change for all who work in them, and that learning is a powerful way to develop reasoned choices about what individuals want from their lives and how they can realise this. However, we cannot ignore the ways in which schools, education systems, and the people who work in them are shaped by complex histories that limit the extent to which they are able to bring about change. To do this is to fail to be attentive enough to the conditions that will help practices in schools contribute to change. It is important to understand how individuals and social groups living with very different conditions negotiate and bring about change in relations of gender and other inequalities, and how the optimism of the first perspective can be tempered by the realism of the second to improve policy and practice in the face of a horrific epidemic.

Conclusion

We have drawn out some differences between two ways of viewing gender: in essentialist terms, as an age-old feature of the identities of girls and boys; and merely commenting on equal levels of provision for girls and boys. We have distinguished these two approaches from more transformational strategies that document and try to change unequal gendered power relations, acknowledging that women and men have the capacity for empowerment and change, but that multi-dimensional approaches are needed. The challenges for the education sector are twofold. Strategies are needed to ensure adequate levels of provision for the needs of learners and teachers that take account of both prevention and care, regardless of gender. But meeting these needs is only a partial response to the epidemic. The wider challenge is to identify and confront the unequal power relations inside and outside school, where gender and other inequalities intersect; to work to change these; and to acknowledge the creativity and concerns about transformation that already exist, and can be further nurtured.

Note

1   Generalised epidemics are defined as epidemics where HIV infections are driven primarily by sexual behaviour patterns in the general population.

References

ActionAid (2007) 'Transforming Education for Girls in Nigeria and Tanzania', report of a meeting to plan a baseline research study, Nairobi: ActionAid.

Aggleton, P. (2004) 'Sexuality, HIV prevention, vulnerability and risk', *Journal of Psychology and Human Sexuality* 16(1): 1–13.

Barnett, T. and A. Whiteside (2002) *AIDS in the 21st Century: Disease and Globalization,* Basingstoke: Palgrave Macmillan.

Bennell, P. (2005) *Teacher Mortality in sub-Saharan Africa,* Brighton: KSD.

Bennell, P., K. Hyde, and N. Swainson (2002) *The Impact of the HIV/AIDS Epidemic on the Education Sector in Sub-Saharan Africa,* Sussex: Centre for International Education, University of Sussex.

Bhana, D. and D. Epstein (2007) '"I don't want to catch it." Boys, girls and sexualities in an HIV/AIDS environment', *Gender and Education* 19(1): 109–25.

Boler, T. (2004) 'Approaches to Estimating the Impact of HIV/AIDS on Teachers', London: Save the Children and ActionAid.

Boler, T. and K. Carroll (2003) 'Addressing the educational needs of orphans and vulnerable children', *Policy and Research* 2, UK Working Group on Education and HIV/AIDS, Save the Children and ActionAid International.

Burns, K. (2002) 'Sexuality education in a girls' school in Eastern Uganda', *Agenda,* No 53.

Casely-Hayford, L. (2008) 'Gendered experiences of teaching in poor rural areas of Ghana', in S. Fennell and M. Arnot (eds.) *Gender, Education and Equality in a Global Context: Conceptual Frameworks and Policy Perspectives,* London: Routledge.

Chapman, D. W. and S. Miske (2007) 'Promoting girls' education in Africa: evidence from the field', in M.A. Maslak (ed.), *The Agency and Structure of Women's Education,* New York: SUNY Press.

Chege, F. (2006) 'Teachers' gendered identities, pedagogy and HIV/AIDS education in African settings within ESAR', *Journal of Education* 38.

Chinouya, M. (2007) 'Ubuntu and the helping hands for Aids', in O. Wambu (ed.) *Under the Tree of Talking: Leadership for Change in Africa,* London: British Council.

Chisholm, L. (2004) *Changing Class: Education and Social Change in Post-apartheid South Africa,* Cape Town: HSRC Press.

Coleman, J., E. Campbell, C. Holson, et al. (1966) *Equality of Educational Opportunity,* Washington: Government Printing Office.

Coombe, C. (2000) *Managing the Impact of HIV/AIDS on the Education Sector,* Pretoria: University of Pretoria.

Coombe, C. (2002) 'Mitigating the Impact of HIV/AIDS on Education Supply, Demand and Quality: a Global Review for UNICEF', Florence: Innocenti Research Institute.

Coombe, C. and M.J. Kelly (2001) 'Education as a Vehicle for Combating HIV/AIDS', Paris: UNESCO, http://lobby.la.psu.edu/_107th/127_Basic_Education/Organizational_State ments/Basic%20Education%20Coalition/BEC_Educ_combating_AIDS.pdf (last accessed January 2008).

Doggett, R. (2005) 'Enabling education for girls: the Loreto Day School Sealdah, India', in S. Aikman and E. Unterhalter (eds.) *Beyond Access: Transforming Policy and Practice for Gender Equality in Education*, Oxford: Oxfam GB.

Duffett, A. (2006) 'Contesting Masculinities: Sport as a Medium for Development in Three HIV/AIDS Initiatives in South Africa', MA dissertation, University of London (Institute of Education).

Global Campaign for Education (2005a) 'Educate to End Poverty', Briefing Paper for the UN Millennium +5 Summit, Johannesburg: Global Campaign for Education.

Global Campaign for Education (2005b) 'Deadly Inertia: A Cross-Country Study of Responses to HIV', Brussels: Global Campaign for Education.

Glynn, J. R., M. Carael, B. Auvert, et al. (2001) 'Why do young women have a much higher prevalence of HIV than young men? A study in Kisumu, Kenya and Ndola, Zambia', *AIDS* 15 (Suppl 4): S51–60.

Gregson, S. and G. P. Garnett (2000) 'Contrasting gender differentials in HIV-prevalence and associated mortality increase in eastern and southern Africa: artefact of data or natural course of epidemics', *AIDS* 14 (Suppl 3): S85–99.

Gregson, S., C. A. Nyamukapa, G. P. Garnett, et al. (2002) 'Sexual mixing patterns and sex-differentials in teenage exposure to HIV infection in rural Zimbabwe', *Lancet* 359(9321): 1896–903.

Grown, C., G. Rao Gupta, and A. Kes (2005) *Taking Action: Achieving Gender Equality and Empowering Women*, London: Earthscan.

Hargreaves, J. and T. Boler (2006) 'Girl Power: the Impact of Girls' Education on HIV and Sexual Behaviour', Johannesburg: ActionAid.

Hunter, M. (2002) 'The materiality of everyday sex: thinking beyond "prostitution"', *African Studies* 61(1): 99–120.

Jukes, M. (2006) 'Early childhood health, nutrition and education', background paper for *EFA Global Monitoring Report 2007*.

Kabeer, N. (1999) 'Resources, agency, achievements: reflections on the measurement of women's empowerment', *Development and Change* 30(3): 435–64.

Kabeer, N. (2003) *Gender Mainstreaming in Poverty Eradication and the Millennium Development Goals: a Handbook for Policy Makers and Other Stakeholders*, London: Commonwealth Secretariat.

Kelly, M. (2000a) 'Planning for Education in the Context of HIV/AIDS', Paris: IIEP, UNESCO.

Kelly, M. (2000b) 'The Encounter between HIV/AIDS and Education', Harare: UNESCO sub regional office for Africa, www.sahims.net/Search_sahims/Sahims_Doc_2004/documents/ The%20encounter%20between%20AIDS%20and%20education_1.pdf (last accessed January 2008).

Kelly, M. (2006) 'The Potential Contribution of Schooling to Rolling Back HIV and AIDS', Commonwealth Youth and Development.

Kelly R. J., R. H. Gray, N. K. Sewankambo, et al. (2003) 'Age differences in sexual partners and risk of HIV-1 infection in rural Uganda', *Journal of Acquired Immune Deficiency Syndromes* 32(4): 446–51.

Kent, A. (2004) 'Living life on the edge: examining space and sexualities within a township highschool in greater Durban in the context of the HIV epidemic', *Transformation*, 54.

Langley Smith, R. (2002) 'The link between health, social issues and secondary education: life skills, health and civic education', Washington: World Bank.

Leach, F. (2006) 'Gender violence in schools in the developing world', in F. Leach and C. Mitchell (eds.) *Combating Gender Violence in and Around Schools,* Stoke-on-Trent: Trentham.

Luke, N. (2005) 'Confronting the "sugar daddy" stereotype: age and economic asymmetries and risky sexual behavior in urban Kenya', *International Family Planning Perspectives* 31(1): 6–14.

Macphail, C., B. Williams, and C. Campbell (2002). 'Relative risk of HIV infection among young men and women in a South African township', *International Journal of STD and AIDS* 13: 331–42.

Magnani, R., K. MacIntyre, A. Karim, L. Brown, P. Hutchinson, C. Kaufman, N. Rutenburg, K. Hallman, J. May, and A. Dallimore (2005) 'The impact of life skills education on adolescent sexual risk behaviors in KwaZulu-Natal, South Africa', *Journal of Adolescent Health* 36(4) 289–304.

Makoni, H. B. (2006) '"Victims for being girls" – forced virginity testing in Zimbabwe', *Equals* 18.

Manchester, J. (2004) 'Hope, involvement and vision', *Transformation*, 54.

Martino, W. M. and Kehler (2006) 'Male teachers and the "boy" problem: an issue of recuperative masculinity politics', *McGill Journal of Education* 41(2): 113–31.

Mirembe, R. and L. Davies (2001) 'Is schooling a risk? Gender, power relations and school culture in Uganda', *Gender and Education* 13/4: 401–16.

Morrell, R. (2003) 'Silence, sexuality and HIV/AIDS in South African schools', *The Australian Education Researcher* 30(1): 41–62.

Morrell, R. (2006) 'Fathers, fatherhood and masculinity in South Africa', in L. Richter and R. Morrell (eds.), *Baba: Men and Fatherhood in South Africa*, Pretoria: HSRC Press.

Morrell, R. and L. Ouzgane (2005) *African Masculinities: Men in Africa from the Late Nineteenth Century to the Present,* New York and Basingstoke: Palgrave Macmillan.

Odora-Hoppers, C. (2005) 'Between "mainstreaming" and transformation: lessons and challenges for institutional change', in L. Chisholm and J. September (eds.) *Gender Equity in South African Education 1994–2004: Perspectives from Research, Government and the Unions*, Cape Town: HSRC.

Page, E. (2004) 'Gender and the Construction of Identities in Indian Elementary Education', Ph.D thesis, University of London (Institute of Education).

Parkes, J. (2005) 'Children's Engagements with Violence: A Study in a South African School', Ph.D thesis, University of London (Institute of Education).

Parkes, J. (2007) 'The multiple meanings of violence: children's talk about life in a South African neighbourhood', *Childhood* 14(4): 401–14.

Pattman, R. and F.Chege (2003) *Finding our Voices: Gendered and Sexual Identities and HIV/AIDS in Education*, Nairobi: UNICEF.

Phaladze, N. and S. Tlou (2006) 'Gender and HIV/AIDS in Botswana: A focus on inequalities and discrimination', *Gender and Development* 14(1): 23–35.

Pronyk, P. M., J. R. Hargreaves, J. C. Kim, L. A. Morison, G. Phetla, C. Watts, J. Busza, and J. D. H. Porter (2006) 'Effect of a structural intervention for the prevention of intimate-partner violence and HIV in rural South Africa: a cluster randomised trial', *Lancet*, 368(9551): 1973–83.

Pulizzi, S. and L. Rosenblum (2007) *Building a Gender Friendly School Environment: A Toolkit for Educators and Their Unions*, Brussels: Education International.

Raynor, J. (2008) 'Schooling girls: an intergenerational study of women's burdens in rural Bangladesh', in S. Fennell and M. Arnot (eds.) *Gender, Education and Equality in a Global Context: Conceptual Frameworks and Policy Perspectives*, London: Routledge.

Reid, G. and L. Walker (2005) *Men Behaving Differently: South African Men Since 1994*, Cape Town: Double Storey/ Juta.

Rooth, E. (2005) 'An Investigation of the Status and Practice of Life Orientation in South African Schools in Two Provinces', unpublished Ph.D thesis, Cape Town: University of the Western Cape.

Royce, R. A., A. Sena, W. Cates Jr., and M. S. Cohen (1997) 'Sexual transmission of HIV', *New England Journal of Medicine* 336(15): 1072–8.

Shaeffer, S. (1994) *The Impact of HIV/AIDS on Education: A Review of Literature and Experience*, Paris: UNESCO.

Stromquist, N. (1995) 'Romancing the state: gender and power in education', *Comparative Education Review*, 39(4): 423–54.

Thorpe, M. (2005) 'Learning about HIV/AIDS in schools: does a gender-equality approach make a difference?', in S. Aikman and E. Unterhalter (eds.) *Beyond Access: Transforming Policy and Practice for Gender Equality in Education*, Oxford: Oxfam GB.

UNAIDS (2004) 'Report on the Global HIV/AIDS Epidemic', Geneva: UNAIDS.

UNAIDS (2006) 'Report on the Global HIV/AIDS Epidemic', Geneva: UNAIDS.

UNAIDS (2007) 'AIDS Epidemic Update', Geneva: UNAIDS.

UNAIDS IATT on Education (2006a) 'Report on the Education Sector Global HIV/AIDS Readiness Survey 2004', Paris: IIEP.

UNAIDS IATT on Education (2006b) *Quality Education and HIV & AIDS*, Paris: IIEP.

UNAIDS IATT on Education (2006c) 'Review of the Evidence: Girls' Education and HIV Prevention', CD-Rom, Paris, UNESCO, www.unesco.org/aids/iatt

UNAIDS IATT on Education (2008) *Toolkit for Mainstreaming HIV and AIDS in the Education Sector: Guidelines for Development Cooperation Agencies*, Paris: UNESCO.

UNESCO (2005) *EFA Global Monitoring Report 2004*, Paris: UNESCO.

UNESCO (2006a) 'Focus', *Education Today* 15.

UNESCO (2006b) *EFA Global Monitoring Report 2007,* Paris: UNESCO.

UNESCO (2007) *EFA Global Monitoring Report 2008,* Paris: UNESCO.

United Nations (2005) 'The Millennium Development Goals Report 2005', New York: United Nations.

Unterhalter, E. (2007) *Gender, Schooling and Global Social Justice*, London: Routledge.

Vavrus, F. (2003) *Desire and Decline: Schooling Amid Crisis in Tanzania*, New York: Peter Lang.

Voluntary Service Overseas (VSO) (2006) *Reducing the Burden of HIV and AIDS Care on Women and Girls*, London: VSO.

Walker, L. (2005) 'Men behaving differently: South African men since 1994', *Culture, Health and Sexuality* 7(3): 225–38.

Wiggins, K. (2007) 'Loving or Lecturing? An Exploration of the Role of Male and Female Teachers in Response to the Educational Needs of Orphans of HIV and AIDS and Vulnerable Children in a South African Community', MA dissertation, University of London (Institute of Education).

2 Girls' education and vulnerability to HIV infection in Africa

James Hargreaves and Tania Boler

AIDS has been a reality in many parts of the world for more than 25 years. As the epidemic evolves and matures across areas of eastern and southern Africa, researchers have tried to keep pace with its changing course. Evidence often conflicts within and across countries and can – at times – lead to a frustrating situation in which the response is forced to rush ahead of the evidence.

In the field of education and HIV and AIDS, there have been two opposing points of view in which some have argued that individuals with higher levels of education are more vulnerable to HIV (Kelly 2006), whereas others argue that more education (especially girls' education) protects against HIV infection (see Global Campaign for Education 2004).

In the middle of this debate is growing evidence of the 'feminisation of the epidemic', in which girls and women are becoming disproportionately infected with the virus. Although there are a number of reasons why women might be more vulnerable to infection (see Glynn *et al.* 2001), many have suggested that underlying gender inequality leaves women vulnerable to HIV. One of the pivotal responses to this claim has been to promote universal girls' education in order to reduce HIV vulnerability.[1]

However, one underlying assumption is that higher levels of education reduce HIV vulnerability for girls. Yet the evidence varies considerably from country to country, over time, and across regions. Moreover, there is little understanding about how simply going to school might reduce HIV vulnerability, or how much schooling is needed: is primary schooling enough, or is it secondary education that really matters?

This chapter attempts to answer some of these questions by first discussing relevant results from recent systematic reviews of the evidence and then going on to discuss in detail the probable reasons behind these trends and potential responses to them.

Findings from the reviews

We and other authors have recently conducted systematic reviews of the association between educational attainment and HIV and sexual behaviour in Africa (Hargreaves and Glynn 2002; Hargreaves and Boler 2006; Hargreaves *et al.* 2008). Here we focus on the findings shown in those reports concerning young women. Therefore we include in our discussion studies reporting on the association between, on the one hand, an indicator of education (such as school attendance, years of schooling, or grade attained) and, on the other, indicators of sexual behaviour and/or prevalence or incidence of HIV infection among populations where young women were a key group. A number of other criteria were also applied in the reviews, summarised in Table 1 below.

Table 1: Criteria for inclusion in the systematic review

Excluded	Included
	Outcome variable = HIV prevalence or reported sexual behaviour
	Exposure variable = educational attainment or attendance in school
'Grey literature' from NGOs, UN agencies, etc.	Peer-reviewed articles in academic journals
Men-only studies	Women-only studies
	Studies on both men and women reported separately
	Studies on mixed-sex groups as long as they also adjusted for gender
Purely descriptive studies (e.g. no adjustment for possible confounders such as age)	Results adjusted for the possible confounding effects of other variables (at the bare minimum: age, gender, and setting)
	Studies that adjusted for factors on the causal pathway ('overadjusted') were also included, though this is not strictly appropriate
Fewer than 500 individuals in the study	More than 500 individuals in the study
Sample drawn from high-risk and minority groups	Sample broadly representative of the general population
Western and northern Africa	Southern, eastern, and central Africa

For the purposes of this chapter we deemed education to have had either a positive impact (more education, less risk), negative impact (more education, more risk), or no impact.

The impact of education on HIV rates

Among the articles reviewed, the outcome variables, education systems, populations, and ages are all different, making comparison highly complicated.

However, initial studies seemed to suggest that the more educated women are, the higher their risk of HIV (supporting the theory that more education leads to higher economic status, higher levels of mobility etc.) (Hargreaves and Glynn 2002). If this is the case, does this mean that the many different organisations campaigning for girls' education as the 'social vaccine' against HIV might be misdirected?

In a later paper, however, the studies were re-analysed and new data were added, considering the period in which they collected data to see if – like an evolving epidemic – the impact of education on HIV was also evolving (Hargreaves *et al.* 2008). This evidence suggested that, before 1996, more education was often related to higher HIV vulnerability. However, after 1996, more education was either not related to HIV vulnerability or was indicative of lower HIV vulnerability. Further, some studies examined the impact of education on HIV rates over time (either as cohort studies or serial cross-sectional surveys).

With few exceptions, the relationship between education and HIV was changing in the same direction: the negative impact of education on HIV (i.e. more educated, more HIV) was weakening over time. This might be caused by decreasing HIV vulnerability among more educated groups or by increasing vulnerability in the least educated groups.

These findings suggest that the following is happening: although girls' education may be linked to higher HIV vulnerability early in the HIV epidemic, this can be expected to change over time as the epidemic matures, with rising HIV vulnerability among uneducated groups and decreasing vulnerability among educated groups.

The impact of education on sexual behaviour

The reviews also examined the impact of girls' education on sexual behaviour such as age of first sexual activity (or sexual debut) and use of condoms (Hargreaves and Boler 2006; see Figure 1). This set of outcomes was more complicated to compare than data for HIV, as the outcomes can be measured in a variety of ways. For example, surveys vary from asking about condom use during last sexual activity to condom use in the last six months, twelve months, etc. To further complicate the analysis, it should be noted that these are *reported* sexual behaviours. It is impossible to know whether a person is telling the truth or saying something that sounds socially desirable.

In terms of sexual debut, there were seven articles that explicitly explored the link between young women's educational attainment and age of sexual debut. Five of these articles showed that more educated young women were more likely to delay sexual debut. The remaining two articles showed no association between education and sexual debut.

Although these results suggest a strong positive benefit of education, it is also possible that the relationship works in the opposite direction, and that girls who are more sexually active are more likely to drop out of school (because they become pregnant, for example).

All the studies on the impact of girls' education on condom use showed strikingly similar findings and provided by far the most conclusive and powerful message: more girls' education increases the chances that young women use condoms. Not a single study suggested that women with less education were more likely to use condoms.

The findings across the studies demonstrates very clearly how girls' education can help women to negotiate safer sex. This finding also flies in the face of an increasingly vocal minority who are claiming that condoms do not work in Africa.

Figure 1: Selected articles reporting associations with condom use

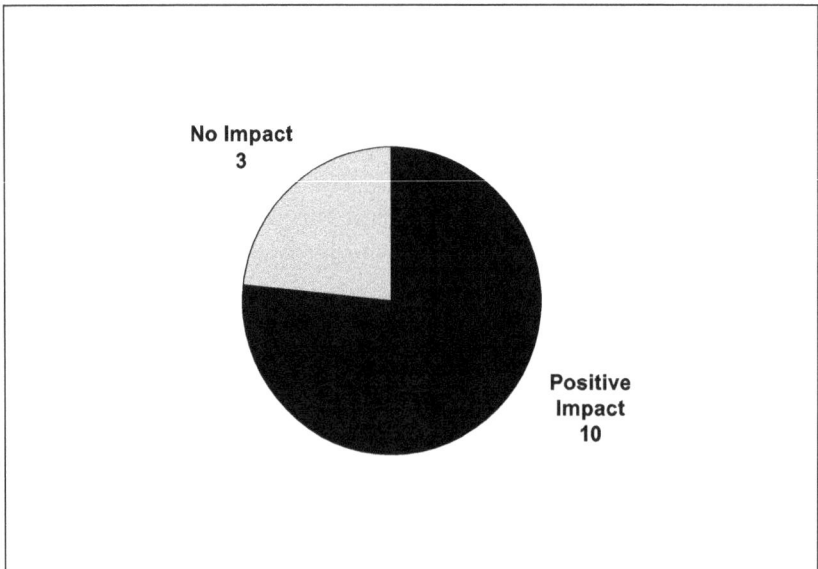

Discussion

The results from the reviews raised a number of questions. The first is to do with the extent to which the impact of education on HIV and sexual behaviour is the same for men and women. Although the review focused on girls' education, it was also possible to study ten gender-disaggregated studies. Seven out of the ten articles showed that the impact of education on HIV rates did not differ between men and women, and the remaining three articles showed highly mixed results. Similarly, the impact of education on sexual behaviour was broadly similar for men and women. Given these findings, it seems that the impact of education on HIV vulnerability does not differ remarkably between men and women.

A second question which arose from the review was whether or not secondary schooling or primary schooling had the largest impact on HIV vulnerability. The review found only six studies which differentiated the results by primary and secondary schooling. The results from these six studies are shown in Figure 2 below. It seems that, in most cases, secondary education had a greater impact on reducing HIV vulnerability for women than primary education (evidenced by increased condom use and reduced HIV rates).

Figure 2: Impact of girls' education on HIV vulnerability

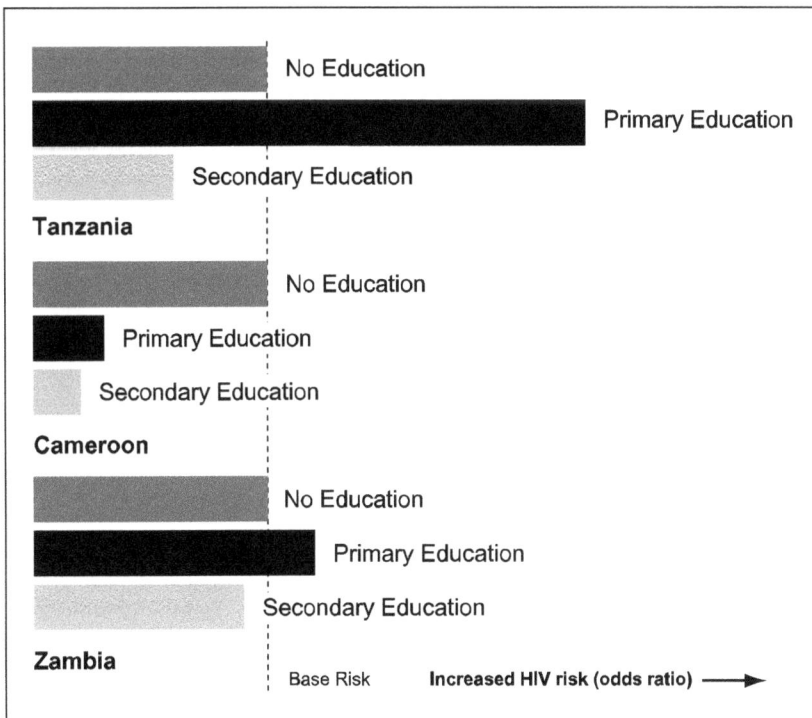

Taken together, these data suggest that as an epidemic matures, having more education reduces vulnerability to HIV. This is the case for both men and women, and it seems that the more education the better. The beneficial effects of education have been shown to work within an individual's lifetime but have also been passed through generations.

These findings are useful but do not quite go far enough. What is actually happening? What are the underlying mechanisms?

Possible mechanisms

Attending school and gaining a higher level of education can influence sexual behaviours in a number of different ways. These pathways are not independent, but for the sake of simplicity can be categorised as follows:

1. Contact with school-based HIV and AIDS education

2. Psychosocial benefits of education

3. Economic and lifestyle impacts of education

4. Power within sexual relationships

5. Social and sexual networks.

School-based HIV and AIDS education

As government and non-government responses to HIV and AIDS gather pace across sub-Saharan Africa, access to HIV-prevention messages has increased dramatically, and the information vacuum that existed a mere ten years ago is more and more of a rarity. Although HIV-prevention messages have taken advantage of a wide range of different media and have targeted many different sub-groups, research by ActionAid shows that the most trusted source for young people to learn about HIV is through schools and teachers (Boler 2003).

A recent survey conducted jointly by the Health Economics and HIV/AIDS Research Division (HEARD) at the University of KwaZulu–Natal and ActionAid shows that 85 per cent of countries with a high HIV prevalence[2] have established some sort of HIV and AIDS curriculum in primary schools (Badcock Walters and Boler 2004). Although the report also highlights the shocking implementation gap, it seems reasonable to conclude that attending school can increase a young person's contact with school-based HIV and AIDS education and thus reduce his or her vulnerability to infection.

Psychosocial benefits of education

Behavioural science and cognitive science have long emphasised the importance of not only providing information on how to change behaviour, but also trying to strengthen women's confidence and capacity to act on these messages. General education, even in the absence of school-based HIV and AIDS education, might help to improve such qualities. Conversely, the least educated members of society may have relatively low self-esteem, self-efficacy, and a negative outlook on the future (Marmot 2003). Consequently, they may be less likely to protect their health by having fewer sexual partners or using condoms. This will be particularly true when peer pressure is exerted in ways contradictory to HIV-prevention messages. A common example of this is being pressured by peers to have sex at an early age.

Economic and lifestyle impacts of education

Numerous studies have shown that increased education has a positive impact on economic prospects for both men and women, as more highly educated individuals are more likely to find regular employment and earn higher wages (Case and Deaton 1999). These economic benefits in turn influence a wide range of factors, including the spread of infectious diseases; more educated individuals are often more geographically and socially mobile.

In this scenario, the more education a person receives, the greater his or her vulnerability to HIV might be. Women with increased education may be more likely to form partnerships with more highly educated and richer men, who may have multiple partners and/or engage in commercial sex, thus increasing women's vulnerability to HIV infection. Greater mobility also puts young women of higher socio-economic status in contact with larger social and sexual networks, which could, in theory, increase their number of potential sexual partners.

On the flip side, among the poorest communities the economic opportunities afforded by a higher education may prevent women from entering into activities that carry a high risk of infection, such as commercial sex work or other relationships that are entered into primarily to provide resources. In this respect, girls' education might help protect women from HIV infection.

Power within sexual relationships

The ways in which girls' education might affect HIV vulnerability can be considered on both an absolute and a relative scale. While absolute levels of education might drive the pathways described above, the level of a young woman's education relative to her male partner's level of education also has important consequences. In many African settings, it remains socially acceptable for men to have many sexual partners, but unacceptable for women to do so (Luke 2003; Varga 1997). Within these same settings, women are often more likely to leave school early, be unemployed, and earn low wages (Gilbert and Walker 2002). These women are therefore entering into sexual relationships characterised by a significant power imbalance.

Such power imbalances within relationships are compounded by the common practice of young women going out with much older men. Older men might be seen to be better options as boyfriends and husbands by women and communities because they are in a better position to provide material support. Gifts and money are seen by many as an intrinsic component of any sexual relationship (Kaufman and Stavrou 2002), thus further increasing women's economic dependence. Both the inferiority in age and the economic dependence of women decrease their power to negotiate within sexual relationships.

What implications does this power imbalance within relationships have for HIV vulnerability? The problem is that it is often the men who dictate when to have sex and how. Since many men prefer not to use condoms (MacPhail and Campbell 2001), their wishes – within an unequal relationship – are very likely to prevail. Scxual violence is an extreme manifestation of this power imbalance within relationships and may particularly affect women who have not received much education, who in turn are less able to negotiate within a relationship.

Each of the scenarios above suggests that education is a positive factor in reducing HIV vulnerability for young women – but this is not always the case. Power imbalances within relationships are never more obvious than in relationships between teachers and students. Although the evidence is currently mostly anecdotal or qualitative in nature, an increasing number of studies suggest that some male teachers in African schools abuse their higher position of power to initiate sex with female students (Wellesley Centers for Research on Women 2003). For the economic and power-related reasons cited above, it may even be the case that some female students and their parents encourage such relationships. Whatever the circumstances, the gross power imbalance between a teacher and a student can place a young woman in a position of high vulnerability.

Social and sexual networks

Another potential pathway between girls' education and HIV vulnerability is related to factors associated with going to school, rather than overall educational attainment.

Attending school influences the social network of a young person, affecting the group of people with whom he or she has contact. In turn, these contact patterns may influence the formation of sexual partnerships. Research suggests that HIV vulnerability is influenced by the size of a person's sexual network and an individual's position within that network (Doherty *et al.* 2005). The effects could be either positive or negative. On the positive side, being at school might limit the pool of potential sexual partners and thus reduce the number of partners. It is also plausible that young women at school are more likely to choose boyfriends within school who are of a similar age and are therefore less sexually experienced than older men (thus reducing their vulnerability to HIV infection).

Some studies have also shown that being at school can lead to positive communication, group bonding, and group negotiating within social networks, which in turn can create more positive attitudes towards sex and HIV (Campbell 2003; Campbell and MacPhail 2002). This group negotiation is thought to occur both within gender groups and across them. School attendance may also encourage the formation of peer groups that understand about HIV and have more positive attitudes towards safer sex (Gregson *et al.* 2004). Conversely, young people who drop out of school are more likely to enter into adult sexual networks where older partners with more experience and power dictate the 'rules' of sexual engagement.

Of course, attendance in school is not always uniformly a good thing for girls. Sometimes schools are institutions that allow gender inequality and discrimination to thrive. They can become places that tolerate violence and sexual abuse, whether by older boys or by teachers. A recent report by ActionAid suggests that sexual violence within schools is a serious problem in a number of countries (ActionAid 2003).

Early in the epidemic, when more highly educated women were more vulnerable to HIV, it is likely that the third pathway was the main mechanism through which education was impacting on HIV: more highly educated people used their higher status and economic powers to have more sexual partners. A strong possibility now is that coming from a richer household means a girl stays in school longer and – independently – means she can protect herself from HIV. In this scenario, the effects of being in school may be confounding the underlying issue, which is poverty.

As the AIDS epidemic has matured, the opposite impact of education is taking place; more highly educated women have lower vulnerability to HIV. Unfortunately, studies have rarely examined what the underlying mechanism for this might be. In general, there is a dearth of evidence on why girls' education influences HIV vulnerability.

The results from the study of the impact of education on sexual behaviour suggest that more education results most notably in increased condom use, so it is very possible that this is the reason why more educated women are now able to protect themselves from HIV. This still leaves us with little understanding of how more education leads to more condom use in the first place. Some exploratory work in South Africa suggests that the creation of positive social networks in school might create enabling environments for condom use (Hargreaves 2006). If this is the case, women will still need a certain level of power within sexual relationships in order to benefit from these social networks.

It is very important to understand what the mechanisms underlying the relationship between girls' education and HIV vulnerability might be. It is possible that there is nothing specific about being in school that affects HIV vulnerability. It could be that girls who stay longer in school come from different social backgrounds and that these background characteristics affect HIV rates. Some of the studies above did control for these background characteristics (e.g. economic status), which suggests that education is having an effect independently of economic status. In turn, this suggests that the impact of education is also operating through some of the psychosocial pathways. Identifying these mechanisms is hugely important in informing our prevention messages more broadly.

Conclusions and recommendations

Early in the AIDS epidemic, higher levels of girls' education were associated with better economic prospects and more mobility. It is likely that these factors increased women's vulnerability to HIV.

However, as the epidemic has evolved, the relationship between girls' education and HIV has also changed. Now, more highly educated girls and young women are more likely to be able to negotiate safer sex and reduce HIV rates. The more education the better – although even the most educated women are still vulnerable to infection. It is not certain what some of the underlying mechanisms might be, but the data on sexual behaviour suggest that increased condom use among more highly educated women might be the answer. However, even if the reason is increased condom use, the question still remains, why are more educated women more able to negotiate safer sex? It may be through more positive attitudes towards condoms being fostered in social networks in school, and/or more power and balance within relationships over how to have sex. Furthermore, if more highly educated women are changing their behaviour because of HIV, then clearly HIV messages are also having an effect.

What seems to become clear is that education can play a key role in enabling girls and women to process and apply messages that they hear about HIV and

AIDS. It is likely that girls outside of school do receive some of the same messages (e.g. through radio, religious groups, etc.), but education can make a difference by providing girls and women with the capacity to apply the messages in their own lives. What is less clear is what kind of education can help build this capacity, and how to ensure that all girls have the opportunity to benefit from education.

This chapter was based on the ActionAid International report 'Girl Power' (2006).[3] Oxfam and the authors are grateful to ActionAid for permission to use material from this report.

Notes

1   For example, UNAIDS Global Coalition on Women and AIDS, Global Campaign for Education, Global AIDS Alliance.

2   Out of 71 countries around the world.

3   J. Hargreaves and T. Boler (2006) 'Girl Power: the impact of girls' education on sexual behaviour and HIV', ActionAid International. Available at: www.actionaid.org.uk/100296/hiv__aids.html

References

ActionAid (2003) 'Global Education Review', London: ActionAid.

Badcock Walters, P. and T. Boler (2004) 'Education Sector Global Readiness HIV and AIDS Survey: Policy Implications for Education and Development', London: Actionaid.

Boler, T. (2003) 'The Sound of Silence', London: ActionAid.

Campbell, C. (2003) *'Letting Them Die': Why HIV/AIDS Prevention Programmes Fail*, Oxford: James Currey.

Campbell, C. and C. Macphail (2002) 'Peer education, gender and the development of critical consciousness: participatory HIV prevention by South African youth', *Social Science and Medicine* 55: 331–45.

Case, A. and A. Deaton (1999) 'School inputs and educational outcomes in South Africa', *Quarterly Journal of Economics* 114(3): 1047–84

Doherty, I.A., N.S. Padian, C. Marlow, and S.O. Aral (2005) 'Determinants and consequences of sexual networks as they affect the spread of sexually transmitted infections', *Journal of Infectious Diseases* 191 Suppl 1: S42–54.

Fylkesnes, K., R.M. Musonda, M. Sichone, Z. Ndhlovu, F. Tembo, and M. Monze (2001) 'Declining HIV prevalence and risk behaviours in Zambia: evidence from surveillance and population based surveys', *AIDS* 15: 907–16.

Gilbert, L. and L. Walker (2002) 'Treading the path of least resistance: HIV/AIDS and social inequalities: a South African case study', *Social Science and Medicine* 54(7): 1093–110.

Global Campaign for Education (2004) 'Learning to Survive: How Education for All Would Save Millions of Young People from HIV/AIDS'.

Glynn, J.R., M. Carael, B. Auvert, et al. (2001) 'Why do young women have a much higher prevalence of HIV than young men? A study in Kisumu, Kenya and Ndola, Zambia', *AIDS* 15 Suppl 4: S51–60.

Gregson, S., N. Terceira, P. Mushati, C. Nyamukapa, and C. Campbell (2004) 'Community group participation: can it help young women to avoid HIV? An exploratory study of social capital and school education in rural Zimbabwe', *Social Science and Medicine* 58(11): 2119–32.

Hargreaves, J.R. (2006) 'The Social Epidemiology of HIV Infection: A Study Among Unmarried Young People in Rural South Africa in 2001', University of London.

Hargreaves J.R. and T. Boler (2006) 'Girl Power: The Impact of Girls' Education on HIV and Sexual Behaviour', London: ActionAid International.

Hargreaves J.R. and J. Glynn (2002) 'Educational attainment and HIV-1 infection in developing countries: a systematic review', *Tropical Medicine and International Health* 7(6): 489–98.

Hargreaves J.R., C.P. Bonell, T. Boler, D. Boccia, I. Birdthistle, A. Fletcher, P.M. Pronyk, and J.R. Glynn (2008) 'Systematic review exploring time trends in the association between educational attainment and risk of HIV infection in sub-Saharan Africa', *AIDS* 22(3): 404–14.

Kaufman, C. and S.E. Stavrou (2002) '"Bus fare, please": the economics of sex and gifts among adolescents in urban South Africa', New York: Population Council.

Kelly, M. (2006) 'The potential contribution of schooling to rolling back HIV and AIDS', Commonwealth Youth and Development.

Luke, N. (2003) 'Age and economic asymmetries in the sexual relationships of adolescent girls in sub-Saharan Africa', *Studies in Family Planning* 34(2): 67–86.

MacPhail, C. and C. Campbell (2001) '"I think condoms are good but, aaai, I hate those things": condom use among adolescents and young people in a Southern African township', *Social Science and Medicine* 52: 1613–27.

Marmot, M. (2003) 'Self esteem and health', *British Medical Journal* 327(7415): 574–5.

Varga, C.A. (1997) 'Sexual decision-making and negotiation in the midst of AIDS: youth in Kwazulu Natal, South Africa', *Health Transition Review* (supplement) 7: 45–67.

3 Gender inequality in primary education in the context of HIV and AIDS: a challenge for Uganda

Doris M. Kakuru

Introduction

In the past decade, access to primary education for pupils in Uganda has increased, leading to the achievement of gender parity in enrolment (i.e. an equal number of girls and boys attending school). However, gender inequalities in school and classroom participation, attendance, and learning outcomes persist (Kakuru 2003; Kasente 2003; Okuni 2003; Kakuru 2006; Kakuru 2007). Over the years, various measures have been implemented to address the inequalities. A number of factors have been considered responsible for the persistence of educational inequalities, including the influence of patriarchal beliefs, values, and practices (Kwesiga 2003). HIV and AIDS have been blamed for reinforcing existing forms of social inequalities, including gender inequalities (Barnett 2004; Mohlahlane 2006; Kakuru 2007).

Gender inequality has been described as a form of denial of equal treatment and opportunity (Unterhalter 2003; Aikman and Unterhalter 2005; Subrahmanian 2005). It is reinforced by poverty which perpetuates unequal access to national, community, and household resources. It is multi-faceted and has numerous causes, and numerous consequences for the economy and social relations. One feature of gender inequality is unequal gender power relations due to the patriarchal nature of cultural beliefs, values, and practices. Gender inequality is a cause as well as a consequence of HIV and AIDS.

In order to explore these issues I draw on small-scale research in rural Uganda that examines the persistence of gender inequalities in the education sector in the context of efforts to address the epidemic. I will argue that although Uganda has done a great deal of work in terms of expanding access to primary education, this has not resulted in gender-equality gains at the grassroots level. One of the reasons for this is a fundamental disjuncture between policy and practice in terms of the education sector's response to HIV. In particular, the Presidential Initiative on AIDS Strategy for Communicating to Young People (PIASCY), with its focus on abstinence and the moral judgements associated with it, has created problems that have acted as barriers to improvements in gender equality.

The study reveals inequalities in children's opportunities to advance to upper primary, and consequently to secondary education. Prior to the implementation of universal primary education (UPE) in Uganda, the tuition-fees requirement was assumed to be the major cause of disparities in school dropout, as those who could afford it continued with schooling, and those who couldn't dropped out. The government of Uganda has achieved remarkable success through the education-promotion campaign launched in 1996 (Cameron 2005). In fact, Uganda has almost achieved gender parity in primary-school enrolment, with national rates at 49.6 per cent for girls and 50.4 per cent for boys (Ministry of Education and Sports 2005). However, one of the greatest challenges for the Ministry of Education and Sports since the implementation of UPE is still school dropout. For example, there was an increase in dropout rates from 12 per cent to 20 per cent between 2001 and 2004, while completion rates declined (Cameron 2005). This is attributable to a multiplicity of factors.

Education and HIV prevalence in Uganda

Education

Formal education in Uganda was introduced by missionaries in the 1880s and supported by the colonial government until 1925. Thereafter, the government took full responsibility, but only a few people had access to education. The need to improve equality in access to education was first pointed out in the Castle Commission of 1963,[1] and later emphasised by the 1992 Government White Paper on Education, which recommended the introduction of UPE. UPE was implemented in 1997, and this led to a rapid expansion of primary education. Primary-school enrolment increased from 2.7 million in 1997 to 7.3 million in 2003, constituting an estimated 85 per cent of all children of primary-school age (Ministry of Education and Sports 2004). The general increase in enrolments was accompanied by a rise in enrolment in areas with the highest illiteracy rates, and a growth in enrolment among girls, children with special needs, and rural children. However, despite the successes of UPE, some children still had no access to school, due to social, economic, and environmental reasons including gender inequality and the consequences of HIV (Ministry of Education and Sports 2004). Primary-school attendance, participation, and completion rates are still inadequate (McGee 2000; Cameron 2005; Kakuru 2006).

HIV prevalence

Uganda has made great progress in reducing the national adult HIV prevalence rate from a high 29 per cent in the 1990s to a current 6.5 per cent (Uganda AIDS

Commission 2006). But currently in some districts there appears to be a rise in HIV infection, with prevalence increasing from six to eight per cent in the last three years (Ministry of Health and ORC Marco 2006; UNAIDS/WHO 2006). Although by December 2006, the national adult HIV prevalence rate still stood at 6.5 per cent (UNAIDS/WHO 2006), there were indications that the rate is increasing among certain subgroups of the population. For example, Shafer's (2006) analysis of antenatal clinic-based surveillance and general-population cohort data shows that between 2001 and 2004, Uganda's HIV prevalence increased from 5.6 per cent to 6.5 per cent among men, and from 6.9 per cent to 8.8 per cent among women. Shafer also shows that prevalence data from 24 antenatal clinics reflect an increase in ten sites, a decline in seven sites, and no change in seven other sites. The rising HIV prevalence is blamed on complacency and decreased intensity of prevention programmes, gaps in funding, and fluctuating political commitment (Ministry of Health and ORC Marco 2006). This all points to a need to acquire new prevention strategies, and intensify those that exist.

The response of the education sector to HIV and AIDS

The education sector has an important role to play in addressing HIV. Education has the potential to reduce both prevalence and stigma, as schools are able to reach millions of young people before they become sexually active. Schools can provide knowledge as well as protection, thereby reducing overall vulnerability to HIV infection (International Institute for Educational Planning/UNESCO 2003). In order to intensify the fight against HIV and AIDS, achievement of gender equality in the education context should be prioritised (*ibid.*), but exactly how gender inequality presents challenges to the education sector in addressing HIV and AIDS has not generally been clearly documented.

Shortfalls in attendance due to gender inequality, HIV, and poverty

Gender is a key feature of shortfalls in school attendance, participation, and completion (Kwesiga 2003; Bitamazire 2005). Although gender equality is one of the objectives of UPE, a recently concluded study shows that inequality persists (Kakuru 2006). One of the major factors fuelling gender inequality in primary education is the impact of HIV and AIDS on household livelihoods. In Zimbabwe and Swaziland, studies show that HIV and AIDS have a negative impact on children's living arrangements and schooling (Mushunje 2006; Poulsen 2006).

Children from households with good economic status are significantly more likely to attend primary as well as secondary school, with boys enjoying a five per cent higher probability than girls (Deininger 2003). The tuition-fee requirement for all secondary-school pupils (in place until January 2007) was one factor which deterred very poor parents from supporting children to complete primary school, as they recognised they would never be able to enrol in secondary school. This particularly affected orphaned children and adolescents who had not managed to make progress in primary school and were in the lower grades, despite being teenagers. In a context of AIDS-induced poverty, fewer girls than boys were able to advance to the secondary level of education. By 2005, there was a gender imbalance in total secondary-school enrolment of 55:45 per cent in favour of boys (Ministry of Education and Sports 2005). Unfortunately, even after the current implementation of universal secondary education (USE) in Uganda, it is most likely that the Ministry of Education and Sports will continue to face challenges similar to those faced in implementing UPE with regard to the achievement of gender equality in school completion, with gender inequality and HIV exacerbating the experience of poverty.

Thus despite some successes in expanding access to education, inequalities, and in particular gender inequalities, persist. Although Uganda has seen some success in tackling HIV rates, this has not been associated with corresponding improvements in school attendance or participation by girls, and, alarmingly, there is evidence that infection rates are rising. What policies and processes in the Ministry of Education are associated with these developments?

Policies and processes

The response of Uganda's education sector to HIV and AIDS is part of the country's multi-sectoral approach to HIV and AIDS prevention and mitigation. Within this approach, HIV and AIDS activities and programmes have been mainstreamed in all government ministries, including the Ministry of Education and Sports. The national strategic framework for HIV and AIDS activities 2001–2005/6 was developed out of a consultation process among stakeholders working towards HIV and AIDS prevention and care. The framework was inspired by the understanding that HIV and AIDS need multi-pronged responses that should be integrated into all aspects of developmental work, service provision, and government plans and activities. The response of the Ministry of Education and Sports to HIV and AIDS consists of an effort to fit into the national HIV and AIDS strategy.

The education-sector response to HIV and AIDS includes the policy that guides workplace interventions, and prevention education carried out through schools and institutions. The response focuses on capacity-building, provision of information on the impact of HIV and AIDS, and strong co-ordination at national and district levels. The work is guided by an assurance that communication on behavioural change is effective in the education system at all levels.

Age-appropriate prevention messages are passed on to young people through curricular and extra-curricular activities. Efforts have also been put into curriculum development and delivery and enhancement of knowledge and skills among teachers and pupils.

Various activities and programmes have been implemented (Ssemakula 2004). The PIASCY programme is one major initiative to provide information, education, and communication (IEC) in schools. This is a nationwide school-based HIV-prevention curriculum aimed at reaching every single pupil in the country's estimated 14,000 primary schools. Through PIASCY, abstinence and life-skills education are promoted among school-aged children. Teachers are given manuals that include chapters on how HIV is transmitted, how to protect oneself from infection, how to 'say no' to sex, and how to avoid sexual violence. There is a PIASCY curriculum for primary and secondary education. Plans are also under way to develop guidelines for teachers on how to deal with HIV and AIDS challenges in schools. However, this programme has been criticised for putting too much emphasis on abstinence and ignoring the importance of advocating safer sex among sexually active adolescents (see Cohen and Tate 2005).

The Ministry of Education and Sports should be commended for the various initiatives put in place to address the AIDS pandemic. However, the threat of possibly rising HIV prevalence rates amidst the current preventive efforts implies that more needs to be done. The extent to which existing HIV-prevention messages in school are relevant to the life situations of their intended audience, and the ways in which they are understood, given existing forms of gender inequality, are two issues that must be addressed.

Researching the impact of HIV on gender inequality in the educational context

To understand some of these issues, a small-scale study was conducted by the author as part of her doctoral research (University of Wageningen) in Luwero district in central rural Uganda between June 2004 and June 2005. It focused on how the impact of HIV and AIDS on rural households contributes to the persistence of gender inequalities despite the introduction of UPE. The research was ethnographic by design, involving three primary schools and their surrounding villages. Two of the schools were government-owned, and the third was a private school. The two government schools were slightly different in terms of size and quality of education. One was bigger and had better infrastructure and human resources. The private school did not have better facilities but had better-trained and motivated teachers.

People in the area depend on subsistence farming. They grow crops for food, and some households have a little surplus for sale. Many households had experience of HIV and AIDS; either they had lost a family member to AIDS, or a member of their family had become infected with the virus, or they were hosting a child or children affected and made vulnerable by HIV and AIDS, or at least supporting or neighbouring an AIDS-afflicted household.

I worked at each of the schools as a teacher and researcher. I observed lessons and other school activities such as assemblies, prayers, general cleaning, and sports. I selected 36 AIDS-afflicted households to participate in the study, and eight of these were used for in-depth study. Data-collection methods included participant observation, life stories, and in-depth interviews. Key informants included representatives of the Ministry of Education and Sports, local council leaders at village, sub-county, and district levels, and representatives of NGOs working in HIV and AIDS and girls' education. I conducted focus groups and conversations within households and with teachers and school children. In addition, I collected and analysed secondary data from a variety of relevant sources.

Reduced opportunity for girls to attend school

Girls in the households studied are denied equal opportunities in several ways. For example, HIV causes cash and labour shortages, and girls are required to work in the household to produce food and cash, as well as to take care of young, elderly, and sick members. There was a gender-biased division of household labour that interfered with girls' schooling. For example, women and girls undertook most household tasks. They also contributed labour for food preparation and associated tasks during village funerals and feasts. Men on the other hand were expected to make contributions in terms of cash, but rarely fulfilled their obligations. As the consequences of HIV and AIDS bite deep, household labour shortage is the order of the day.

Girls have less bargaining power within the household than boys. Whereas all pupils undertook household tasks before school, boys could easily just refuse, unlike girls. Boys also had fewer responsibilities, and this was an advantage because they normally left the house before girls. Girls therefore did the last-minute tasks which were often identified only when the boys had already left. This is a demonstration of failure of the household to provide equal opportunities for all children to be at school in time for learning. The situation is of course worse in AIDS-afflicted households, where loss of labour has led to an increase in children's participation in household chores, and where children also join in with cropping and income-earning activities before school. It is thus not surprising that gender inequalities in primary schooling persist, and their persistence is reinforced by the impact of HIV and AIDS on rural households.

Some children from AIDS-affected households experienced food and income insufficiency. In addition, they alleged that they were mistreated at home.

> *Sometimes when we come from school, we don't find any food to eat at home. Instead, we are allocated work to do. Even when you have a problem to tell the adults at home, nobody can listen to you before you complete the task allocated to you.*
> (Orphan, Tumo)

This quotation shows that there were differences in children's access to basic needs like food. This was particularly true for girls who lived with relatives as fostered children. They were engaged in all sorts of household chores and sometimes went without food, especially when they were out fetching water at meal times. None of the parents/guardians admitted to discriminating between their own and fostered children, although it was a common complaint among the children. Such girls were therefore vulnerable to giving in to the temptation of exchanging sex for gifts and money, which often led to their dropping out of school.

In the study area, inequality in primary education was perceived to take various forms, and the impact of the HIV epidemic featured in each of them. For example, the study findings show that girls were less able to attend school than boys, due to gender imbalances in the household division of labour. Girls were automatically required to fill any labour gaps resulting from illness of a household member or a funeral in the neighbourhood, even if this meant missing school for days or weeks. Girls from households with a bed-ridden AIDS patient(s), those whose parents had died of AIDS (and were therefore fostered by relatives), and those whose households had fostered orphans were most vulnerable to irregular school attendance. The following statement is an example of a typical explanation for irregular attendance:

> *If there is a sick person at home, I cannot go to school until the patient recovers. In case the person wants something to eat or drink, I have to improvise even if there is nothing in the house. Sometimes our patient soils her bed and I have to clean it because I am the 'outsider' in the home.*
> (13-year-old orphan girl at Tulo)

This quotation shows that in that particular household there was discrimination between biological and fostered children. Orphans in particular bear a disproportionate burden of labour. Such discrimination was also reflected in the provision of opportunities to attend school. AIDS and related orphanhood contributed to inequalities in opportunities to attend school daily.

Girls were more likely to be late for school than boys, due to last-minute requests. Girls in AIDS-affected households normally arrived at school later than other children, and therefore faced associated consequences in learning and achievement, as well as punishment by teachers. All schools that participated in this study had strict schedules, and all children were equally required to adhere to them. However, it was not always possible for everybody to fulfil the promptness requirement. Children in all three schools walked varying distances to school. Whereas variations in distances walked can be perceived as a justification for differences in tardiness, it is not the sole reason for the observed gender differences. In reality, gender differences in tardiness can largely be attributed to the household livelihood situation, including the unequal division of labour. Girls often pointed out that it was quite common for them to be asked to undertake some last-minute tasks before they left for school. Such tasks include fetching water, food from the garden, or something from the shop:

> *Usually I wake up and plan my time knowing it takes about 50 minutes to reach school. Then sometimes just before I set off, someone calls me and sends me to the well or to the shops. Remember the shops are not near! Or they can ask you to go to collect food from the garden. And by the time I return, if it's already too late I decide to stay at home that day.*
> (11-year-old schoolgirl at Tumo)

> *I stay in a home with little children who depend on me for assistance in many ways because my aunt is never at home. She wakes up early to go to work in her gardens every day. I have to do all the household work alone, which includes taking care of the children. I fetch water, clean the house, cook the food, and wash the dishes for everybody. On week days, I have to do all this including cooking food for the little ones before I go to school…In case one of them [children] is sick, I have to stay at home and sometimes my aunt tells me to take the sick child to the health centre for treatment instead of going to school.*
> (12-year-old orphan girl at Tulo)

Meeting children's needs

In the schools studied, it was discovered that apart from tuition fees, children's survival in education depended on their ability to have their material and non-material needs met. Pupils were in need of materials such as stationery, clothes, and meals, as well as intangible things such as psychosocial support. Psychosocial needs were particularly pressing for orphans and other children made vulnerable by HIV and AIDS who were fostered by relatives or lived in child-headed households.

Girls were vulnerable to school dropout as a result of pregnancy. Some of them were tempted to engage in sexual relations with older men in the village in order to satisfy their material needs. Such girls thought these things would make them happy, but were unable to access them because of their household economic situation. Next to one of the schools, there was a bicycle/motorcycle taxi (commonly known as *boda-boda*) stage. The *boda-boda* cyclists were identified as posing the biggest temptation for schoolgirls, since they got a daily income and could afford to buy small gifts for the girls. This explains why pregnancy was found to be a major cause of dropout among girls in the study schools. In a study of secondary-school children in Masaka, Uganda, Hardon (2005) found that girls' engagement in commercial sex was linked to the need to 'prove themselves' as normal adolescents. However, this did not come up in the Luwero research. Girls' and their parents/guardians perceived their engagement in commercial sex as a desperate measure, because parents and guardians were unable to fulfil their children's desire for material things:

> *We as parents try to give children equal opportunities, but girls get spoilt easily. Girls of these days don't have patience. They want to have shoes and nice clothes. That's why I think girls need to study when they are still young. We have children here who are 16 years and are still in primary schools. They meet many men on the way who disturb [seduce] them. Our children get spoilt because they delay in primary schools, yet they have no patience. They lose hope quickly and think that the easy means for them to have shoes is through accepting money from someone. All mothers are worried because girls don't listen.*
> (Parent at Tumo)

The desire for material items such as shoes was also driven by the need to earn some prestige and peer influence:

> *Some children are proud and abuse others. Many children at school don't have shoes. Some people have shoes but don't want to wear them every day. The few who put on shoes usually abuse us and even step on us. For example on speech day, I came and I also participated in singing, but other children shouted at me saying, 'You are embarrassing us'. Moreover, some girls who were shouting at us got money to buy shoes from boyfriends. There is a girl who missed PLE [Primary Leaving Examinations] the other year [2003] after she got pregnant; but she used to wear shoes every day.*
> (Girl orphan at Tulo)

Going to school without shoes attracted some form of harassment and embarrassment specifically in upper classes. The above quotation shows that it was not unusual for some schoolgirls to get gifts like shoes from men, and that pregnancy sometimes occurred. Many girls who had dropped out of school due to pregnancy got married at a young age.

For boys in difficult economic situations, the major cause of dropout was the temptation to work for money through providing labour or engaging in some petty trade. However, boys generally found it easy to re-enrol in school. Girls' vulnerability to school dropout is higher than that of boys, since it is associated with sex for commercial gain, leading to pregnancy. Free education alone does not protect against this.

AIDS-induced poverty

In the villages studied, there was a connection between household livelihoods and the teaching/learning environment. Many households had suffered loss of labour and income due to AIDS-related morbidity and mortality. Indeed, household sizes for many had increased due to the constant influx of orphans as foster children. Such households were literally overwhelmed as they became increasingly vulnerable to food and income insecurity whenever they had to take on an extra member. Their poverty became more serious as a result of HIV and AIDS. They experienced a sort of 'AIDS-induced poverty'. In response, AIDS-afflicted households tend to reduce their expenditure on education and also increase children's involvement in income-earning. Reduced expenditure on education compelled affected children to go to school without the required learning materials such as stationery, lunch, and clothing. Whereas boys had opportunities to earn income either through providing labour or engaging in petty trade, girls were confined to the household, where their tasks were essential to daily survival. Boys, in effect, had access to income to spend on their school needs, unlike girls. Gender inequalities in access to financial capital/income to cater for school and individual needs also yielded inequalities in classroom participation and learning outcomes.

Implications for HIV prevention and care

The persistence of gender inequality as a result of AIDS-induced poverty is a challenge for the education sector in various ways. Gender inequality contributes to the social conditions that facilitate the spread of HIV and AIDS. These include poverty, unequal access to information, inadequate access to health care, and discrimination. The role of education in HIV prevention is hampered by the nature of gender inequalities, because they affect sexual attitudes, practices, and behaviour. Females tend to remain more vulnerable to HIV infection despite the existence of HIV-prevention programmes. For example, school AIDS-education messages continue to be undermined by society-wide gender relations and associated educational inequalities. Consequently, such messages do not make the intended impact. Some girls continue to engage in sexual relationships with older men, not necessarily because they are ignorant of the consequences. The major existing school-based programme PIASCY is implemented by teachers in school assemblies, without much community involvement. Schools could partner with the community in implementing AIDS and sex education, as a means to discourage adult males who lure girls into sex. Increased community involvement could reduce the scare about community complacency regarding HIV and AIDS education messages, since it acts as a constant reminder of the reality of AIDS and the need to take precautions (Kakuru and Mulder 2007).

In rural areas such as Luwero, the consequences of the interface between HIV and poverty fall differently on schoolchildren of different sexes. The education sector faces the challenge of how to counteract processes in households and schools that perpetuate gender inequalities, which undermine the effectiveness of responses to the epidemic. The Ministry of Education and Sports has put in place measures to educate children about the dangers associated with engaging in sexual relations. For example, various messages are displayed on posts in school compounds. Most HIV-prevention messages in schools are abstinence-orientated: 'choose to abstain', 'say no to sex', 'virginity is healthy', 'say no to bad touches', and 'say no to gifts for sex'. Despite the fundamental importance of knowledge in the fight against HIV, and despite the fact that access to HIV and AIDS information is a human right (Cohen and Tate 2005), safer-sex information is withheld from primary-school children in Uganda. In fact Cohen and Tate (2005) document a recent removal of condom-use information from the HIV and AIDS curricula on the grounds that pupils received 'too much' or unnecessary awareness. The reason for the emphasis on abstinence at the expense of safer sex in primary schools is to avoid conflict between the two strategies. The Luwero research shows that some primary-school pupils are sexually active and are thus in need of this information. The emphasis on abstinence seems to be based on the assumption that all children's life situations are similar. The differences in children's individual values and circumstances, such as economic disadvantage and desperation, are ignored. There is a need to promote widespread awareness of HIV and AIDS while bearing in mind that 'one size does not fit all'. The Ministry of Education and Sports must revise the existing HIV-education messages to avoid excluding children who are already sexually active.

The increasing rate of school dropouts has implications for children's vulnerability to HIV and AIDS. Large numbers of children who have dropped out of school, many of them girls, are not accessing the prevention messages associated with the school-based initiatives.

Teachers are not yet trained well enough on how to deal with problems experienced by children who are affected and made vulnerable by HIV and AIDS. The research revealed the gendered nature of children's psychosocial and material needs, of which teachers were generally ignorant. The challenge for the education sector is not only how to adjust primary teacher education to the rural context of HIV and AIDS, but also how to educate the current teachers about the best ways of dealing with children affected and made vulnerable by HIV and AIDS. There are particular challenges entailed in supporting girls and boys for which teachers need sustained support.

Conclusions

Some of the measures that Uganda has taken to address HIV and AIDS in the education sector include mainstreaming concern with HIV and AIDS in all government ministries, the national strategic framework for HIV and AIDS activities 2001–2005/6, and PIASCY, through which abstinence and life-skills education are promoted among school-aged children. But these measures do not take account of contextual issues such as gender inequalities in schools and the wider society.

Despite government efforts to achieve gender equality, even after the implementation of UPE, the problem of children's access to school is still far from being solved, and the consequences of the HIV and AIDS epidemic entail extra effort in particular sectors. Although girls are enrolled in schools in large numbers, they continue to drop out at high rates, are unable to attend school daily, and often do not participate fully in classroom activities. Gender parity therefore does not guarantee equality in any way. HIV is both a cause and a consequence of girls' dropout and irregular attendance. HIV in the family is a cause of dropout because of its tendency to reduce household income, which requires girls to stay at home to seek employment or take on domestic and caring work. In addition, girls who are not attending and learning at school are more vulnerable to HIV because they have less access to information about HIV and may be more vulnerable to beginning sexual relationships with men in return for money or gifts.

The persistence of gender inequalities despite UPE is sustained by problems associated with poverty, discrimination, and girls' vulnerability. PIASCY's focus on abstinence fails to address the particular circumstances in which young people are living, including their economic circumstances, their own values, and the cultural beliefs and practices within their families, communities, schools, and broader society. Epstein (2005) argues that Ugandan culture does not fit easily with the message of abstinence, and that policy makers are demonstrating a degree of hypocrisy in promoting this policy. In addition, there is no evidence from any country to support the argument that abstinence is effective in reducing HIV infection rates; indeed, there is evidence to suggest that condoms have helped to control Uganda's epidemic.

There is a need to mitigate the impact of AIDS on the education sector in general and on children in particular. This requires a multi-pronged approach capable of addressing the obstacles in communities and families alongside the in-school factors. One way forward is to forge a partnership between communities and schools, with common objectives such as facilitating girls' schooling and reducing everybody's vulnerability to HIV infection. This could in the long run break the vicious cycle of HIV and gender inequalities in schooling and society. The implication of this is that the government's HIV-prevention strategy must be linked in with broader poverty-reduction and gender-equality strategies, with the aim of enabling more girls to stay in school longer.

Note

1   Castle was appointed in the first year after independence by the new government; see Uganda, Ministry of Education and Sports (1999): 'The Ugandan experience of universal primary education', Dakar: Association for the Development of Education in Africa.

References

Aikman, S. and E. Unterhalter (2005) 'Introduction' in S. Aikman and E.Unterhalter (eds). *Beyond Access: Transforming Policy and Practice for Gender Equality in Education*, Oxford, Oxfam GB, 1–12.

Barnett, T. (2004) 'HIV/AIDS and Development Concern Us All', *Journal of International Development* 16 (7), 943–9.

Bitamazire, G. (2005) 'Status of Education for Rural People in Uganda', presentation at the Ministerial Seminar on Education for Rural People in Africa 7–9 September 2005, Addis Ababa.

Cameron, L. (2005) 'Primary Completion Rates', technical paper WP-09-01, Washington, DC: Education Policy and Data Centre, Academy for Educational Development.

Cohen, J. and T. Tate (2005) 'The less they know, the better: abstinence-only education programs in Uganda', *Human Rights Watch* 17 (4A).

Deininger, K. (2003) 'Does the cost of schooling affect enrolment by the poor? Universal Primary Education in Uganda', *Economics of Education Review* 22 (3), 291–305.

Epstein, H. (2005) 'God and the fight against AIDS', *New York Review of Books* 52(7), available at: www.nybooks.com/articles/17963 (last accessed January 2008).

Hardon, A (2005) 'Confronting the HIV/AIDS epidemic in sub-Saharan Africa: policy versus practice', *International Social Science Journal* 57 (186), 601–8.

International Institute for Educational Planning/UNESCO (2003) *HIV/AIDS: A Strategic Approach*, Paris: International Institute for Educational Planning /UNESCO.

Kakuru, D.M. (2003) 'Gender Sensitive Educational Policy and Practice: Uganda Case Study', background paper for the UNESCO 'EFA Global Monitoring Report 2003/4'.

Kakuru, D.M. (2006) 'The Combat for Gender Equality in Education: Rural Livelihood Pathways in the Context of HIV/AIDS', Wageningen: University of Wageningen.

Kakuru, D. M. (2007) 'HIV/AIDS, children's rights and gender equality in Uganda's Universal Primary Education', *International Journal of Learning* 14(2): 137–48.

Kakuru, D.M. and M. Mulder (2007) 'The Need to Involve the Community in Implementing Sustainable School HIV/AIDS Education Programs in Uganda', unpublished working paper.

Kasente, D. (2003) 'Gender and Education in Uganda', background paper for the UNESCO 'EFA Global Monitoring Report 2003/4'.

Kebba, A. (2006) 'Antiretroviral therapy in sub-Saharan Africa: myth or reality?', *Journal of Antimicrobial Chemotherapy* 52(5): 747–9.

Kwesiga, J. C. (2003) 'Review of the 2005 Education Gender Parity Millennium Development Goal in Uganda and Proposed Strategies for Achieving this Target', Kampala: UNICEF Uganda Country Office.

McGee, R. (2000) 'Meeting the international poverty targets in Uganda: halving poverty and achieving universal primary education', *Development Policy Review* 18(1): 85–106.

Ministry of Education and Sports (2004) 'The National Report on the Development of Education in Uganda at the Beginning of the 21st Century', report on the 47th session on the International Conference on Education, Geneva, Switzerland, 8–11 September 2004.

Ministry of Education and Sports (2005) '2005 Education Statistics Abstract', available at: www.education.go.ug/statistics_abstracts.htm (last accessed July 2007).

Ministry of Health and ORC Marco (2006) 'Uganda HIV/AIDS Sero-behavioural Survey 2004–2005', Calverton, Maryland: Ministry of Health and ORC Marco.

Mohlahlane, R. (2006) 'Gender, the Girl Child and Strategies for Action', paper presented at the regional workshop on good practices in education-sector responses to HIV and AIDS in Africa, Johannesburg, South Africa, 12–14 September 2006.

Mushunje, M. T. (2006) 'Challenges and opportunities for promoting the girl child's rights in the face of HIV/AIDS', *Gender and Development* 14(1): 115–25.

Okuni, A. (2003) 'EFA policies, strategies and reforms in Uganda: assessment of the current potential for sustainable progress towards achieving the EFA goals by 2015', background paper for the UNESCO 'EFA Global Monitoring Report 2003/4'.

Poulsen, H. (2006) 'The gendered impact of HIV/AIDS on education in South Africa and Swaziland: Save the Children's experiences', *Gender and Development* 14(1): 47–56.

Shafer, L. A. (2006) 'HIV Prevalence and Incidence are No Longer Falling in Uganda – a Case for Renewed Prevention Efforts: Evidence from a Rural Population cohort 1989–2005, and from ANC Surveillance', paper presented at the XVI International AIDS Conference 13–18 August 2006, Toronto, Canada.

Ssemakula, J. B. (2004) 'Uganda's Ministry of Education and Sports Response to the HIV/AIDS Epidemic', International symposium on HIV/AIDS workplace policies and programmes for the public and the private sectors, Dar-Es-Salaam, 26–28 May 2004.

Subrahmanian, R. (2005) 'Gender equality in education: definitions and measurements', *International Journal of Educational Development* 25(4): 395–407.

Uganda AIDS Commission (2006) 'The Uganda HIV/AIDS Status Report July 2004–December 2005'.

UNAIDS/WHO (2006) 'The AIDS Epidemic Update 2006', Geneva: UNAIDS/WHO.

Unterhalter, E. (2003) 'The capabilities approach and gendered education: an examination of South African complexities', *Theory and Research in Education* 1 (1): 7–22.

Yamano, T., Y. Shimamura, and D. Sserunkuuma (2006) 'Living arrangements and schooling of orphaned children and adolescents in Uganda', *Economic Development and Cultural Change* 54: 833–56.

4 Violence against girls: are schools doing enough to protect them against HIV and AIDS?

Fiona Leach

Introduction

It is now generally acknowledged that HIV prevalence rates among school-going youth are significantly lower than among those out of school, and that education reduces vulnerability to HIV infection in some way (Hargreaves and Boler 2006; Pridmore and Yates 2005; Jukes and Desai 2005). This is an especially important finding for girls, being the group at most risk. However, we need to avoid overstating claims about the link between schooling and HIV, as the nature of this relationship is not well understood. Even if we do accept that schooling has an impact on vulnerability to HIV in some complex and not fully understood way, it is important to consider the extent to which schools are *actively* working to protect students, girls in particular, from exposure to the virus, rather than merely passing on messages about safe sex.

This chapter focuses on one particular aspect of schooling that has been largely ignored in assessments of the link between schooling and exposure to HIV. This is the existence of sexual violence in schools, which until recently was an under-researched and poorly recognised global phenomenon. The chapter discusses some of the findings of a small number of school-based studies of gender violence in developing countries, most of which were conducted in sub-Saharan Africa. This research concentration on Africa can be explained in part by the high level of donor funding for education in the region, and in part by the urgent need to examine the effectiveness of locating HIV and AIDS awareness-raising programmes in schools. We need to recognise, however, that the problem is confined neither to Africa nor to developing countries but is a global phenomenon, as a recent collection of country case studies testifies (Leach and Mitchell 2006).

There is an expanding literature in the developing world on the way in which the school provides an important arena for the construction of masculine and feminine identities (Dunne *et al.* 2005; Pattman and Chege 2003; Kakuru 2006). This chapter provides evidence to suggest that, by promoting certain norms and practices which reinforce gender hierarchies, and by failing to tackle violent incidents that result from this unequal gender regime, school authorities are in fact encouraging male sexual violence against girls. This inaction not only presents risks to girls' sexual health, it also undermines health messages, including those about HIV, being passed on in schools. As research in Uganda reveals, the messages imparted through the AIDS curriculum about safe sex, negotiated sex, and equal partnership in sexual relationships are in conflict with, and neutralised by, an informal school culture which permits widespread sexual harassment and abuse of girls (Mirembe and Davies 2001). The chapter concludes that schools could do much more to reduce the vulnerability of both girls and boys to HIV by working vigorously to eliminate sexual violence and gender inequalities within their walls.

Links between sexual violence and other forms of violence

The presence of violence in schools has been acknowledged for some time, and various studies have been carried out, in both industrialised and developing countries (e.g. Smith 2003; Akiba *et al.* 2002; Ohsako 1997). Such studies have uncovered a wide range of violent behaviours, including physical and verbal assaults, the use of guns and knives, gang fights, damage to school property, arson, and rape. However, they tend to conceptualise school violence in terms of male delinquency and youth crime, failing to make the link between the violence observed and the gendered nature of schooling (one exception is the AAUW 2001 *Hostile Hallways* study in the USA; see also the 'Bullying. No Way!' website in Australia). Most studies of bullying (e.g. Olweus 1993, Smith *et al.* 2004) and corporal punishment (e.g. Hart 2005) also fail to apply a gender lens; hence the policies and interventions designed to address abuses in school ignore this important dimension (exceptions are Duncan 1999, on sexual bullying, and Humphreys 2006 and Morrell 2001, on corporal punishment).

We need to recognise that all acts of violence are gendered in some way (Leach and Humphreys 2007), regardless of how they are labelled. Gender interacts in different settings with other social markers, such as class, race, caste, ethnicity, and religion, to create multi-layered patterns of discrimination. Violent acts may be prompted by a complex response to perceived difference, in which gender may not always be the most salient feature. The failure to recognise the gender dimension of school violence has meant that some forms of sexual violence have remained largely hidden. These include homophobic violence (see for example Meyer 2006; HRW/IGLHRC 2003) and the sexual abuse of boys by Catholic priests in religious schools (see for example John Jay College 2004, in the USA). Even in societies where sexual matters are almost never discussed in the media, the sexual abuse of children, e.g. by clerics in koranic schools, has now been acknowledged (Anderson 2004; Murphy 2005). Student violence against teachers, which usually comprises male students behaving violently towards young female teachers, is also emerging as a serious issue for school authorities (see West 2007, in Australia).

Research into sexual violence has tended not only to exclude consideration of boys as victims of violence but also to treat girls and boys as homogeneous and oppositional groups. There may in fact be as much variation in attitude and behaviour concerning sex, sexuality, and sexual violence *within* groups of girls or boys as *between* girls and boys. Nevertheless, the evidence is clear that girls are overwhelmingly the target of sexual violence, and it is here that their vulnerability to HIV is greatest. This chapter focuses on this issue, while not wishing to undermine the importance of other forms of violence, or to deny the fact that boys, as well as girls, can be victims of physical and sexual violence.

At the same time, we need to recognise the links between differing manifestations of violence in educational institutions. An environment which tolerates one type of violence against children is likely to condone others. So, for example, the often excessive and unauthorised use of corporal punishment in schools may help to legitimise sexual abuse. Indeed, the two can be linked: in schools where sexual relationships between teachers and schoolgirls are tolerated, a girl may have sex with a teacher to avoid being beaten, whereas a girl who has resisted a teacher's advances may risk being singled out for punishment (Leach *et al.* 2003).

Difficulties of definition and scope of sexual violence

We have no clear picture of the scale of sexual violence in schools around the world (Mirksy 2003). There are numerous reasons for this. First, it is a sensitive area to investigate, and those in positions of authority have been reluctant to recognise that schools, the very place where we expect our children to be most protected, can be an unsafe environment. Relatively few studies have been carried out and many of these have small sample sizes, making it impossible to generalise.

Second, different studies are defined variously as investigations of sexual harassment, sexual abuse, sexual violence, or bullying,[1] and terms may be used interchangeably or inconsistently. How violence is conceptualised and labelled inevitably has a bearing on the data gathered. In an attempt at clarification, in this chapter sexual violence is taken to be a 'blanket' term, which includes sexual harassment and sexual abuse (whether of a physical, verbal, emotional, or psychological nature), sexual assault, and rape. In turn, sexual violence is considered part of a broader cycle of gender violence which also includes more subtle forms of violence, what Debarbieux *et al.* (2003) in a French study called 'incivilities' or 'micro-violence'. Subtle messages about gender conformity and gender power relations, and the penalties for not conforming, are passed on through the daily informal practices and hidden curriculum of schooling.

Third, there is the question of finding an appropriate research methodology for exploring sensitive matters of sex and sexuality. Data collected in a one-to-one interview may deliver very different findings from an anonymous questionnaire. In interviews, whether as individuals or in groups, girls are likely to under-report their experiences of sexual violence, given societal disapproval of women engaging in pre-marital sexual activity (despite evidence that in many settings age at first sexual experience is very young). In contrast, it is widely believed that boys tend to over-report sexual activity (Mensch *et al.* 2003), as male sexual experience is often considered a rite of passage to adulthood. It is also a source of competitiveness and bragging between boys. Both boys and girls are also likely to respond differently depending on whether the researcher is male or female.[2]

Anonymous surveys which probe sensitive personal topics using questionnaires present other difficulties, including inexplicable inconsistencies both within and across countries. For example, Mensch *et al.* (2003) noted that in one survey of pre-marital sex in sub-Saharan Africa, 13 per cent of young women aged 20–24 in Zimbabwe who had never married reported sexual experience before the age of 20, in contrast to 43 per cent in Zambia. Whether there is a genuine difference of behaviour between girls in the two countries or merely a greater willingness to acknowledge sexual behaviour in Zambia is debatable.

Finally, there is massive under-reporting of sexual violence. It is well known that women and girls often remain silent for fear of the stigma attached to it and because they expect to be blamed for having invited the attack. In one study of over 2000 girls and young women aged 13 and above in Ghana (Coker-Appiah and Cusack 1999), two-thirds of all those who had experienced sexual violence (not just in school) had not reported the incidents, due to feelings of shame and a belief that no action would be taken against the culprits. Another deterrent is the widespread attitude that a woman was 'asking for it' by dressing or behaving provocatively, as noted in the African context by Wible (2004), Terefe and Mengistu (1997), and Pattman and Chege (2003). However, this attitude is not confined to Africa: a 1998 survey in the UK of attitudes towards violence, sex, and relationships among 2000 young people aged 14–21 found that more than half thought that women provoke violence, for example by the way they dress or by flirting.[3]

Levels of sexual violence will of course vary between countries, locations, and schools. Individual students within any one school or class will also have differing experiences, with some having no exposure at all while others may be subjected to violence routinely. Social class, race, ethnicity, religion, physical appearance, personality, and (dis)ability are all factors which influence exposure:

factors which are poorly captured in the studies carried out to date. This makes mapping tight connections between forms of sexual violence and experience of HIV difficult (but not impossible) to explore.

Scale of the problem

Although it is impossible to gauge the scale of sexual violence in schools with any certainty, there is compelling evidence that many girls across the world experience varying degrees of sexual violence in school. The recently published report of the two-year UN global study of 'Violence against Children' (United Nations 2006) has added significantly to existing knowledge and confirmed just how widespread all forms of violence are in schools. Recent studies in Europe, including in Scandinavia (Sunnari *et al.* 2003), the UK (Duncan 1999; Osler 2006), and Eastern Europe (e.g. UNICEF 2005, in Kosovo, and Zdravomyslova and Gorshkova 2006, in Russia) provide valuable new insights into gendered aspects of violence in schools.

Looking at the research across the developing world, in sub-Saharan Africa there are now studies in at least ten countries (USAID 2003; Wible 2004). These focus almost exclusively on heterosexual violence by male students and teachers against female students, although the studies by Burton (2005) in Malawi and Rossetti (2001) in Botswana also report some boys being sexually abused. Backed up by frequent media reports, they confirm that sexual violence in the region is widespread and that teachers, albeit a small minority, are frequent perpetrators. The public nature of teachers' sexual advances to girls in school without fear of being disciplined suggests that it has become, if not endemic, at least accepted as a 'normal' part of school life. Indeed, some teachers state openly that they consider sex with schoolgirls to be a 'perk' of the job, what Botswana teachers call 'harvesting' (Bennell *et al.* 2001). We also know that this tends to be worse in rural schools and in schools serving poor communities. This is because such schools are often staffed with less well-trained or even untrained teachers, with male rather than female teachers, and with less competent head teachers (Dunne *et al.* 2005). This documentation of sexual violence in a number of schools in Africa needs to be read alongside figures on high prevalence rates of HIV and AIDS. Although we do not have data on causal relations, the connection merits further research.

The issue of girls as perpetrators of violence, which has emerged as a less well-recognised but significant aspect of violence in schools in the West (e.g. Duncan 2006; Chesney-Lind and Shelden 2004), is as yet not directly addressed in the African literature. However, one phenomenon that is highlighted (e.g. Leach and Machakanja 2000) is that of adult men (sometimes called 'sugar daddies', a term which belies their exploitative intent) who prey on girls for sex.

In searching for evidence of sexual violence, we should not ignore the Asian region simply because the evidence is thin. This is a particularly difficult topic to investigate in societies where matters of sex and sexual abuse are rarely discussed either in public or in private, and where female sexuality and sexual purity are fiercely guarded. However, a few exploratory studies have been carried out recently in South Asia, for example in Nepal (Standing *et al.* 2006), Pakistan (Brohi and Anjaib 2006), and India (Leach and Sitaram 2007). These have highlighted girls' fear and experience of harassment on the way to and from school, especially when using crowded public transport, rather than in school itself. One UNICEF study in Nepal also indicated that 9 per cent of children had experienced severe sexual abuse (kissing of sensitive parts, oral sex, and penetration) and 18 per cent of the abusers were teachers (UNICEF 2006), although it is not known whether the children who were abused were boys or girls. In East Asia, evidence is also emerging of teachers sexually abusing students (e.g. French 2003 in Japan, and Tang 2002 in Hong Kong, cited in United Nations 2006). Whether there are any connections between these contexts and those where HIV is a risk requires investigation.

In Latin America, where school violence has usually been framed as the product of youth gangs involved with guns and drugs, some evidence of sexual violence comes from Brazil (Abramovy and Rua 2005), while a World Bank study in Ecuador (World Bank 2000) reported 22 per cent of adolescent girls being sexually abused in school. The UN World Report on Violence against Children (2006) also cites a desk study indicating that many girls in Latin America experience sexual coercion from teachers, sometimes with threats that their grades will suffer if they do not co-operate (UNICEF 2006). Levels of HIV infection in Latin America are lower than in Africa, and the extent to which different forms of sexual violence link with different patterns of infection is suggestive.

Research evidence from sub-Saharan Africa

This section provides a brief overview of some of the studies from Africa. In particular it focuses on evidence of sexual violence by teachers against female students, for it is these relationships that put girls at risk of HIV infection, not least because they are likely to involve multiple partners (although Bennell [2003] disputes the claim that teachers constitute a high-risk group for HIV, citing lack of reliable mortality data, erroneous stereotyping of the African teacher as predominantly male, married, and living apart from his wife or partner, and media sensationalism as the cause of exaggerated projections of AIDS-related deaths among teachers). The studies show considerable variation in the reported frequency of incidents of sexual violence.

Rossetti's (2001) survey of 560 secondary-school students in Botswana revealed the highest levels of sexual violence by teachers. Using a combination of questionnaire, interviews, and focus-group discussions, she found that 67 per cent of girls said they had been sexually harassed by teachers, including unsolicited touching, patting, and pinching; dirty jokes and sexual innuendoes; pressure for dates; and whistles. Twenty-five per cent said they had been subjected to such harassment on a regular basis, and 20 per cent (112 girls) said teachers had asked them to have sexual relations; almost half of these (47 girls) accepted, mainly because they feared lower grades if they refused. In another survey in Botswana by Rivers (2000) using structured interviews, 800 students aged 13–16 living in remote areas were asked about 'unwanted sexual activity'. This revealed lower but still significant levels of sexual harassment, with 40 per cent of girls and 28 per cent of boys reporting having been made uncomfortable by talk about sex or being touched in a sexual manner without their consent, usually by their peers. Only three girls reported having sex with their teachers, despite the fact that 27 per cent had visited a teacher's home, in contravention of Ministry of Education regulations.[4]

One study in Ghana (Brown 2002), which was framed in terms of sexual abuse and based on interviews and focus-group discussions, produced much lower figures than either of the Botswana studies, possibly because it included a younger age group. Out of a total of 490 students aged 7–17 (of whom 75 per cent were female), 11.2 per cent (47 girls and five boys) reported having been sexually abused at school, mostly by other students. Out of the total sample, 14.9 per cent reported having been subjected to unwelcome sexual advances at school, 15.7 per cent to requests for sexual favours, and 10.8 per cent had been fondled, touched, grabbed, or pinched in a sexual way. Only three admitted that they had been abused by a teacher, while 4.5 per cent said that they had been threatened by a teacher that their school life would suffer if they did not have sex with them.

Although most of the studies carried out have been at the (junior) secondary level, two other recent studies have included, and reported separately on, the primary level. They provide disturbing evidence that sexual violence is widespread here too. Wible's (2004) small study of gender-based violence in Benin, based on participatory workshops followed by individual interviews with 30 primary and 40 secondary schoolgirls, reported that over half the primary pupils had experienced inappropriate touching, inappropriate requests and/or offensive jokes and gestures, while 40 per cent said they experienced pressure for sex and 33 per cent thought that teachers engaged in such behaviour. At the secondary level, the figures were somewhat higher, and 63 per cent identified teachers and other school personnel as most often responsible.

A much larger interview survey in Malawi (Burton 2005) of 4,412 children aged 9–18 also found that unwanted physical touching, forced sex, and bullying were common among the younger age group, although not all incidents took place in school, and the perpetrators were said to be mostly other students. Of the 1,650 children aged 9–13 in the sample, 71.5 per cent reported having been bullied (53.5 per cent at school or on the way to school), 9.3 per cent had been touched on the genitals or breasts against their will (of whom 56.8 per cent at school), 6.6 per cent had experienced forced penetrative and non-penetrative sex (of whom 71.1 per cent at school). For the majority, this targeting occurred more than once. Disturbingly, a much higher number of younger children reported knowing someone who had been sexually abused by a teacher in return for good grades (83.6 per cent) than older children (33.8 per cent), suggesting that perhaps teachers targeted younger children due to their greater vulnerability or their likelihood of being free of the HIV virus.

Not surprisingly, levels of sexual violence in school mirror to a large extent those in the wider society. South Africa therefore presents a picture of extreme sexual violence in schools, as documented most disturbingly in the Human Rights Watch report *Scared at School* (Human Rights Watch 2001), which found that sexual harassment and abuse of girls by teachers and students was widespread, and that girls were raped in school toilets, empty classrooms, and hostels. In another study, which focused on rape among a sample of 11,735 South African women aged 15–49 in 1998, out of the 159 women who had been victims of rape as children (those below the age of 15), 33 per cent said that they had been raped by teachers (Jewkes *et al.* 2002).

Another setting where girls are particularly vulnerable is in Namibia, where many secondary-school students have to live in school hostels or boarding houses because their homes are in remote areas with scattered populations. One prominent manifestation of adolescent male violence is the ritual of 'hunting', where boys break into the girls' hostels at night and rape them; gang rape is referred to as 'the tournament' (Kandirikirira 2002). Such violence is perceived by boys and men to be a form of masculinity-affirming entertainment, which, through the inaction of parents, teachers, and hostel wardens, has come over the years to be seen as normal 'boys-will-be-boys' behaviour. Even if students do not have to live in hostels, some have to travel long distances to school. In Zimbabwe, some of the girls interviewed lived as far as 15km from the school and they sometimes took lifts with truck drivers (Leach and Machakanja 2000), while in Malawi it was reported that girls had affairs with mini-bus drivers so as to get free lifts to and from school (Leach *et al.* 2003).

Sexual violence against girls is also a significant problem in refugee camps, as evidenced by the scandal of humanitarian aid workers and teachers in camps in West Africa engaging girls in transactional sex (UNHCR/Save the Children UK 2002). Evidence from elsewhere confirms that, where communities experience high levels of civil unrest, lawlessness or war, female students are likely to be at particular risk. In Nepal during the recent Maoist insurgency, the fear of abduction and rape and the use of girls as sex slaves by both government and Maoist armed forces were serious deterrents to girls' continued schooling (and also led to an increase in child marriages) (Standing *et al.* 2006).

The above brief account provides a convincing, if varying, picture of sexual violence against girls, and most strikingly of the widespread practice of teachers demanding sexual favours of schoolgirls. Although the total numbers involved may not be as high as media reports sometimes suggest, the fact that any teacher is able to abuse with impunity the trust placed in them by parents and education authorities, by offering to trade high grades, exam questions, money, or promises of marriage for sex is a shocking indictment of the low level of professionalism and accountability in many school systems.

Despite the evidence from these sources of the scale of teachers' sexual misconduct, it is in fact from boys' gratuitously aggressive 'performances of masculinity' (Butler 1990) in their school and community that girls face the greater risk on a daily basis. In one qualitative study in Zimbabwe (Leach and Machakanja 2000), 34 out of 50 girls (68 per cent) in three co-educational junior secondary schools who were asked to describe their experiences of violent behaviour by boys reported having their breasts or buttocks groped, grabbed, or pinched, and even being hit or beaten. Some girls described how they were regularly ambushed by groups of boys while leaving school, with other boys looking on and laughing. Girls also reported having to suffer demeaning obscenities, sexist comments, and name-calling. Showing condoms or pornographic pictures and drawings in class were other ways in which boys embarrassed girls. In a follow-up study (Leach *et al.* 2003) in Ghana and Malawi, girls gave examples of boys cornering them in the school grounds or intercepting them on the way to the toilets, where they would try to fondle their breasts or peek at them.

Beyond the school gates, in many sub-Saharan African countries, older men are found to target schoolgirls in the belief that they are less likely to be infected with the HIV virus or, worse, that they can be cured of AIDS by having sex with a virgin. Older men engaging young girls in sexual relationships has a cultural history in parts of Africa (Luke and Kurz 2002), but the risk of contracting AIDS in this way makes such a practice life-threatening. It is well known that for many girls, staying on in secondary school is a struggle because of the requirement to pay fees, and this makes them an easy target. In Leach and Machakanja's (2000) Zimbabwe study, out of a total of 112 girls interviewed in four schools, 103 girls (92 per cent) said that they had been propositioned by adult men, whether strangers, neighbours, or relatives, and over half said that they had experienced unsolicited physical contact or assault from strange men or out-of-school boys, of whom 13 had been grabbed or pinched on the breast and seven grabbed by the buttocks (18 per cent).

Why does sexual violence exist in schools?

Violence in schools cannot be divorced from violence in the home, the community, and the workplace. The school, alongside the family, is a prime site for the construction of gender identity and the institutionalisation of a socially sanctioned gender hierarchy framed by a 'compulsory heterosexuality' (Mirembe and Davies 2001; Dunne *et al.* 2006). The structures and practices which guide and regulate behaviour during the school day through explicit and implicit rules, norms, and symbols reinforce and perpetuate the unequal gender relations already reproduced in the home. Teacher tolerance of male students' domination of classroom space at the expense of girls' participation in lessons, the celebration of masculine competitiveness, and the allocation of more public and higher-status tasks and responsibilities to male students and teachers all teach children that masculinity is associated with aggression and superiority, while femininity requires obedience, acquiescence, and making oneself attractive to boys (Leach and Machakanja 2000; Dunne *et al.* 2006). The vignette from Uganda in Box 1 gives some indication of how unpleasant an aggressively masculine school environment can be for girls.

Box 1: How gendered practices can undermine HIV messages

An ethnographic study* of an elite co-educational government boarding school in Uganda revealed extensive gendered practices which undermined the HIV messages contained in the new AIDS curriculum and neutralised Ugandan schoolchildren's relatively high knowledge of the disease. These gendered practices included:

- preference for male pupils and male teachers in leadership roles
- restricted access for girls to high-status knowledge, e.g. science
- the use of different disciplinary measures on boys and girls
- strict 'policing' of girls' sexuality by the school authorities, e.g. what to wear, how to sit in public, how to talk to boys
- sexual harassment of girls by boys, which went unchallenged by staff
- boys' control of classroom language and physical space, which forced girls to face insults whenever they spoke up – or to remain silent

continued overleaf

Box 1: How gendered practices can undermine HIV messages continued

Outside the classroom, girls were routinely subjected to unsolicited touching, groping, and pinching by boys. Intense competition over girls meant that a girl who refused a boy's sexual advances risked taunts, abusive language, and/or assault. This sexual harassment was reinforced by sexually explicit graffiti on school walls.

The study showed that social conformity to ideals of male domination, leadership, and manhood, and a perceived male entitlement to sex, was integral to the school culture. Yet, central to the 'official' AIDS message in the Ugandan curriculum was that negotiation and partnership in sexual relationships are essential to HIV prevention. This, however, requires equal power and status between partners. The endemic harassment in the school denied girls the right to make choices or voice independence in relationships.

The study suggested that a better understanding of patriarchy and gender roles in Uganda, and their contribution to the AIDS epidemic, was needed if schooling was to play an effective role in teaching about HIV and AIDS. Equally important was for the Ministry of Education to address gender inequality within schools and to promote democratic learning in sex- and AIDS-education programmes within the curriculum.

The researcher concluded that there was an urgent need to:

- address a wide concept of sexual health, including positive aspects (such as sexual orientation and the good sides of sex) within the school curriculum

- teach sex education in single-sex groups to give pupils greater freedom to discuss sensitive issues and greater control of their learning

- adopt a whole-school approach (human rights, family planning, democratic learning) that challenges the social injustices brought about by gender discrimination

- initiate teacher-training courses that explore ways in which gender discrimination can be challenged within schools

- embark on serious gender-mainstreaming initiatives offering equal opportunity for all.

*R. Mirembe (1998) 'AIDS Education and Gender in Ugandan Schools', unpublished PhD thesis, University of Birmingham (adapted from *Gender Violence in Schools* newsletter No. 1, www.sussex.ac.uk/education/1-4-30-1.html)

This male privileging leads to violence because, as part of the gender socialisation process in schools, students learn to recognise, and to police, the boundaries of acceptable gender behaviour. Those who transgress these boundaries may be targeted for punishment, both by teachers and students (boys who do not conform are also at risk). While teachers indirectly regulate gendered behaviour through disciplinary measures, students resort either to overtly violent means or less visible forms of violence which are 'normalised' as 'teasing', 'playing', or 'gossiping' (Dunne *et al.* 2006). For example, a boy who is perceived as cowardly or effeminate, or a girl who does not behave sufficiently modestly or who scorns a boy's advances, may be punished by being bullied, victimised, or gossiped about in a malicious or destructive way. Teachers often consider student-initiated incidents as not worthy of reprimand, and so, by tolerating or ignoring them, they are implicitly sanctioning violence and ensuring that it becomes accepted in adolescent relationships and thus perpetuated into adulthood. The perception that male violence against women is acceptable is surprisingly widespread among adolescents.[5]

The role of peer pressure in sustaining male violence is observed in the Zimbabwe study (Leach and Machakanja 2000). Having girlfriends, or at least being seen to have girlfriends, and boasting about 'winning' girls through (hetero)sexual prowess were important means of enhancing a boy's status in the peer group (physical prowess in fighting being another). It should not be surprising that, if boys' initial overtures to girls (usually through writing a 'love letter') are rejected, their demands for attention can be unsolicited and aggressive. Observing male teachers making sexist or derogatory comments to female students and teachers, and engaging in unnecessary and unsolicited physical contact with girls during lessons, provides an unhelpful role model for boys.

Girls were not exempt from peer pressure; for example the study found that they made themselves attractive to boys and developed a recognisably pliant femininity. However, girls can be confused by their desire to adopt the 'modern' forms of femininity portrayed so compellingly through media images, while still conforming to traditional expectations and roles. Having a boyfriend and receiving gifts may give a girl a desirable status within the female peer group, but it is also risky as she may be labelled 'loose' or 'a prostitute'. Bastien (2005) suggests that sexual violence against girls may be symptomatic of the frustrations and confusions brought on by such tensions between modernity and tradition in shaping adolescent gender and sexual identities, since, when the gender boundaries become blurred, boys and men may attempt to symbolically and physically solidify their status.

This suggests that it is misleading to assume that girls' relationships with boys and older men are always coercive and that female agency plays no part in informal school life. Many girls may decide to have sex on the grounds of physical attraction or feelings, but for others, poverty may make this an unavailable luxury. Some boys in the above cited studies were of the opinion that it was often girls who made sexual advances, in particular with a view to obtaining gifts or money. There is indeed a large literature on transactional sex between adolescent girls and older men (e.g. Luke and Kurz 2002), especially in South Africa (Dunkle *et al.* 2004; Hunter 2002), and also between school-going adolescents (Nyanzi *et al.* 2000, in Uganda). Many girls find it harder to continue their education than boys, not only because of family poverty and preference for educating boys, but because of the difficulty of obtaining casual work. Opportunities to obtain a small regular income through gardening, farming, washing cars, portering, and so on are unlikely to be available to girls, while the demands of domestic chores and the social disapproval of unmarried girls working outside the home impose further constraints. The desire to complete their schooling and improve their lives may therefore oblige some girls to rely on their only economic asset, their body. Under such circumstances, a relationship with an older man (or men) may appear as a rational, even an attractive, choice, albeit one which places them in a dependent relationship, which men can all too easily exploit.

Sexual violence, along with other forms of violent behaviour including unauthorised corporal punishment, is facilitated by government failure to implement regulations on teachers' professional conduct, punish perpetrators, and enforce child protection and anti-discrimination laws where they exist. In many parts of the world, there are poor levels of accountability in the educational system and a lack of good management and professional commitment, whether due to poor training, low salaries, poor support from the authorities, poverty, or other factors. Evidence from sub-Saharan Africa suggests that teachers who exploit their authority by having sexual relations with students are rarely expelled from the teaching profession, even in cases where a girl is made pregnant; at most, an offending teacher will be transferred to another school (Leach *et al.* 2003; Dunne *et al.* 2006). High levels of bureaucracy, apathy among officials, ignorance by parents and students as to how to lodge a complaint, and a reluctance to believe students who make allegations are contributory factors. To complicate matters, not all parents, teachers, and girls in sub-Saharan Africa disapprove of teachers or older men having sexual liaisons with schoolgirls, whether for economic or cultural reasons (Leach *et al.* 2003).

The consequences for girls of sexual violence in schools

High levels of sexual violence, and fear of such violence, have a number of consequences for girls' schooling, some with a direct impact on their exposure to HIV.

Dropout

Dropout inevitably means lost opportunities for cognitive development, for future careers, and for improved socio-economic status. There are of course many reasons for girls and boys choosing to, or being obliged to, leave school – family poverty, early marriage, societal perceptions that girls do not need as much education as boys, and the requirement for girls to look after orphan siblings or ailing parents in AIDS-afflicted households. However, violence also plays a part. A girl who experiences sexual violence at school may start missing lessons and may finally drop out; sustained verbal abuse or malicious gossiping may be sufficient for her to wish to leave. In sub-Saharan Africa in particular, parental fear that girls will be exposed to the predatory sexual behaviour of male teachers and students at school is exacerbated by media reports and may persuade parents to remove their daughters (Leach *et al.* 2003). If adolescent girls drop out of school, the evidence of higher prevalence rates among out-of-school youth suggests that their vulnerability to HIV will increase.

The risk of sexual impropriety is even more serious for a girl in South Asia, where the fierce control of female sexuality and fear of family scandal means that the slightest hint of a girl being exposed to inappropriate contact with men or even young boys outside the family can be enough for her to be withdrawn from school. Moreover, the level of secrecy and denial around any incident of even mild harassment involving a girl is likely to be much higher than in sub-Saharan Africa, and therefore the more difficult it is to assess the scale of the problem. According to Leach and Sitaram (2007), some officials in India admit to hearing of occasional cases of teachers having sexual relations with girls, and of schoolgirl rape, but nobody wants to talk openly about it. Likewise, despite rising HIV rates in India and an estimated 55,000 children aged 0–14 with HIV in 2003 (Ministry of Women and Child Development, India 2007), there is little attempt to increase knowledge of the nature and cause of the disease among children either in or out of school.

Low achievement

Evidence also exists to confirm that violence in schools, however defined (sexual violence, bullying, corporal punishment), has harmful psychological effects on children, leads to stress which distracts them from learning, and lowers their motivation to do well. Lower achievement may increase the risk of dropout and undermine future economic prospects. Wible (2004) reported that girls in Benin believed that avoiding advances by teachers creates a hostile and intimidating learning environment and contributes to poor performance. Some girls also report that the fear of attracting unwanted attention either from the teacher, or from male students not wanting to be outshone by a girl in class, deters them from participating actively in lessons (Dunne *et al.* 2005; Human Rights Watch 2001). In a study from Ghana (Leach *et al.* 2003), 79.2 per cent of girls reported that they were troubled by boys' aggressive behaviour and 39.5 per cent felt it affected their studies.

Pregnancy

Some countries in sub-Saharan Africa have very high teenage pregnancy rates (Chilisa 2002; Kadzamira *et al.* 2001; Mensch *et al.* 1999). Studies in Ghana in 1997 indicated that 41 per cent of all junior secondary-school dropouts are caused by pregnancy (cited in FAWE 2004), while Chilisa (2002) estimates that in Botswana about 3 per cent of newly enrolled girls (1,200 girls) drop out of school (or are expelled) annually due to pregnancy. Despite legislation in many countries permitting girls to return to school after giving birth, socio-economic circumstances, stigma, and head teachers' reluctance to allow young mothers back for fear of setting a bad example to other girls prevent many young mothers from doing so.

Gordon (2002), in an unpublished study in Zimbabwe, interviewed 36 young women who had dropped out of school due to pregnancy. She found that the psychological, emotional, social, and economic costs to the girls were high: the majority were rejected by their parents, the fathers of their children, their teachers and their peers, and were labelled as loose and immoral. Some attempted illegal abortions and others contemplated suicide. Her findings suggest that unmarried teenage mothers usually live in poverty, and are often forced to enter sexual relationships with older men in order to support themselves and their child(ren). Their circumstances and their lack of self-esteem increase their indebtedness to sexual partners who provide them with the material benefits that they cannot earn for themselves. This makes it much more difficult for young women to insist on condom use and hence makes them more vulnerable to HIV, which, if pregnancy follows, may result in an HIV-positive baby.

Risky friendships

Mensch *et al.* (1999) cite several studies which argue that the expansion in school enrolments in sub-Saharan Africa, mostly in co-educational establishments, has led to increased sexual activity among adolescents as schooling removes young people from the supervision of traditional carers and exposes them to daily interaction with the opposite sex and to peer pressure. Ironically, however, while parents fear the close proximity of boys *within* school, an aggressive institutional atmosphere may make genuine friendship between a girl and a boy difficult, and encourage girls who feel vulnerable to seek protection and/or comfort from older boys and men *outside* the school. This goes against the view (Hargreaves and Boler 2006) that one benefit of girls' education is the greater likelihood of girls choosing boyfriends within the school who are of a similar age and are therefore less likely to be infected with HIV than older men. However, many of the boys interviewed expressed views that older men, including teachers, were more attractive sexual partners to girls (and presented unfair competition to themselves) because of their ability to offer material support (Leach and Machakanja 2000). Clearly, the connection between friendships and HIV is, like the role of the peer group in encouraging risky sexual behaviour, complex, and requires further research.

Health, psychological, and social impacts

In addition to educational impacts, there are negative consequences of sexual violence in terms of the health, state of mind, and social relations of the person who has become the victim of the violence. The immediate risk of physical harm and of sexually transmitted infections, including HIV, may be accompanied by psychological damage, including impairment of emotional development and long-term mental distress and ill-health, which can contribute to physical ill-health. Sexually abused children often develop eating disorders, depression, insomnia, feelings of guilt, anxiety, and suicidal tendencies. They may react by engaging in such dysfunctional behaviours as self-harm, use of psychoactive substances, and highly aggressive behaviour, often of a sexual nature (WHO *et al.* 1998).

Negative impact on portrayal of women and girls in society

Girls interviewed in Wible's study (2004) in Benin believed that sexual violence in schools, especially that perpetrated by teachers, damages the social fabric of the school and devalues it in the eyes of the community. To boys, the knowledge of teacher–schoolgirl relationships creates the impression that all girls are materialistic and that they seek preferential treatment by selling their bodies to teachers to compensate for their lesser abilities. This breeds resentment and scorn in boys, who are then more likely to act aggressively towards girls. 'Boys sometimes accuse girls of being "friends" with the teacher when they see that a girl has taken what they think is their place among the passing grades' (Wible 2004: 17). The perception that girls are seen as achieving on the basis of their sexuality rather than their intellect does nothing to promote more equal gender relations or more consensual sexual relationships. This in turn aggravates the already widely held view in many societies that women are inferior to men, that they are the property of men, and that they are expected to gratify male sexual desire. This can only increase their exposure to sexual violence and to HIV.

Conclusions

This chapter has provided an overview of the scale and nature of sexual violence in schools, focusing primarily on studies from the sub-Saharan African region, where the HIV prevalence rate among adolescent girls is alarmingly high. It has also highlighted some of the methodological and practical problems of trying to accurately assess the level of sexual violence in schools. It notes that the scale is probably grossly under-estimated, due to the reluctance of young women to report incidents – and also of young men to report homophobic violence – and that poverty plays a major role in exposing young girls to sexual violence and sexual health risks.

The question was posed at the start of the chapter as to whether schools could do more to protect students, especially girls, from exposure to HIV. From the evidence provided, the chapter concludes that the unsafe and hostile environment created in many schools by widespread sexual violence targeted especially at girls (and at boys who do not conform to dominant versions of masculinity) reduces the potential benefits of schooling and contributes to truancy, low achievement, and dropout, and to a range of negative health, psychological, and social impacts. In particular, the institutionalisation of male privilege and hierarchy, peer pressure to conform to certain types of gendered behaviour, and the tolerance of other forms of school violence such as bullying and corporal punishment encourage the view that violence against young women is acceptable. A school culture based on unequal and at times violent gender relations undermines the messages about safe sex and sexual health contained in lessons on HIV and AIDS. It also serves to present coercive relationships and forced sexual encounters both within and outside the school as the norm, making it difficult for young women to exercise choice, articulate expectations of sexual fidelity from male partners, and insist on condom use. This increases their vulnerability to HIV infection.

The claim that schooling helps build up girls' capacity to act on HIV-prevention messages and influences the level of power within sexual relationships is therefore difficult to reconcile with the evidence. As Hargreaves and Boler (2006) recognise, we just do not know enough about the underlying mechanisms through which girls' education might affect HIV vulnerability. However, it would seem that a school environment dominated by an aggressive and competitive heterosexuality is likely to act as a disincentive to girls continuing their education, whereas a more collaborative, egalitarian, and supportive school culture in which boys and girls mutually support each other's learning is more likely to keep both groups in school, strengthen shared interests and understandings, and develop the more mutually responsive and respectful relationships that the HIV and AIDS messages seek to impart.

The evidence suggests that education authorities could do much more to reduce the vulnerability of both girls and boys to HIV by meeting more fully their responsibilities to protect children and by working vigorously to eliminate sexual violence and gender inequalities inside their schools. Education officials, head teachers, and teachers need to report and, where appropriate, take action against any perpetrator of violence, whether student, teacher, or other adult. Effective school leadership and greater awareness among teachers of the harmful effects that their decisions, actions, and inactions may have in reinforcing stereotypical gender views are crucial. This requires that much greater attention be paid to gender awareness-raising during pre-service and in-service training and to ensuring that trainee teachers are familiar with, and understand the implications of, the principles of professional and ethical conduct.

Despite the claims made about the impact of HIV and AIDS education on adolescent sexual behaviour, schools face a huge challenge in trying to implement it in meaningful ways within an authoritarian and often violent school environment. To be effective, HIV and AIDS education must address the broader context of gender differentiation and hierarchies, power in sexual relationships, and the effects of stigma and discrimination. Much has been written about the need for schooling to promote life skills such as critical thinking, problem solving, and interpersonal and communication skills. To do this requires moving from the authoritarian school culture, which dominates in much of the world, to a more open and democratic culture which creates space for pupils, teachers, and parents to discuss such issues openly. Such a school culture cannot accommodate the continuing use of corporal punishment as a form of discipline, since this encourages the perception among young people that violence of any kind is permissible, and expected, in school. Such a culture requires effective, transparent, and accessible procedures and mechanisms for children, parents, and carers to report incidents of violence affecting children both in and outside school.

The above survey of the field also suggests that more research is needed into all forms of violence in school, as well as into the link between education and HIV. If we are to capture young people's views and concerns honestly and explore effective ways of changing adolescent sexual behaviour, we need to develop new research methodologies. These might include some of the participatory methodologies that have already been tried out with children and young people such as peer-led focus-group discussions, diary and narrative essay writing, memory work, drama, and arts-based visual work, including photography and video documentary (see Leach and Mitchell 2006 for examples). In this way, we may come to a better understanding of how to assist young people to protect themselves against sexual violence and HIV and AIDS.

Notes

1   The term 'sexual harassment' applies to any unwelcome conduct of a sexual nature intended to offend, humiliate, or intimidate, including sexual advances and remarks with sexual connotations. It tends to be associated with adults, although some studies reviewed here use the term. In contrast, 'sexual abuse' is a legal term which refers to the sexual exploitation of a child by an adult by virtue of his/her superior power, and for his/her own benefit or gratification. 'Bullying' is the label given to peer-on-peer violence in schools in much of the industrialised world.

2   See Zwiers and Morrissette (1999), Jones (2003), and Christensen and James (2000) for a general discussion about interviewing children. Several studies in African countries (Leach *et al.* 2003; Wible 2004) found that while girls (and sometimes boys) were reluctant to talk of their own personal sexual experiences, especially where teachers might be involved, they were on the whole happy to comment on the sexual activities of others or to talk impersonally about issues of sexuality.

3   Zero Tolerance Trust, Respect Campaign, www.zerotolerance.org.uk/campaigns/camp.php?pg=61 (last accessed August 2007).

4   The methodology used in this study is questionable. Students were interviewed individually, with the researcher instructed to ask the closed-item questions exactly as they were written on the schedule and not to add anything (intimidating to say the least!).

5   In a survey conducted in Johannesburg with 30,000 youth (CIET 2000), one in four males claimed to have had sex without the girl's consent before the age of 18, and at least half of those interviewed, both female and male, believed that forced sex was not sexual violence, it was just 'rough sex'. The survey by the Zero Tolerance Trust among 2000 young people in the UK found that one in two boys and one in three girls thought it acceptable to hit a woman in certain circumstances (e.g. if they nag), that both boys and girls found forced sex more acceptable than hitting, and that half knew someone who had been sexually assaulted (www.zerotolerance.org.uk).

References

AAUW (2001) 'Hostile Hallways: Bullying, Teasing and Sexual Harassment in School', Washington DC: American Association of University Women.

Abromavay, M. and M. Rua (2005) *Violences in Schools*, Brasilia: UNESCO.

Akiba, M., G.K. LeTendre, D.P. Baker, and B. Goesling (2002) 'School victimization: national and school system effects on school violence in 37 nations', *American Educational Research Journal* 39(4): 829–53.

Anderson, P. (2004) 'Madrassas hit by sex abuse claims', BBC News, http://news.bbc.co.uk/1/hi/world/south_asia/4084951.stm (last accessed December 2007).

Bastien, S. (2005) 'The Construction of Gender in Times of Change: A Case Study of School-Based HIV/AIDS Education in Kilimanjaro', unpublished M.Phil thesis, University of Oslo.

Bennell, P. (2003) 'The Impact of the AIDS Epidemic on Schooling in sub-Saharan Africa', background paper for the Biennial Meeting of the Association for the Development of Education in Africa, December.

Bennell, P., B. Chilisa, K. Hyde, A. Makgothi, E. Molobe, and L. Mpotokwane (2001) 'The Impact of HIV/AIDS on Primary and Secondary Education in Botswana: Developing a Comprehensive Strategic Response', Education Research No. 45, London: Department for International Development.

Brohi, N. and Ajaib, A. (2006) 'Violence against girls in the education system of Pakistan', in F. Leach and C. Mitchell (eds.) *Combating Gender Violence in and around Schools,* Stoke-on-Trent: Trentham, 81–9.

Brown, C. (2002) 'Sexual Abuse of School Children in Ghana', Cape Coast, Ghana, Centre for Development Studies, University of Cape Coast, and UNICEF.

'Bullying. No Way!', www.bullyingnoway.com.au (last accessed August 2007).

Burton, P. (2005) 'Suffering at School: Results of the Malawi Gender-based Violence in Schools Survey', National Statistical Office, Malawi.

Butler, J. (1990) *Gender Trouble, Feminism and the Subversion of Identity,* London: Routledge.

Chesney-Lind, M. and R.G. Shelden (2004) *Girls, Delinquency and Juvenile Justice,* Belmont CA: Wadsworth.

Chilisa, B. (2002) 'National policies on pregnancy in education systems in sub-Saharan Africa', *Gender and Education* 14(1): 21–35.

Christensen, P. and A. James (2000) *Research with Children: Perspectives and Practices,* London and New York: Falmer Press.

CIET (2000) 'Beyond Victims and Villains: the Culture of Sexual Violence in South Johannesburg', Johannesburg: Community Information Empowerment and Transparency Foundation (CIET).

Coker-Appiah, D. and K. Cusack (1999) 'Violence against Women and Children in Ghana: Report of a National Study on Violence', Accra: Gender Studies and Human Rights Documentation Centre.

Debarbieux, B. C. and D. Vidal (2003) 'Tackling violence in schools: a report from France', in P.K. Smith (ed.) *Violence in Schools: the Response in Europe,* London and New York: RoutledgeFalmer, 17–32.

Duncan, N. (1999) *Sexual Bullying: Gender Conflict and Pupil Culture in Secondary Schools,* London: Routledge.

Duncan, N. (2006) 'Girls' violence and aggression against other girls: femininity and bullying in UK schools', in F. Leach and C. Mitchell (eds.) *Combating Gender Violence in and around Schools,* Stoke-on-Trent: Trentham Books, 51–9.

Dunkle, K.L., R.K. Jewkes, H.C. Brown, G.E. Gray, J.A. McIntryre, and S.D. Harlow (2004) 'Transactional sex among women in Soweto, South Africa: prevalence, risk factors and association with HIV infection', *Social Science and Medicine* 59(8): 1581–92.

Dunne, M., S. Humphreys, and F. Leach (2006) 'Gender violence in schools in the developing world', *Gender and Education* 18(1): 75–98.

Dunne, M. and F. Leach, with B. Chilisa, T. Maundeni, R. Tabulawa, N. Kutor, L.D. Forde, and A. Asamoah (2005) 'Gendered Experiences of Schooling: the Impact on Retention and Achievement', Education Research Report No. 56, London: Department for International Development.

FAWE (2004) 'Stop the abuse: combating gender violence in schools', *FAWE News*, 12(3), July–September, Nairobi: Forum for African Women Educationalists (FAWE).

French, H.W. (2003) 'Victims say Japan ignores sex crimes committed by teachers', *New York Times*, June 29.

Gordon, R. (2002) 'A Preliminary Investigation of the Causes and Consequences of Schoolgirl Pregnancy and Dropout in Zimbabwe', Harare: Department for International Development.

Hargreaves, J. and Boler, T. (2006) 'Girl Power: the Impact of Girls' Education on Sexual Behaviour and HIV', London: ActionAid International.

Hart, S.N. (2005) 'Eliminating Corporal Punishment: the Way Forward to Constructive Child Discipline', Paris: UNESCO.

Human Rights Watch (2001) 'Scared at School: Sexual Violence against Girls in South African Schools', New York: Human Rights Watch.

Human Rights Watch and the International Gay and Lesbian Human Rights Commission (2003) 'More than a Name: State-Sponsored Homophobia and its Consequences in Southern Africa', New York: Human Rights Watch.

Humphreys, S. (2006) 'Corporal punishment as gendered practice – not simply a human rights issue', in F. Leach and C. Mitchell (eds.) *Combating Gender Violence in and around Schools*, Stoke-on-Trent: Trentham, 61–9.

Hunter, M. (2002) 'The materiality of everyday sex: thinking beyond "prostitution"', *African Studies* 61(1): 99–120.

Jewkes, R., J. Levin, N. Mbananga, and D. Bradshaw (2002) 'Rape of girls in South Africa', *The Lancet* 359: 319–20.

John Jay College (2004) 'The Nature and Scope of the Problem of Sexual Abuse of Minors by Catholic Priests and Deacons in the United States', The City University of New York: John Jay College of Criminal Justice, www.nccbuscc.org/nrb/johnjaystudy/ (last accessed August 2007).

Jones, D.P.H. (2003) *Communicating with Vulnerable Children: A Guide for Practitioners*, London: Royal College of Psychiatrists Publications.

Jukes, M. and Desai, K. (2005) 'Education and HIV/AIDS: UNESCO Global Monitoring Report 2005', Paris: UNESCO.

Kadzamira, E.C., N. Swainson, D. Mauluwa-Banda, and A. Kamlongera (2001) 'The Impact of HIV/AIDS on Formal Schooling in Malawi', Brighton: Centre for International Education, University of Sussex.

Kakuru, D.M. (2006) *The Combat for Gender Equality in Education: Rural Livelihood Pathways in the Context of HIV/AIDS*, The Netherlands: Wageningen Academic Publishers.

Kandirikirira, N. (2002) 'Deconstructing domination: gender disempowerment and the legacy of colonialism and apartheid in Omaheke, Namibia', in F. Cleaver (ed.) *Masculinities Matter! Men, Gender and Development*, London and New York: Zed Books/Cape Town: David Philip.

Leach, F. and S. Humphreys (2007) 'Gender violence in schools: taking the "girls-as-victims" discourse forward', *Gender and Development* 15(1): 51–65.

Leach, F. and P. Machakanja (2000) 'Preliminary Investigation into the Abuse of Girls in Zimbabwean Junior Secondary Schools', Education Research Report No. 39, London: Department for International Development.

Leach, F. and C. Mitchell (2006) *Combating Gender Violence in and around Schools*, Stoke-on-Trent: Trentham.

Leach, F. and M. Sitaram (2007) 'The sexual harassment of adolescent schoolgirls in South India', *Journal of Education, Citizenship and Social Justice*, 2(3): 257–77.

Leach, F., V. Fiscian, E. Kadzamira, E. Lemani, and P. Machakanja (2003) 'An Investigative Study of the Abuse of Girls in African Schools', Education Research Report No. 56, London: Department for International Development.

Luke, N. and K.M. Kurz (2002) 'Cross-generational and Transactional Sexual Relations in Sub-Saharan Africa: Prevalence of Behavior and Implications for Negotiating Safer Sexual Practices', Washington DC: International Center for Research on Women.

Mensch, B.S., W.H. Clark, C.B. Lloyd, and A.S. Erulkar (1999) 'Premarital Sex and School Dropout in Kenya: Can Schools Make a Difference?', World Bank Working Paper No. 124, Washington DC: World Bank.

Mensch, B., P.C. Hewett, and A.S. Erulkar (2003) 'The reporting of sensitive behaviour by adolescents: a methodological experiment in Kenya', *Demography* 40(2): 247–68.

Meyer, E. (2006) 'Gendered harassment in North America: recognising homophobia and heterosexism among students', in F. Leach and C. Mitchell (eds.) *Combating Gender Violence in and around Schools*, Stoke-on-Trent: Trentham Books, 43–50.

Ministry of Women and Child Development, India (2007) 'Study on Child Abuse: India', New Delhi: Ministry of Women and Child Development, Government of India.

Mirembe, R., and L. Davies (2001) 'Is schooling a risk? Gender, power relations and school culture in Uganda', *Gender and Education* 13(4): 401–16.

Mirsky, J. (2003) 'Beyond Victims and Villains: Addressing Sexual Violence in the Education Sector', London: Panos.

Morrell, R. (2001) 'Corporal punishment and masculinity in South African schools', *Men and Masculinities* 4(2): 140–57.

Murphy, B. (2005) 'Sex abuse in Islamic schools', FrontPageMag, Associated Press, www.frontpagemag.com/Articles/ReadArticle.asp?ID=19530 (last accessed December 2007).

Nyanzi, S., R. Pool, and J. Kinsman (2000) 'The negotiation of sexual relationships among school pupils in south-western Uganda', *AIDS Care* 13(1): 83–98.

Ohsako, T. (1997) 'Violence at School: Global Issues and Intervention', Paris: UNESCO/IBE.

Olweus, D. (1993) *Bullying at School: What We Know and What We Can Do*, Oxford: Blackwell.

Osler, A. (2006) 'Excluded girls: interpersonal, institutional and structural violence in schooling', *Gender and Education* 18(6): 571–89.

Pattman, R. and F. Chege (2003) 'Finding our Voices: Gendered and Sexual Identities and HIV/AIDS in Education', Nairobi: UNICEF.

Pridmore, P. and C. Yates (2005) 'Combating AIDS in South Africa and Mozambique: The Role of Open, Distance, and Flexible Learning (ODFL)', *Comparative Education Review* 49(4): 490–511.

Rivers, R. and Associates (2000) 'Shattered Hopes: Study of Sexual Abuse of Girls', Methaetsile Women's Information Centre, Botswana/UNICEF.

Rossetti, S. (2001) 'Children in School: A Safe Place?', Botswana: UNESCO.

Save the Children (2004) 'So You Want to Involve Young Children in Research? A Toolkit Supporting Children's Meaningful and Ethical Participation in Research Relating to Violence against Children', London: Save the Children.

Smith, P. (2003) *Violence in Schools: the Response in Europe*, Abingdon: RoutledgeFalmer.

Smith, P., D. Pepler, and K. Rigby (2004) *Bullying in Schools: How Successful Can Interventions Be? Global Perspectives on Interventions*, Cambridge: Cambridge University Press.

Standing, K., S. Parker, and L. Dhital (2006) 'Schools in Nepal: "zones of peace" or sites of gendered conflict?', in F. Leach and C. Mitchell (eds.), *Combating Gender Violence in and around Schools*, Stoke-on-Trent: Trentham, 91–9.

Sunnari, V., J. Kangasvuo, and M. Heikkinen (2003) 'Gendered and Sexualised Violence in Educational Environments', University of Oulu, Finland.

Tang, C. (2002) 'Childhood experience of sexual abuse among Hong Kong Chinese college students', *Child Abuse and Neglect* 26(1): 23–37.

Terefe, D. and D. Mengistu (1997) 'Violence in Ethiopian schools: a study of some schools in Addis Ababa', in T. Ohsako (ed.), *Violence at School: Global Issues and Interventions*, Paris: UNESCO/IBE.

UNHCR/Save the Children UK (2002) 'Note for Implementing and Operational Partners on Sexual Violence and Exploitation: the Experience of Refugee Children in Guinea, Liberia and Sierra Leone', www.unhcr.org/partners/PARTNERS/3c7cf89a4.pdf (last accessed August 2007).

UNICEF (2005) 'Research into Violence against Children in Schools in Kosovo', UNICEF with the Ministry of Education, Science and Technology and Care International, Kosovo.

UNICEF (2006) 'Regional Study on Violence against Children in South Asia', desk review for the UN report on Violence against Children.

United Nations (2006) 'The United Nations Secretary-General's Study on Violence against Children', www.violencestudy.org (last accessed August 2007).

USAID (2003) 'Unsafe Schools: a Literature Review of School-Related Gender-Based Violence in Developing Countries', Washington DC: Wellesley Centers for Research on Women & DTS/USAID.

West, D. (2007) 'The impact of student violence on teachers: a South Australian study', in F. Leach and M. Dunne (eds.), *Education, Conflict and Reconciliation: International Perspectives*, Bern: Peter Lang.

WHO/UNESCO/Education International (1998) 'WHO Information Series on School Health – Document 3. Violence Prevention: An Important Element of a Health Promoting School', Geneva: WHO, www.who.int/school_youth_health/resources/en/ (last accessed August 2007).

Wible, B. (2004) 'Making Schools Safe for Girls: Combating Gender-Based Violence in Benin', US Academy for Educational Development, www.aed.org/ToolsandPublications/upload/g18937english.pdf (last accessed August 2007).

World Bank (2000) 'Ecuador Gender Review: Issues and Recommendations', Washington DC: World Bank.

Zdravomyslova, O. and I. Gorshkova (2006) 'The "usual evil": gender violence in Russian schools', in F. Leach and C. Mitchell (eds.), *Combating Gender Violence in and around Schools*, Stoke-on-Trent: Trentham, 71–89.

Zwiers, M.L. and P.J. Morrissette (1999) *Effective Interviewing of Children*, Philadelphia: Accelerated Development and Taylor & Francis.

5 The gendered impact of AIDS on orphans and education in KwaZulu-Natal, South Africa[1]

Tania Boler

This chapter examines the gendered dimensions of the impact of AIDS on orphans' education, drawing on data from KwaZulu-Natal, one of the provinces in South Africa with extremely high levels of HIV infection. In sub-Saharan Africa, there are currently an estimated 11.4 million children orphaned by AIDS,[2] and 1.2 million in South Africa alone. If a child is orphaned, what difference does it make if the child is a boy or a girl? How is education affected differently if the mother dies or if the father dies?

Methodological issues and the question of impact

The 'impact of HIV and AIDS' refers to the consequences of increased chronic illness and death due to HIV and AIDS (Barnett and Whiteside 2002). Each person is embedded in a network of family, peers, communities, and society. As a person becomes ill and dies, there are important consequences for his or her family – particularly for any dependants such as children or the elderly. When enough individuals become infected with HIV, the consequences begin to affect whole communities. The next development – some researchers argue – is that whole societies begin to feel the impact of unprecedented levels of death (Whiteside 2000).

Politically, the potentially devastating impact of AIDS epidemics around the world has been used to mobilise resources and action. The international donor community has been lobbying African governments, arguing that the very institutions holding society together are under threat: health systems, education systems, and industries (Coombe 2000; Kelly 2000). However, these systemic impacts have been difficult to show empirically (Bennell *et al.* 2002; Barnett and Whiteside 2002). One possible reason for this is that many of these systems are already dysfunctional, and although AIDS is making matters worse, the systems still continue to function (or dysfunction) (Badcock-Walters *et al.* 2003). Given the complexities which determine the extent to which an education system is functioning, the shortage of any longitudinal data partly explains why – to date – there has been little evidence of systemic impacts.

It has been easier for researchers to show the consequences of increased illness and death at the household level by surveying affected households. Questions such as 'what happens to children when one or two parents die?' (Ainsworth and Filmer 2002; Bicego *et al.* 2003; Foster 1997) and 'what is the effect of adult death on household levels of income?' (Barnett and Whiteside 2002; Wyss *et al.* 2004; Yamano and Jayne 2005) are asked. Whiteside – among others – argues that the impact of HIV and AIDS is felt as an immediate and severe shock (short-term impact); and later by more complex, gradual, and long-term changes (long-term impact) (Barnett and Whiteside 2002; Whiteside 1998). For instance, when a parent dies, a child might have to move house – a sharp and perceptible consequence. A few years later, that child might drop out of school because of emotional stress and poverty – both of which were indirectly triggered by their parent dying. There is a need to see how short-term and long-term impacts feed into each other. The only way to do this is through longitudinal studies.

Orphans and education in South Africa

Given the low level of access to anti-retroviral treatment in South Africa, for the majority of HIV-positive people, the infection inevitably leads to death, preceded by chronic illness (Cohen 2002; Coombe 2000; Kelly 2000). In South Africa, the main mode of transmission of HIV is through sexual intercourse (UNAIDS 2002). Consequently, most of those who are dying are adults in the most productive part of the human life cycle (both in terms of procreation and economically).

According to the Actuarial Society of South Africa's model, there are an estimated one million children in South Africa whose mother has died and 2.13 million children whose father has died (Giese 2004). Upon the death of a parent, a coping system is activated in which the extended family traditionally takes over responsibility for the welfare of the orphans (Foster 1997). Given the rise in the number of orphans, it appears that these coping systems are becoming over-stretched (Nyambedha *et al.* 2003; Foster 2004). In many cases, orphans are being cared for by grandparents (Bicego *et al.* 2003; Foster 1997; Ntozi and Nakamany 1999), or looking after themselves – evidenced by the increase in the number of child-headed households (Gregson *et al.* 2001; Sengendo and Nambi 1997). The physical well-being of children is also at risk, with sick parents less likely to take children for immunisations or for more general health-care services (Foster 1998; Shetty and Powell 2003; Mishra *et al.* 2005).

Although the rapid increase in the number of orphans in South Africa cannot be disputed, it is far from clear whether or not these orphans are disadvantaged in ways which will undermine their well-being. One group of researchers in South

Africa has recently argued that the psychological impacts of AIDS on children may have been exaggerated and based on assumptions which are supported neither by research in psychology nor by the realities of growing up in Africa (Killian 2004; Pharoah 2004; Richter 2004).

Drawing from psychological literature on resilience, Killian argues that between 50 and 66 per cent of children growing up in circumstances of multiple risk overcome their adverse conditions and show strong signs of coping and resilience (Killian 2004). The author goes on to argue that resilience is often over-looked in the literature on orphans and is an important process in adapting successfully, despite difficult circumstances. Clearly, it cannot be assumed that orphanhood automatically undermines the well-being of children, and its effects are likely to be context-specific. Yet there is a dearth of evidence on the circumstances under which orphanhood might lead to adverse outcomes.

Barnett and Whiteside review the literature on the impact of HIV and AIDS on household levels of poverty. They conclude that impact will depend on (1) the number of AIDS cases a household experiences; (2) the characteristics of dead individuals; (3) community attitudes; and (4) the household's wealth (Barnett and Whiteside 2002). The implication is that future impact studies should take into account these socio-demographic factors. Moreover, the authors suggest that more longitudinal research is needed to understand how the impact of parental illness and death is felt by households. Finally, they – and others – criticise the small sample sizes of many impact studies (*ibid.*; Booysen and Arntz 2003).

Three different sets of researchers have analysed data from around 19 Demographic and Health Surveys (DHS). One group found that orphans in Africa live, on average, in poorer households than non-orphans (Case *et al.* 2003). Conversely, Bicego *et al.*'s analysis of the data suggests that orphans are no more economically disadvantaged than non-orphans (2003). The answer may be that impact will be felt differently in different countries, and at different times (Ainsworth and Filmer 2002). However, these contrasting results from the same datasets are also due to the different ways in which the researchers measured the variables.

In South Africa, a longitudinal study in Free State showed that AIDS-affected households were poorer at baseline, but also that over a six-month period their household expenditure and income decreased more rapidly than unaffected households (Bachmann and Booysen 2003). Although this study shows the importance of using longitudinal data to understand the dynamic nature of the impact of AIDS, the baseline survey did not differentiate between the stages of impact that the households were experiencing.

Impact of AIDS on orphans' education

Internationally, a received wisdom has sprung up which claims that girl orphans are more educationally disadvantaged than boy orphans, and that the death of a mother has more of an impact on education than the death of a father. However, several systematic reviews and analyses of multiple datasets suggest otherwise.

Four different groups of researchers have analysed DHS data from a number of countries in order to explore cross-country correlations between enrolment and orphanhood (Ainsworth and Filmer 2002; Bicego *et al.* 2003; Case *et al.* 2003; Monasch and Boerma 2004). In one of the largest of the four studies, Ainsworth and Filmer (2002) compared DHS data from 28 countries and argue that it is impossible to make cross-country generalisations, because the relationship between orphanhood and economic status is not uniform. Although orphanhood has an effect on enrolment in some countries, by far the more important factor was poverty.

Case *et al.*'s 2003 analysis of the same datasets suggests that orphans are less likely to be enrolled in school, even once economic background is controlled for. Combining both DHS and Multiple Indicator Cluster Surveys, Monasch and Boerma (2004) analyse datasets from 37 countries and also find that in 30 of these countries orphans are less likely to be enrolled. Like other researchers, they found no clear pattern relating to the type or sex of the orphan.

A recent systematic review on the impact of orphanhood on educational outcomes in sub-Saharan Africa (Schierhout *et al.* 2004) found 17 studies, of which 12 were household studies and the remaining five were school-based surveys. Across the 17 studies, Schierhout *et al.* generalised that orphans have lower enrolment than unorphaned children, especially older orphans. However, it is not always the case that orphans are educationally disadvantaged in terms of a range of educational outcomes (Bicego *et al.* 2003; Gould and Huber 2002).

In terms of gender, although some evidence exists that girls' educational outcomes are more affected by being orphans, evidence also exists that boys are affected too (Schierhout *et al.* 2004; Case and Ardington 2005; Urassa *et al.* 2001), and that any gender differences among orphans simply reflect underlying gender differentials in enrolment (Ainsworth and Filmer 2002). Similarly, although some studies show that maternal death has a greater impact than paternal death (Bicego *et al.* 2003; Case and Ardington 2005; Nyamukapa and Gregson 2005), contrary evidence exists that paternal death has a similar effect (Schierhout *et al.* 2004). Some researchers have found dual orphans to be particularly educationally disadvantaged (Bicego *et al.* 2003), while others suggest dual orphans might actually be advantaged because of the scholarship criteria of many NGOs (Bennell *et al.* 2002; Mishra *et al.* 2005).

The other dimension to the debate is whether orphans are disadvantaged because they are poorer (Ainsworth *et al.* 2002; Serpell 1999) or through some other factor such as increased stigma and discrimination (Schonteich 1999). One study suggests that orphans – particularly maternal orphans – were angry and depressed when having to live with a foster family, and that this in turn impacted on their education (Sengendo and Nambi 1997). A demographic approach is taken by Case *et al.,* who argue that educational outcomes for orphans depend largely on the degree of relatedness of the child to the head of the household (Case *et al.* 2003; Case and Ardington 2005). The importance of socio-demographic factors was also highlighted by Gould and Huber (2002) and Mishra *et al.* (2005), who show that children from one-parent households could be as disadvantaged at school as orphans.

Research into which educational outcomes are affected by orphanhood also yields mixed results. The majority of the studies have focused on enrolment (Ainsworth and Filmer 2002; Case *et al.* 2003; Serpell 1999; Carr-Hill and Peart 2003; Carr-Hill *et al.* 2002; Booysen 2001), while others have also included primary-school completion (Nyamukapa and Gregson 2005), school fees (Case and Ardington 2005), delayed enrolment (Ainsworth *et al.* 2002), and attendance (Bennell *et al.* 2002; Schierhout *et al.* 2004; Gould and Huber 2002). Many of the researchers contributing to this literature are not educationalists but rather researchers who are interested in children's well-being, and see the impact of AIDS on education as both a way to assess well-being and a way to estimate the long-term economic impact of the AIDS epidemic. Although some of this research has yielded important results, one of the limitations of many studies is that the prevailing educational policy context has been ignored. As Carr-Hill and Peart (2003) point out, the impact of AIDS on enrolment has been masked in many countries by the concurrent policy of abolishing user fees in primary education, which causes a huge surge in the number of children enrolling in primary schools. This increase can hide a decrease in enrolments among orphans.

Implications of the literature

Despite the establishment of democracy, growing up in South Africa still remains, for many, a difficult and vulnerable period. Apartheid undermined the African family structure through forced labour migration, which historically led to high numbers of children being fostered or living in female-headed households. Children are facing multiple vulnerabilities, with only a minority living in a two-parent nuclear family.

This pre-existing vulnerability of many children in South Africa is increased through the impact of AIDS. How the impact is felt will depend on how households respond, which in itself is determined by complex factors such as resilience, fostering, and local customs relating to child-rearing.

The impact of AIDS on children is a dynamic process and can thus be observed at different stages: from when a parent becomes ill, to when the parent dies, and the longer-term impact after parental death. Although there are many ways in which AIDS impacts on children, the bulk of the research focuses on studying the well-being of orphans, as this sub-group is one of the easiest groups of vulnerable children to identify. This remains one of the most easily identifiable approaches to studying the impact of AIDS.

Research has attempted to untangle the links between poverty, HIV, gender, and children's well-being, but a lack of longitudinal data has obstructed an understanding of the causal mechanisms underlying the impact of AIDS on children. Clearly, a need exists for longitudinal studies that combine strong socio-economic indicators as well as detailed demographic information.

Existing studies of the impact of AIDS on education have produced very mixed results. Links between orphanhood and enrolment are not straightforward, and seem to depend on a number of different factors. What is surprising though is how few studies have looked into the possible mechanisms through which HIV and AIDS impacts on educational outcomes. The only factors which have been investigated are poverty, relationship to head, and family composition. More longitudinal studies are needed to understand these potential mechanisms and also to investigate the sequence of events that leads to educational disadvantage. Many studies have relied on sampling through schools, which excludes some of the most disadvantaged children who have already dropped out of the formal education system. Sample sizes have also, on occasions, been small. There is a need for large-scale household surveys. The research agenda also needs to be broadened to look at a wider range of educational outcomes – not just enrolment. These outcomes need to be looked at by age and gender, taking into account the overarching policy context.

A study of orphans' educational outcomes in KwaZulu-Natal, South Africa

In response to some of the gaps identified above, a research team from the London School of Hygiene and Tropical Medicine collaborated on a longitudinal study of households and children in KwaZulu-Natal, South Africa. The remainder of this chapter describes the findings *vis-à-vis* the gendered impact of being an orphan on educational outcomes.[3] The research took place in KwaZulu-Natal, where just over one-fifth of South Africa's 44.8 million inhabitants live. Data from the census in 2001 show that the largest population group in the province is Black South African (84.9 per cent), followed by the Indian population (8.5 per cent) (Census 2001).

KwaZulu-Natal has experienced a very severe HIV and AIDS epidemic, with prevalence rates increasing from an estimated 7.1 per cent in 1990 to 36.5 per cent in 2000 (UNAIDS 2002). Recent analysis of a demographic surveillance system of a rural population in northern KwaZulu-Natal (Africa Centre Demographic Information System) suggests that AIDS is now the leading cause of death in adulthood: responsible for 48 per cent of deaths in 2000 in the study region (Hosegood *et al.* 2004). Although KwaZulu-Natal is not the poorest of South Africa's nine provinces, two-fifths of its residents live in poverty (Carter and May 2001).

KwaZulu-Natal Income Dynamics Study (KIDS)

Research design and questionnaire

The study analysed educational outcomes of a cohort of children who were surveyed in 1998 and 2004. The cohort included 1635 children who were aged between 7 and 20 in 2004 (school-going age), and who formed part of a wider household survey known as the KwaZulu-Natal Income Dynamics Study, or KIDS.

KIDS is a panel of households which has been re-interviewed twice since it was first surveyed in 1993. During the first wave (KIDS 1), the sample was representative at the national and provincial levels, and, at the time, KIDS 1 was the first fully representative household survey to be conducted in South Africa (Roberts 2000). Given the sweeping changes in policy since 1993, a group of economists at the University of Natal (now the University of KwaZulu-Natal) and elsewhere decided to revisit the households in 1998. The white and coloured populations were excluded from the 1998 wave because of doubts over the representativeness of the small and highly clustered samples of these population groups interviewed in 1993, and their low response rates. In 2002, plans for a third wave of data collection were developed between the University of KwaZulu-Natal, University of Wisconsin, and the London School of Hygiene and Tropical Medicine (by Ian Timæus and the author).

KIDS covers an 11-year span – the same 11-year period which has seen huge increases in AIDS-related death in the region (Hosegood *et al.* 2004). KIDS is therefore perfectly placed for analysing the long-term gendered impacts of parental death.

All three waves of KIDS have collected demographic and household expenditure data. In addition, the 2004 wave collected detailed information on children's schooling. This dataset has been linked to official statistics on schools in order also to study the role of school factors in determining educational outcomes. Logistic regression modelling[4] is used to control for confounding factors and identify causal pathways. In this way, the educational outcomes of children orphaned by 2004 are compared with the educational outcomes of non-orphaned children in 2004, controlling for a wide range of socio-demographic and economic factors.

Main findings

The findings are structured around the living conditions of orphans (under the age of 21 in 2004) and then how educational outcomes of orphans compare with unorphaned children.

Orphans, fostering, and gender in KwaZulu-Natal

A very high number of children in the study are orphans – more than one-third (see Table 1). The most common type of orphan is a paternal orphan (when the father has died). The table below shows the number of orphans by age group: it is obvious that the older the children, the higher the proportion of orphans. This is expected, because the proportion of children who are orphaned can only increase with age.

Table 1: Percentage of children aged 7 to 20 in 2004 according to parental survival and residency status by age group

Parental status (Number)	All ages	Percentages of children by age group		
		7 to 10	11 to 15	16 to 20
Parents alive Of which:	1072	71.5	66.9	60.8
Parents resident	376	19.1	26.0	23.0
Father absent	380	30.8	21.8	19.6
Mother absent	56	4.2	2.9	3.4
Both absent	260	17.4	16.2	14.7
Orphaned child Of which:	555	28.5	33.1	39.2
Paternal orphan	352	18.6	21.1	24.4
Paternal orphans, living with mother	238	12.0	14.5	16.7
Fostered-out paternal orphan	114	6.6	6.7	7.7
Maternal orphan	109	5.9	6.8	7.2
Maternal orphan, living with father	16	0.5	1.3	1.0
Fostered-out maternal orphan	93	5.4	5.5	6.1
Dual orphan	94	4.0	5.2	7.7

Overall, orphans tend to live in poorer households than other children, but they also tend to come from urban areas and to have relatively educated parents. For example, 34 per cent of all unorphaned children are classified as very poor,[5] compared with 41 per cent of orphaned children. In particular, it is the paternal and dual orphans who are living in the poorest households. In families where children are living with their father (because the mother is either absent or dead), less than 23 per cent fall into this extremely poor category. This suggests that living with a father can have protective benefits. Maternal orphans are not living in poorer households.

Identifying which children are orphans is not a straightforward process. It involved cross-checking parental status between the waves of data collection. Through this longitudinal approach it was possible to identify a significant number of orphans who would not have been categorised correctly if only the data from 2004 had been used. The main reason for this appears to be that respondents tend to say a step-parent of an orphan is – erroneously – their real parent. It is possible that this bias is particular to Zulu culture but, given the awkwardness involved in talking about death in most countries, it is likely that under-counting of orphans is fairly commonplace. Indeed, this under-counting of orphans has been pointed out by a number of demographers who term it 'the adoption effect' – referring to the phenomenon of step-parents adopting orphaned children (Brass 1975; Hill 2000; Timaeus 1991). Although this bias is fairly well recognised in demographic research, it has largely been ignored by AIDS researchers.

Gendered differences in fostering patterns

In many ways, orphans are living in different conditions from unorphaned children. Paternal and dual orphans live in poorer households. The research shows that fostering of children will depend on the gender of the surviving parent. If the father dies, then most children continue to live with the mother. However, if the mother dies, most children are not living with their father. These children might have been fostered out or – as is common among unorphaned children – may never have resided with their father.

There are, therefore, strong gender dimensions to the fostering arrangements of orphans. However, these fostering patterns need to be interpreted within a context where only a minority of children are living in a nuclear family with both their parents. Absence of the father is very common, as is sending children to live with relatives. In the former case children are living in more impoverished households, whereas in the latter case children appear to be relatively advantaged. These results indicate that the common assumption that fostering has a negative impact on children needs to be revisited. More qualitative studies are needed to understand the circumstances and gendered reasons why a child might be fostered out, and the sexual division of labour between fostered and non-fostered children.

Gendered impact of AIDS on educational outcomes

There are striking gender differences both in terms of which parent dies and how children are affected. Table 2 summarises the main results from the study and collates the main ways in which orphanhood impacts on education in KwaZulu-Natal by gender, age group, and educational outcome.

Table 2: Summary of gendered findings

Educational outcome	Paternal or maternal death effect?	Gender of child	Age group	Timing of orphan effect
Delayed enrolment	Both	Boys and girls	Under 9	Short-term only
Attendance long-term	Paternal	Boys only	11–13	Short-term and
Repetition	Paternal	Girls only	11–15	Short-term only
Primary-school completion	Paternal	Girls only	13–16	Short-term only
Dropout and long-term	Paternal	Girls only	16–20	Medium-term

The KIDS 3 study found that a father dying has a larger impact on educational outcomes than if a mother dies, especially for girls. When a mother dies, there is a small negative effect on younger children (both boys and girls) in terms of delayed enrolment into primary school (see Table 2), but the impact is much smaller than if a father dies. Boys are also affected, but in different ways: for boys, being orphaned leads to poorer daily attendance and delayed enrolment, whereas for girls the impact is on primary-school completion, repetition, dropout, and delayed enrolment.

Nevertheless, the results presented here suggest that orphanhood has worse implications for girls than boys: after all, dropping out of school is a worse outcome than poor attendance. Although the impact of orphanhood on education is more severe for girls, the overarching gender inequality in educational outcomes must also be considered. In South Africa, boys generally perform worse than girls, and on outcomes such as repetition or primary-school completion girl orphans perform no worse than unorphaned boys. This is demonstrated in Figure 1 by examining the differences between boys and girls in completing primary school. Girls appear to be completing primary school earlier than boys, which also fits in with the finding that girls are less likely to repeat a grade than boys. Boys, in general, are disadvantaged educationally compared with girls.

Figure 1: Percentage of boys and girls aged 11 to 16 in the KIDS panel who have completed primary school

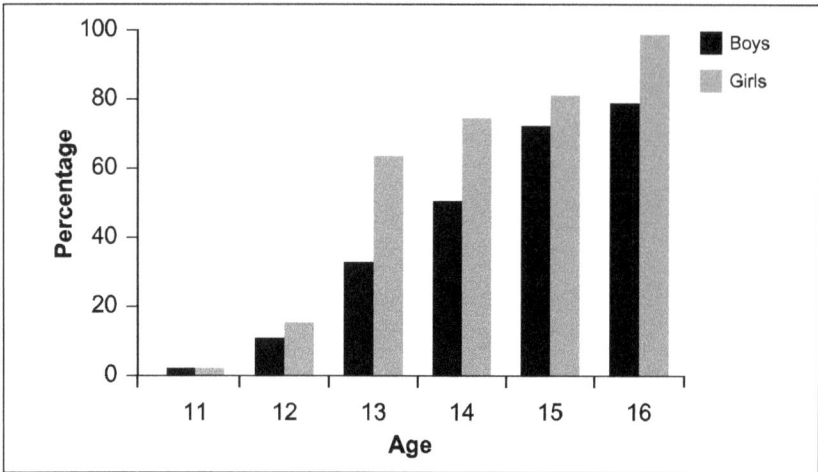

These results were analysed using logistic regression modelling. Researchers looked at what the effects were for girls and boys of the death of a father, mother, or both parents. The results from this modelling (Table 3) show that when a parent dies, primary-school completion is adversely affected, but only if a father dies and only for girls. If a father dies, a girl aged 13 to 16 is 3.85 times more likely not to have completed primary school, compared with similar girls whose fathers have not died (see final column, third row).

AIDS impacts disproportionately on girls' education, especially if the father dies. But why is this happening? Is it because of poverty? Further modelling shows that poverty explains some, but not all, of the relationship between orphanhood and educational outcomes. Even once poverty was controlled for in the analysis, being orphaned was associated with negative educational outcomes for girls on all the relevant educational outcomes (Boler 2006), as measured through delayed enrolment into primary school, repetition rates, primary-school completion, and dropout. In other words, girl orphans were disadvantaged on the whole spectrum of educational outcomes regardless of their level of poverty.

The finding that poverty does not completely explain the impact of AIDS on education highlights the importance of not simply relying on economic interventions, such as cash transfers of bursaries, in responding to the orphan crisis. The disadvantage faced by orphans in KwaZulu-Natal is not purely economic in nature; there are other factors which influence orphaned girls to drop out of school. In fact, it appears that one of the main reasons why girl orphans are disadvantaged at school is because of increased rates of pregnancy and sexual vulnerability.

Table 3: Odds of not having completed primary school in 2004 for boys and girls aged 13 to 16 in 2004, by sex, age and survival and residency status of parents

	Both boys and girls		Boys only		Girls only	
	Odds ratio	P*	Odds ratio	P	Odds ratio	P
Father resident	1		1		1	
Father absent	1.45	0.17	1.16	0.68	2.20	0.09
Father dead	1.84	0.04	1.11	0.78	3.85	0.01
Mother resident	1					
Mother absent	0.88	0.60	0.63	0.16	1.23	0.61
Mother dead	1.45	0.25	1.62	0.28	1.19	0.72
Age						
13	1		2.21	0.03	2.21	0.07
14	0.57	0.03			1.56	0.32
15	0.27	<0.01	0.42	0.04		
16	0.13	<0.01	0.33	<0.01	0.13	0.01
Gender						
Boys	1					
Girls	0.31	<0.01				

*The P value in the table shows what the probability is that the result is the result of random chance. If the P value is below 0.05, this means that the probability is less than 5 per cent that the effect is due to chance, or, in other words, the effect is significant at the 5 per cent significance level.

Sexual vulnerability as a reason for dropping out of school

In addition to poverty, the study looked at other reasons why orphaned girls are more likely drop out of school and found that the main reason for older girls is pregnancy, as shown in Figure 2.

This finding has important ramifications. First, it challenges the dominant idea that staying in school reduces sexual vulnerability and sexual activity. It suggests, instead, that the relationship might be operating in the opposite direction – that those who are sexually active are more likely to drop out of school. Of 37 girls in the study who had been pregnant and had dropped out, 23 (62 per cent) stated that they had dropped out because they were pregnant. In other words, the majority of girls are getting pregnant and then dropping out of school, rather than dropping out first and then becoming pregnant. Second, it appears that although the South African government has policies in place to protect and support the educational rights of teenage mothers, as schools are legally not allowed to refuse

Figure 2: Reasons for dropout for boys and girls in KIDS 3 study

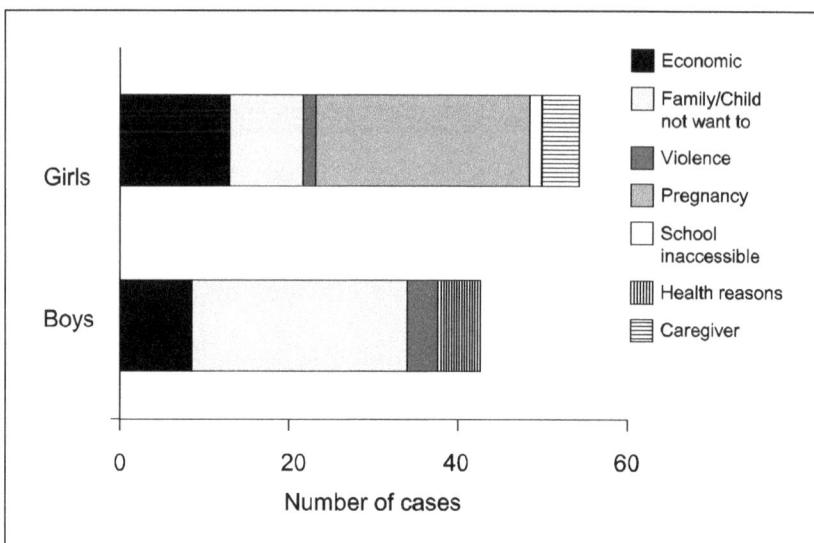

to enrol them, in reality, pregnancy is still a major cause of dropout. As part of wider efforts towards Education for All, schools need to look more closely at how to retain female students who become pregnant.

The study suggests that girl orphans are more sexually vulnerable than their female peers who are not orphaned. However, it is not clear if – as Jewkes *et al.* argue (2001) – the determinants of teenage pregnancy are unique to South Africa's specific cultural and historical context, or if they are more generalisable. Exploratory discussions with researchers in the field suggest the following possible explanations for why paternal death might increase the probability of pregnancy:

- Paternal death might decrease the social capital available to girls, which increases their sexual vulnerability.

- Fathers may play an important role in protecting their daughters from sexual relationships and if they are not present, boys and men might be more likely to try to have sex with the girls.

- A psychological reaction to parental death by the girls might be an urge to create new life.

- Children are psychologically scarred through parental death and likely to behave in socially deviant ways (perhaps boys through truancy and girls through having sexual relationships).

- Girls might be seeking substitute father figures through boyfriends.

In order to examine some of these hypotheses, in-depth qualitative studies are needed, as well as more studies which explicitly focus on the determinants of teenage pregnancy. This finding on pregnancy also shows the importance of linking together studies of sexual health and education outcomes with strong economic data. Many household surveys focus on one of these areas (according to the research interests of the group), but may inadvertently foster a one-dimensional view of the impact of AIDS and thus over-emphasise the poverty or educational dimensions while ignoring some of the social dimensions.

In effect, a vicious cycle has been set up in which AIDS impacts on the daughters of dead men to make them more sexually vulnerable (increasing their risk of HIV), which in turn impacts negatively on their education. The resulting reduction in educational attainment may in turn further increase the risk of HIV infection, as HIV vulnerability has shifted from more educated to less educated populations. A similar cycle is set up with the economic pathway in which, when a father dies, the household becomes more economically vulnerable, which causes girls to drop out. The resulting lower levels of education increase the economic vulnerability of the girl, which in turn will increase her risk of HIV infection.

Conclusions

This study has shown strong gender differences in terms of how the educational outcomes of orphans differ. In KwaZulu-Natal, a father dying has a larger impact on educational outcomes than if a mother dies.

This study has been instrumental, therefore, in highlighting the importance of fathers in determining the well-being of children. This importance goes beyond an economic role and is likely to include psycho-social factors. However, it should be noted that, broadly speaking, the family structure in South Africa differs from many other African countries, and it may therefore be the case that the importance attributed to fathers in this analysis is not generalisable across the region. In poorer countries, the economic role of fathers may be more important as a determinant of educational outcomes. Similarly, in countries where most children live with their father, the impact of the father dying may be even larger than in South Africa.

Orphaned children are, on the whole, performing worse than unorphaned children. The other important gendered finding of this study is that orphanhood affects boys and girls in different ways: for boys, being orphaned leads to poorer daily attendance and delayed enrolment, whereas for girls the impact is on delayed enrolment, as well as on primary-school completion, repetition, and dropout.

Although the impact of orphanhood on education is more severe for girls, the overarching gender inequality in educational outcomes must also be considered.

In South Africa, boys generally perform worse than girls, and on outcomes such as repetition or primary-school completion, girl orphans perform no worse than unorphaned boys. Any South African response should therefore address boys' low educational outcomes and not merely target girls. This gender pattern is different from that of many other African countries where girls generally perform worse than boys, and therefore the gender patterns identified in this analysis are unlikely to be replicated in all countries across the continent.

One of the most important findings from the studies is that the impact of orphanhood negatively affects children's education for reasons which are not wholly economic; particularly through increased sexual vulnerability and pregnancy for older girls. The policy implication is that responses for orphans need to do more than address their economic needs. More attention needs to be paid to how orphans are becoming educationally disadvantaged in school, and measures need to be taken to deal with low attendance and grade repetition.

Notes

1   The study is based on doctoral research undertaken with Professor Ian Timæus at the London School of Hygiene and Tropical Medicine.

2   See UNAIDS update: www.unaids.org/en/HIV_data/2007EpiUpdate/default.asp and UNICEF: www.unicef.org/infobycountry/southafrica_statistics.html (both last accessed April 2008).

3   The findings are drawn from the author's doctoral research and thesis (Boler 2006).

4   Logistic regression modelling involves examining the effect of certain factors that can be ascertained while controlling for other factors.

5   Very poor children were identified as those who have a household per capita expenditure below half the poverty line (196 Rand in 2004).

References

Ainsworth, M., K. Beegle, and G. Koda (2002) 'The Impact of Adult Mortality on Primary School Enrollment in Northwestern Tanzania', Washington DC: The World Bank, 23.

Ainsworth, M. and D. Filmer (2002) 'Poverty, AIDS, and Children's Schooling', Washington DC: World Bank, 41.

Bachmann, M.O. and F.L. Booysen (2003) 'Health and economic impact of HIV/AIDS on South African households: a cohort study', *BMC Public Health* 3: 14.

Badcock-Walters, P., C. Desmond, D. Wilson, and W. Heard (2003) 'Educator Mortality In-service in KwaZulu-Natal', Durban: University of Natal.

Barnett, T. and A. Whiteside (2002a) *AIDS in the Twenty-First Century,* New York: Palgrave Macmillan.

Barnett, T. and A. Whiteside (2002b) 'Poverty and HIV/AIDS: impact, coping and mitigation policy', Florence: UNICEF.

Bennell, P., K. Hyde, and N. Swainson (2002) 'The Impact of the HIV/AIDS Epidemic on the Education Sector in Sub-Saharan Africa', Sussex: Centre for International Education, University of Sussex.

Bicego, G., S. Rutstein, and K. Johnson (2003) 'Dimensions of the emerging orphan crisis in sub-Saharan Africa', *Social Science and Medicine* 56(6): 1235–47.

Boler, T. (2006) 'Facing the consequences of AIDS: orphans, cash grants and educational outcomes in South Africa', London School of Hygiene and Tropical Medicine.

Booysen, F. (2001) 'The socio-economic impact of HIV/AIDS in the Free State Province', Centre of Health Systems Research and Development, University of Free State, South Africa.

Booysen, F. and T. Arntz (2003) 'The methodology of HIV/AIDS impact studies: a review of current practices', *Social Science and Medicine* 56(12): 2391–405.

Brass, W. (1975) 'Methods for estimating fertility and mortality from limited and defective data', Chapel Hill: International Program of Laboratories for Population Statistics.

Carr-Hill, R., K. Katabaro, A. Katahoire, and D. Oulai (2002) 'The Impact of HIV/AIDS on Education and Institutionalising Preventive Education', Paris: IIEP.

Carr-Hill, R. and E. Peart (2003) 'Understanding the Impact of HIV/AIDS on Education Systems in Selected Eastern and Southern African Countries', London: Department for International Development.

Carter, M. and J. May (2001) 'One kind of freedom: poverty dynamics in post-apartheid South Africa', *World Development* 29(12): 1987–2006.

Case, A. and C. Ardington (2005) 'The Impact of Parental Death on School Enrollment and Achievement: Longitudinal Evidence from South Africa', Working Paper 43.

Case, A., C. Paxman, and J. Abledinger (2003) 'Orphans in Africa', Princeton: Centre for Health and Wellbeing, Princeton University.

Census (2001) 'Primary Tables KwaZulu Natal: Census '96 and 2001 Compared', Statistics South Africa, 2004.

CIA (2003) *The World Factbook*, Washington DC: Central Intelligence Agency, https://www.cia.gov/library/publications/the-world-factbook/ (last accessed May 2008).

Cohen, D. (2002) 'Human Capital and the HIV Epidemic in Sub-Saharan Africa', Geneva: International Labour Organization.

Coombe, C. (2000) 'Managing the Impact of HIV/AIDS on the Education Sector', Pretoria, South Africa: University of Pretoria.

Dorrington, R., D. Bradshaw, L. Johnson, and D. Budlender (2004) 'The Demographic Impact of HIV/AIDS in South Africa: National Indicators for 2004', Cape Town: Centre for Actuarial Research, South African Medical Reserach Council and Actuarial Society of South Africa.

Foster, G. (1997) 'Africa's children and AIDS – a continent in crisis. The devastation of the HIV / AIDS pandemic', *AIDSlink* 45: 4–5.

Foster, G. (1998) 'Children affected by HIV', *Child Health Dialogue* 12: 3.

Foster, G. (2004) 'Safety nets for children affected by HIV/AIDS in Southern Africa', in R. Pharoah (ed.) *A Generation at Risk? HIV/AIDS, Vulnerable Children and Security in Southern Africa*, Pretoria: Institute for Security Studies.

Giese, S. (2004) 'Health', in J. Gow and C. Desmond (eds.), *Impacts and Interventions: The HIV/AIDS Epidemic and the Children of South Africa*, Pietermaritzberg: University of Natal Press.

Gould, B. and U. Huber (2002) 'Primary School Attendance in Tanzania – How Far is it Affected by Orphanhood?', Annual Conference of the British Society for Population Studies, University of Liverpool.

Gregson, S., H. Waddell, and S. Chandiwana (2001) 'School Education and HIV Control in Sub-Saharan Africa: From Discord to Harmony?', *Journal of International Development* 13: 467–85.

Hill, K. (2000) 'Methods for measuring adult mortality in developing countries: a comparative review', *The Global Burden of Disease 2000 in Aging Populations*, Research Paper 01.13, Boston: Harvard Burden of Disease Unit.

Horizons (2004) 'Poverty, Educational Attainment and Livelihoods: how well do young people fare in KwaZulu Natal, South Africa?', research update, Washington DC: Horizons/Population Council.

Hosegood, V., A.M. Vanneste, and I.M. Timæus (2004) 'Levels and causes of adult mortality in rural South Africa: the impact of AIDS', *AIDS* 18(4): 663–71.

Jewkes, R., C. Vundule, F. Maforah, and F. Jordaan (2001) 'Relationship dynamics and teenage pregnancy in South Africa', *Sociology, Science and Medicine* 52(5): 733–44.

Kelly, M. (2000) 'Planning for Education in the Context of HIV/AIDS', Paris: IIEP/ UNESCO.

Killian, B. (2004) 'Risk and resilience', in R. Pharoah (ed.), *A Generation at Risk? HIV/AIDS, Vulnerable Children and Security in Southern Africa*, Pretoria: Institute for Security Studies.

Mishra, V., F. Arnold, F. Otieno, A. Cross, and R. Hong (2005) 'Education and Nutritional Status of Orphans and Children of HIV-infected Parents in Kenya', DHS working papers.

Monasch, R. and J.T. Boerma (2004) 'Orphanhood and childcare patterns in sub-Saharan Africa: an analysis of national surveys from 40 countries', *AIDS* 18 Suppl 2: S55–65.

Ntozi, J. and S. Nakamany (1999) 'AIDS in Uganda: how has the household coped with the epidemic?', in I. Orubuloye, J. Caldwell, and J. Ntozi (eds.), *The Continuing HIV/AIDS Epidemic in Africa*, Canberra: Health Transition Centre.

Nyambedha, E.O., S. Wandibba, and J. Aagaard-Hansen (2003) 'Changing patterns of orphan care due to the HIV epidemic in western Kenya', *Sociology, Science and Medicine* 57(2): 301–11.

Nyamukapa, C. and S. Gregson (2005) 'Extended family's and women's roles in safeguarding orphans' education in AIDS-afflicted rural Zimbabwe', *Sociology, Science and Medicine* 60(10): 2155–67.

Pharoah, R. (2004) 'Introduction', in R. Pharoah (ed.), *A Generation at Risk? HIV/AIDS, Vulnerable Children and Security in Southern Africa*, Pretoria: Institute for Security Studies.

Richter, L. (2004) 'The impact of HIV/AIDS on the development of children', in R. Pharoah (ed.), *A Generation at Risk? HIV/AIDS, Vulnerable Children and Security in Southern Africa*, Pretoria: Institute for Security Studies.

Roberts, B. (2000) 'Chronic and Transitory Poverty in Post-apartheid South Africa', Durban: School of Development Studies, University of Natal.

Schierhout, G., A. Kinghorn, R. Govender, J. Mungani, and J. Morely (2004) 'Quantifying Effects of Illness and Death on Education at School Level: Implications for HIV/AIDS Response', Johannesburg: Health and Development Africa.

Schonteich, M. (1999) 'AIDS and age: South Africa's crime time bomb?', *AIDS Analysis Africa* 10(2): 1, 3–4.

Sengendo, J. and J. Nambi (1997) 'The psychological effect of orphanhood: a study of orphans in Rakai district', *Health Transition Review* 7 Suppl: 105–24.

Serpell, N. (1999) 'Children Orphaned by HIV/AIDS in Zambia: Risk Factors from Premature Parental Death and Policy Implications', doctoral dissertation degree, University of Maryland.

Shetty, A.K. and G. Powell (2003) 'Children orphaned by AIDS: a global perspective', *Seminars in Pediatric Infectious Diseases* 14(1): 25–31.

Timaeus, I. (1991) 'Estimation of adult mortality from orphanhood before and since marriage', *Population Studies* 45(3).

UNAIDS (2002) 'AIDS Epidemic Update', Geneva: UNAIDS.

UNAIDS (2003) 'National Response Brief', South Africa: UNAIDS.

UNAIDS (2006) 'Report on the Global AIDS epidemic', Geneva: UNAIDS.

Urassa, M., J.T. Boerma, R. Isingo, et al. (2001) 'The impact of HIV/AIDS on mortality and household mobility in rural Tanzania', *AIDS* 15(15): 2017–23.

Whiteside, A. (1998) 'Monitoring the AIDS pandemic', *AIDS Analysis Africa* 8(5): 4–5.

Whiteside, A. (2000) 'The real challenges: the orphan generation and employment creation', *AIDS Analysis Africa* 10(4): 14–15.

Wood, K. and R. Jewkes (1997) 'Violence, rape, and sexual coercion: everyday love in a South African township', *Gender and Development* 5(2): 41–6.

Wyss, K., G. Hutton, and Y. N'Diekhor (2004) 'Costs attributable to AIDS at household level in Chad', *AIDS Care* 16(7): 808–16.

Yamano, T. and T.S. Jayne (2005) 'Measuring the impacts of prime-age adult death on rural households in Kenya', *Economic Development and Cultural Change*.

Part 2

Building the Evidence Base to
Meet the Challenges

6 The road less travelled: gender-based interventions in the education-sector response to HIV

David Clarke

> *Two roads diverged in a wood, and I –*
> *I took the one less traveled by,*
> *And that has made all the difference.*
> (From *The Road Not Taken* by Robert Frost)
>
> *Gender roles and relations have a significant influence on the course and impact of the HIV epidemic in every region of the world. Understanding the influence of gender roles and relations on individuals' and communities' ability to protect themselves from HIV and effectively cope with the impact of AIDS is crucial for expanding the response to the epidemic.*
> (UNAIDS 1998)

Introduction

This chapter takes stock of the experience of nearly two decades of responding to HIV through the education sector and considers how gender issues have been addressed. It seeks to identify what interventions might be effective, and points to the steps that need to be taken by ministries of education to put these in place. In summary, it concludes that responses to HIV need to prioritise maximising the synergies between concerns with gender, education, and the HIV response. In particular there are lessons to be learned from gender-disaggregated data, and consideration of the ways in which masculinities and femininities shape experiences of education. There is a long way to go in most education systems in relation to developing an evidence base through monitoring and evaluation of gender issues and developing gender-sensitive practices in administration and in learning about HIV. However, there are some islands of good practice which give pointers to developments that can take place.

Since HIV is spread primarily through sex, addressing gender norms, the societal scripts or messages that dictate what is appropriate or expected behaviour for males and females, is increasingly recognised as an important strategy to prevent the spread of HIV infection (Pulerwitz *et al.*). An effective response to the epidemic must be built on understanding those influences in their social context. HIV vulnerability and risks are gender-specific (see Box 1) and specific attention to related gender issues will be a hallmark of an appropriate education programme.

Box 1: HIV vulnerability and risks are gender-specific

- Unequal power relations give women a subordinate position and make them socially dependent on male family members: women have less access to health care, employment, education, information, etc. Thus women are in a poorer position to control when, with whom, or in what circumstances they have sex.

- The ideology of fidelity, love, and trust within marriages/relationships often leads couples of all ages to neglect or abandon condom use. Marriage and long-term relationships are proving high-risk conditions for long-term partners, especially women, to contract HIV.

- Acceptance of double standards for men and women normalises men seeking multiple partners and encourages men to go into sexual circulation without commitment to sexual safety.

- Early marriage forces girls to have sex before their bodies are fully developed, which heightens the risk.

- Young girls are forced or lured into unsafe sex with HIV-positive men, because the men assume the girls are not HIV-positive and/or they mistakenly believe that sex with a virgin can cure HIV.

- Young women are kept ignorant about sexual matters as this is often viewed as a sign of purity and innocence.

- In sexual relations, both men and women often learn to prioritise men's sexual pleasure and disregard women's sexual agency.

- Common attitudes about gender differences that associate masculinity with risk-taking, aggression, and disregard for possible damaging consequences reinforce men's neglect of sexual safety and promote sexual irresponsibility.

- Expected 'masculine' behaviours interfere with the ability of boys/men to clarify incomplete knowledge about sex, and discourage them from expressing uncertainty and exploring safer sexual behaviour.

- Both men and women often have expectations of 'masculine' behaviour that discourage boys/men from discussing problems and feelings, and exclude them from active participation in caring practices (for the young, the elderly, the ill). As a result, men more readily deal with sexual and HIV situations using violence, or with high-risk actions, dissociating themselves from both the problem and the solution.

- Homophobia inhibits many men from taking responsibility for their sexual practices, associating unsafe practices with 'other kinds of men', rather than the risk activity of sexual intercourse itself. Men who live as 'heterosexuals' but also have sex with men are often ill-prepared to practise safer sex.

Source: Norwegian Working Group on HIV/AIDS and Gender (2001) 'HIV/AIDS and Gender: An Awareness Folder', Oslo.

Sophisticated gender analysis is required

The data on HIV infection rates among women and men have led to a discourse on the 'feminisation' of the epidemic, a potentially misleading concept, since the spread of HIV among women is not fully a result of female agency, as exemplified by increasing numbers of monogamous married women infected by their husbands. A strong focus on women and HIV is convergent with a developing emphasis on girls' education (Department for International Development 2005), coinciding with specific attention to girls' education and HIV (UNICEF 2005). Enrolling and retaining girls at school, particularly until secondary level, will contribute to reducing their vulnerability to HIV. Whether these insights are considered in the formulation of national policies and strategies and whether these enable sustained progress towards gender equality in education and appropriate HIV education should be continuously and objectively reviewed.

Concern with girls' education can be considered as necessary, but not sufficient for comprehensive changes in the status of women. The strong emphasis on girls' education risks neglecting the contribution that boys and men make to gender inequality at school and in wider society. A more holistic perspective on education would analyse the social practices of males as well as females. A more sophisticated gender analysis is required; one which includes attention to aggressive male behaviours, sexuality, and violence to women. Research in sub-Saharan Africa has found that many young men view violence against women, including verbal threats and coercive sex, as a socially acceptable dimension of male authority (Barker and Ricardo 2005).

The prevalence of gender-based violence (GBV) in and around the school setting should be a concern from an Education for All perspective, as well as for preventing HIV. In some contexts, girls may be subject to routine sexual advances from older male students and even from male teachers (Leach *et al.* 2000, Leach, this volume). In the vicinity of schools, girls may be preyed on by older men, so-called 'sugar daddies' who seek sex in return for gifts or money to pay school fees (*ibid.*). The role of masculinities in encouraging and legitimising violence to obtain sexual access or dominance may be reinforced in school through peer interactions and conversations (Kenyway and Fitzclarence 1997). The study of masculinity is emerging as an important issue in education (Dillabough 2006) revealing multiple and competing forms. This has facilitated the emergence of a broader understanding of equity issues in educational discourse and practices.

However, in many countries school-related GBV goes unchecked in the face of indifference from school administrators, the larger community, and the Ministry of Education (USAID 2004). By failing to punish sexual aggression or turning a blind eye to teachers having sexual relationships with their pupils, schools may foster harmful gendered practices which will likely stay with a child through to adult life (Leach *et al.* 2003). There is evidence that GBV has short- and long-term consequences, including physical and psychological damage as well as social repercussions, including school drop-out (USAID 2007).

Transmission of HIV by males who have sex with males constitutes a field of gender analysis and response that is seldom included in education-sector practice. Similarly the nexus between homophobia, bullying, and HIV-related stigmatisation is one that is conspicuously neglected in contexts where this ought to be a social-policy issue. The UK is one of a very few countries that have recently taken a policy stand on homophobia in schools (Department for Children, Schools and Families 2006).

It is hard to evade the conclusion that only when education policies and strategies are more fully informed by a more comprehensive gender analysis that includes an understanding of masculinities will educational opportunity for all become a reality rather than an aspiration, and the education response to HIV become meaningful to the learner. The persistence of gender inequality in education is a result of inequitable societal norms and values, and the education system may function as a means of reproducing them (Clarke 2005). How then should Ministries of Education develop a more comprehensive response?

The continuum of response

WHO (WHO 2003) has identified a range of technical approaches for integrating gender into HIV programmes that form a continuum, including 'harmful' responses that negate any potential programme improvements through incorporating discriminatory gender distinctions. In addition the following approaches are identified:

- *Do no harm.* This approach involves the elimination of damaging assumptions and stereotypes concerning men and women. It constitutes a first step along the continuum.

- *Gender-sensitive programmes.* Gender-sensitive responses involve the recognition that the various HIV-related needs of men and women are often different, not only because of physiology, but more importantly on account of gender norms and relations.

- *Transformative interventions.* These are interventions that seek to transform gender roles and create more gender-equitable norms and relationships. They seek to change the underlying conditions that cause gender inequalities.

- *Interventions that empower.* Empowering interventions are those which seek to equalise the balance of power between men and women.

This continuum of response is highly applicable to the education sector in relation, not only to HIV education, but also to education service delivery in general. It is important that Ministries of Education understand the different approaches and are able to place themselves on the response continuum. Whether their position is appropriate to the context of the epidemic is the next question, and this involves the ministry understanding the gendered factors of vulnerability and risk among the student population, and what education can do about them.

The role of education in HIV prevention

It is now routinely asserted that in the absence of a vaccine or a cure for HIV, education constitutes one of the priority approaches to HIV prevention and for dealing with its adverse social consequences, especially among young people (UNAIDS IATT on Education 2003). The education sector has become important in the national multi-sectoral response to the epidemic as it offers a cost-effective vehicle for providing knowledge (World Bank 2002), shaping attitudes and, under certain conditions (Kirby *et al.* 2006), the development of skills on a large scale. Most importantly, it can provide significant learning before most young people are exposed to sexual risk, the main mode of HIV transmission. Hence it can play a role in supporting behaviours that assist them in remaining uninfected.

Experience gathered over more than a decade in education-sector responses to HIV permit the identification of four key benefits arising from effective programmes. These are:

- vulnerability reduction;
- risk reduction;
- reduction in HIV-related stigma and discrimination; and
- impact mitigation on children and staff.

Vulnerability to HIV is highly context-specific. Responses need to be prepared based on comprehensive assessments of child and adolescent vulnerability to social situations that may expose them to HIV. Children and adolescents who are especially vulnerable need to be identified. Vulnerability reduction can be achieved through increasing access to education for poor children at all levels, especially for girls, and putting in place strategies to ensure that they attend, complete, and achieve learning outcomes. Schools and places of learning help to reduce vulnerability to sexual exploitation by increasing the social connectedness of students (UNAIDS IATT on Education 2003). Vulnerability can also be addressed through education, which aims to promote gender equality through changing discriminatory gender norms and harmful practices of masculinity. Interventions such as 'child-friendly schools' may also contribute to vulnerability reduction. Vulnerability reduction through education is in part a structural intervention, but may also include specific targeted interventions to raise awareness of vulnerability factors as well as contribute to changing norms and behaviours.

Risk reduction can be achieved through life-skills education which specifically addresses those risks that confront a target group. Not all adolescents are at the same risk. Thus, age-appropriate programmes need to be based on assessments of risk and identify those adolescents 'most at risk'. These represent a priority for HIV-specific resources and are typically children out of school (UNICEF *et al.* 2007). School-based programmes offer a very large target population and provide an opportunity for interventions to reach a very large number of young people before or around the time when they become sexually active and engage in high-risk behaviours. They encourage young people to delay the onset of sexual activity, while reducing the number of partners and increasing the use of condoms by young people who are already sexually active. School-based programmes are less useful in contexts where the majority of adolescents are out of school.

HIV-related stigma can be reduced through education programmes which can contribute to dispelling myths and misconceptions about HIV, as well as building compassion for those infected and affected. Education programmes that involve people living with HIV appear to be particularly effective in reducing stigma. Workplace policies have a key role in addressing HIV-related stigma and discrimination.

In generalised epidemics over time, HIV can impact on the supply of education staff; the demand for education among affected families, especially where orphaning has taken place; and the quality of education service delivery. In these contexts, impact mitigation is critical to safeguard the functions of the sector.

The balance of interventions should be tailored to match the nature and dynamics of a national HIV epidemic. In all cases, the highest priority needs to be given to HIV prevention through education programmes that aim to reduce vulnerability and risk to HIV. These programmes need to be evidence-based, considering the factors of vulnerability and risk behaviours of the target group and what constitutes an effective response in delivering an intervention.

There is a strong tendency for education responses to HIV to be developed outside the education mainstream on the margins of curriculum and practice. This is due to the perception that HIV is a health issue and not an educational issue. It may also be because funding tends to be external and accessed through HIV budgets rather than education-assistance budgets. A third factor is that many educators tend to stigmatise HIV education and frequently do not understand the specialised field. What needs to be better understood is that HIV education responses can contribute significantly to improving the general quality of education, educational access, and equity. They need to become part of the educational mainstream.

The gender dimensions of HIV and education

This potential of the education sector must be assessed together with its complex relationship with gender inequalities. Education policies that aim at gender equality are contested. Educational opportunity is strongly affected by gender, with girls and women having less access to education in most countries. The school is a gendered environment where girls can be exposed to discrimination and violence (Leach *et al.* 2000). An understanding of gender is central to understanding HIV vulnerability and risk. These assessments are true as much inside the education sector, with its potential to contribute to protection against the epidemic, as outside.

On top of the difficulties entailed in negotiating gender inequality in education, the role of education in tackling HIV is imperfectly understood by those who most need to take action. Although the ministry of education is pivotal in responding to HIV, many ministries are not yet fully engaged in tackling HIV (World Bank 2004c). Not all HIV-related education interventions are effective (Kirby *et al.* 1994). Most countries have tended to develop a piecemeal approach to HIV in the education sector, based on small-scale projects, often donor-funded and driven. These have often led to a fragmented set of interventions requiring considerable investments in terms of co-ordination and scaling up. How then should ministries of education develop a comprehensive response to HIV which takes account of the gender dimensions of the epidemic?

A ministry of education has to respond to the following key questions:

1. How can the education system be most effectively and efficiently harnessed for HIV prevention and for building coping skills in the context of a generalised epidemic?

2. How can the education system safeguard itself in the face of threats to education demand and supply arising out of the impacts of HIV on sector personnel, children, and the community?

3. How can the rights of all children and education staff who are either infected with or affected by HIV be assured?

4. How can education build competencies across society to prevent HIV-related stigma and discrimination?

The questions are straightforward enough; however, an evidence-based approach is required to arrive at the most appropriate solutions to the problem, and one that takes adequate account of gender dynamics. Thus to what extent are girls and boys vulnerable through contextual, environmental, and social factors to HIV exposure? To what extent are children and young adults at risk from HIV transmission on account of their behaviours? How is risk-taking conditioned by gender? What role does the social construction of masculinity play? What beliefs and practices promote the stigmatisation of people living with or affected by HIV? How are stigma and discrimination affected by gender norms and practices? How is the education system responding strategically to gender inequality? What needs to be done to build capacity to develop, implement, and sustain an effective response, and how do HIV interventions mesh with this? What is the extent of the threat to education service delivery posed by the current and projected national HIV epidemic, and what are the gender dynamics? Which impacts can be prevented and which are unavoidable and will need to be mitigated? Which interventions will be most cost-effective?

The evidence base on gender and the education response to HIV is woefully inadequate in terms of providing a clear guide to which interventions are likely to be effective. A number of key interventions can be identified where gender can be addressed. These are:

• education-sector policy;

• institutional capacity;

• the curriculum; and

• teacher training.

Education-sector policy

A coherent, comprehensive, and scaled-up response to HIV is considerably more problematic to achieve without a specific policy in place. Policy is required to define priorities, rights, entitlements, and responsibilities with regard to the HIV response in the education sector. It should specify clearly responsibilities for implementation and monitoring/review. An important aspect of having a policy in place is that it demonstrates ownership by the ministry of the issue and the response. It permits greater accountability by civil society, assuming of course that it is readily accessible to all through a national dissemination process. Policy on HIV for the education sector needs to be fully aligned with existing sector policies as well as other national policies on HIV and AIDS. An initial exercise therefore is often needed to review existing policy to establish how it currently supports and conditions the education response to HIV. Policy, once approved, needs to be disseminated across the entire sector. Guidance and resources need to be made available to schools for implementation. Systems need to be in place to monitor and review periodically the implementation and its intended outcomes in the sector.

Education-sector policy on HIV may be contained in a range of instruments which include the National AIDS Policy (e.g. Bangladesh; see Directorate General of Health Services *et al.* 1996), National AIDS Law (e.g. Cambodia), Policy Framework for Children and AIDS (e.g. India; see National AIDS Control Organisation 2007), National HIV/AIDS Strategy (e.g. Indonesia; see Office of the Co-ordinating Minister for People's Welfare and National AIDS Commission 2003), or in education-sector-specific policy (Namibia; see Ministry of Basic Education, Sport and Culture and Ministry of Higher Education, Training and Employment Creation 2003). It is the latter which will provide the most detailed policy guidance for the sector. Putting in place a specific education-sector policy for HIV is a litmus test of a government's political engagement with the issue and its technical capacity to respond to the challenge.

A key component of any education-sector policy on HIV is a comprehensive workplace policy consistent with ILO and UNESCO guidance (International Labour Organization and UNESCO 2006). Such a document should address issues of sexual abuse (Kelly and Bain 2005). It should clearly specify responsibilities for implementation and monitoring/review. An important aspect of having a policy in place is that it demonstrates ownership by the ministry of the issue and the response. It also permits greater transparency and accountability to civil society.

HIV prevention

In developing a policy, a number of gender issues need to be considered. First, in terms of HIV prevention, what are the needs of young people (e.g. knowledge and skills, vulnerability and risk reduction) that can be met through school education? How are these gendered? At which age should HIV education be introduced in the curriculum? How should HIV education be included in the curriculum and the co-curriculum? What should be the content, pedagogy, and time allocation? Should girls and boys be taught separately or together? What teaching and learning resources will be required? Are any different resources required for boys and girls? How do teachers need to be prepared to teach effectively about HIV (through in-service and pre-service training)? What are the gender considerations that must be addressed with regard to pre-service and in-service training? How are parents/guardians and the community, including people living with HIV and AIDS, to be involved? How can gender power relations in the community be addressed? How can schools be made safer places (from abuse, violence, exploitation, HIV transmission through accidents, HIV-related stigma, and homophobia, etc.)? How can the ways in which schools might encourage harmful gender divisions be addressed? How can schools be made healthier places of learning? What gender-related interventions are needed such as providing separate toilets for boys and girls?

Treatment, care, and support

What are the issues concerning the education of HIV-positive children? Do girls and boys have different needs? Why? What are the issues concerning the education of children whose parents are living with HIV or who have lost a parent/parents to AIDS? Does the loss of a father or mother have different implications, and what might appropriate policy be? What are the issues concerning teachers continuing to work while living with HIV? Are the issues different for men and women teachers? How do schools provide linkages with health services for testing and counselling and anti-retroviral therapy (ART)? What are the gender differences entailed, for example, in making transport to health centres easier for men or for women? Why? How do schools provide linkages with social services (for children infected and affected by HIV and AIDS)? Do social services have different policies for boys and girls?

Workplace support

What kinds of policy support does a teacher living with HIV need, in order to continue working at school? Are there differences for men and women? Do any codes of professional ethics or conduct protect staff and students from sexual harassment? How are these implemented? How do teachers need to be supported to enable them to remain uninfected by HIV? How do assumptions about masculinity and femininity affect this? How should schools ensure that there is no HIV-related discrimination in schools/education? How does this work with wider gender-equality policy? How can teachers' unions support teachers with regard to their work and HIV and AIDS? Are there different issues about work and pay for men and women?

Management of response

Who in the ministry of education is responsible for the implementation of its response to HIV and AIDS? How is gender analysis implemented? What additional capacity needs to be built or existing capacity strengthened to respond to HIV effectively? What capacity is required to mainstream gender and HIV?

Once approved, policy needs to be disseminated across the entire sector. The Ministry of Education and Youth in Jamaica, for example, developed a national workshop-based dissemination process for its education-sector policy (Ministry of Education, Youth and Culture 2001) involving its HIV Resource Team (UNESCO 2005). It has also placed the policy on its website. Implementation concerns the whole sector, and systems need to be in place to monitor and review periodically implementation and its associated outcomes in the sector. The challenges of policy implementation are graphically illustrated by research undertaken in Kenya which found that most schools were not implementing the Education Sector HIV Policy (Republic of Kenya 2005), and most teachers did not know about the policy (CfBT 2006).

Comprehensive evidence on how education policy on HIV has best addressed gender issues is as yet unavailable. Relatively few countries have developed specific detailed policies on HIV for the education sector, and even fewer have done detailed work on gender in those policies. Through a rapid content analysis, it was found that gender is addressed inconsistently, but in all cases there is limited coverage of gender-related issues and specific interventions.

Table 1: Gender component of education-sector policy on HIV in selected countries

Country	Gender in education-sector HIV policy
South Africa (1999)	No mention.
Jamaica (2001)	No mention.
Namibia (2003)	Zero tolerance of sexual abuse, harassment, exploitation, and assault of students. Appropriate systems and safeguards to be put in place.
Kenya (2005)	Principle of gender responsiveness. Application of all aspects of the policy should be responsive to the different needs of women and men, boys and girls.
	Learning institutions will create rape and sexual harassment awareness through sensitisation among girls and boys, men and women, to enhance safety, protection, and prompt action on post-exposure prophylaxis where available.
	Recruitment and deployment of staff. The ministry of education will ensure that partners and spouses are not separated unnecessarily.
Sierra Leone (2005)	Gender sensitivity is a guiding principle.
	Strategy for building gender-sensitive workplace HIV and AIDS peer education.
	Development and distribution of age-specific and gender-sensitive background and curriculum materials to all schools and institutions.

Table 1: Gender component of education-sector policy on HIV in selected countries continued

Country	Gender in education-sector HIV policy
Uganda (2006)	Ensure that access to information, communication, and education on HIV and AIDS is universal and appropriate, taking cognizance of the age, gender, culture, and religion of beneficiaries of the sector.
	Gender is a guiding principle.
	Ensure that vulnerabilities and susceptibilities are analysed in the context of men and women, as well as promoting sensitivity to unique challenges experienced by both sexes in the sector as a result of their differences and the existing social expectations. In particular, the unique factors affecting women and the girl child in context of HIV and AIDS will be given special focus.
	Sexual harassment, abuse, exploitation, or assault of fellow students or learners are prohibited and shall be severely punished.
UNESCO 'Gold Star' (2005)	Not a single reference to any gender-related issue or response in this hypothetical state, developed to exemplify 'best practice'.

Sources: Department of Education 1999; Government of Sierra Leone 2005; UNESCO 2005.

It can be seen that gender is a key concern in only a handful of education-sector policies on HIV. Within these there is considerable diversity in how the sector will respond at all levels of the education system to institutionalise the HIV response.

Institutional capacity

In a central ministry of education, gender-analysis capacity needs to be developed with a full-time focal point or co-ordinator, or the establishment of a team within a unit specialising in HIV to deal with policy and implementation, including monitoring and evaluation (M&E) and tackling any abuse of pupils in schools. In education regions/districts there needs to be similar capacity developed with emphasis on implementation, including M&E. In curriculum-development centres (school health/life skills/HIV education), capacity in gender analysis needs to be supported and sustained. In teacher training institutions gender analysis and research skills need to be developed. In schools (school management boards, parent–teacher associations, school principals, nodal or focal teachers, and peer educators), capacity to ensure that schools are, at a minimum, gender-sensitive in the teaching and learning environment (UNICEF 2002) needs to be developed. A whole-school approach is most likely to be successful in achieving this. Teacher training is a key area for investment. Teachers need to be trained to be more aware of their responsibilities as role models and not to abuse their position, while pupils need access to counselling services. School cultures need to be less authoritarian and more open and democratic (Leach 2004).

The curriculum

The curriculum is likely to be the main vehicle for school-based HIV education. Six key sets of issues need to be addressed (UNAIDS IATT on Education 2003): understanding the nature of HIV infection, knowing which behaviours to avoid, knowing how to avoid risk, adopting attitudes of respect for human rights, understanding the nature and dynamics of human relationships, and skills development. These factors are often described from a bio-medical perspective. In developing a clear understanding of the gender dynamics in each of these areas, each needs to be put in a social context to develop understanding of gender norms, sexuality, and risk-taking behaviours. These will vary significantly from context to context.

To develop a relevant and appropriate curriculum, there needs to be a comprehensive knowledge base on HIV-related vulnerability and risk behaviours of children and young people. An assessment of the motivation, knowledge, and skills of the teachers who would deliver the HIV-related curriculum is also needed. HIV should be integrated into a wider skills-based health programme.[1]

The curriculum content should address age, gender, and culturally appropriate HIV-prevention methods, and promote non-discriminatory behaviours and attitudes to people living with HIV. It should address gender inequality and power issues, including violence and non-consensual sex, and stigma and discrimination. Good-quality teaching and learning materials need to be developed and used at all levels in the education system. The provision of good-quality teacher training to implement the curriculum as designed is an essential component of the response. Classroom teaching may require separate sessions for boys and girls, as is the current practice in India in the Adolescence Education Programme. In other contexts it may be possible to address the needs of both boys and girls in mixed groups (Schneker and Nyirenda 2002). In practice, it is likely that a combination of both single and mixed groups may be the most effective to meet their different practical and strategic gender needs. The evidence base is weak in this regard, and more research is required into gender and the pedagogy of HIV-preventive education.

The UNAIDS Interagency Task Team on Young People has undertaken a systematic review of the evidence from developing countries on preventing HIV in young people (UNAIDS IATT on Young People 2006). It concluded that there is a sufficiently strong evidence base to support the widespread implementation of school-based interventions that incorporate the characteristics of effective programmes, which have been derived from available research results. There is strong evidence that these programmes reduce sexual risk behaviour. Nearly all school-based programmes have strong evidence for increasing knowledge (Kirby *et al.* 2006), though this can be contentious (Stover and Johnston 1999).

The actions needed to achieve effective curriculum-based HIV education programmes are presented below in Table 2, with comments on how to enhance this dimension from a gender perspective. The original table paid scant attention to gender, and an attempt has been made to rectify this, highlighting the centrality of gender to curriculum development, goals and objectives, teaching and learning approaches, and methods and implementation. However, the majority of curriculum-based programmes have paid limited attention to the issues. This is exemplified in the *Sourcebook of HIV Prevention Programmes in Sub-Saharan Africa* (World Bank 2004a). In 13 different programmes, only two (from Senegal and Zambia) explicitly mention gender. The Senegal programme (GEEP) attempts to be transformative in that it challenges young people's attitudes on gender. The Zambian programme (CHEP) includes gender-specific objectives and strategies. In drawing up the table I have synthesised good practice, but implementation remains to be researched.

Table 2: Actions for effective curriculum-based HIV education programmes

Developing the curriculum	
Actions	**Enhancing the centrality of gender**
Involve multiple people with different backgrounds in theory, research, and HIV education	Should involve gender specialists
Assess relevant needs and assets of target group	Assessment should involve comprehensive gender analysis
Use a logic model to develop the curriculum which specifies the health goals, the risk, and the protective factors affecting those behaviours, and the activities addressing those risk and protective factors	Curriculum-development process should be informed by analysis of gendered vulnerability, risk, and protective factors
Design activities consistent with community values and available resources (such as staff time, staff skills, facility space, and supplies)	Community values need to be assessed from a gender perspective Harmful norms need to be addressed
Pilot-test the programme	The pilot programme needs to be assessed for evidence of its effectiveness The assessment needs to be conducted on a gender-sensitive basis

Table 2: Actions for effective curriculum-based HIV education programmes
continued

Content: curriculum goals and objectives	
Actions	**Enhancing the centrality of gender**
Focus on clear health goals such as the prevention of sexually transmitted infections (STIs) and HIV	To be informed by gender analysis of practices that protect against STIs and HIV
Focus narrowly on specific behaviours leading to those health goals (such as abstaining from sex or using condoms or other contraceptives) Give clear messages about these behaviours and address situations that might lead to them and how to avoid them	To be informed by gender analysis (e.g. of which behaviours may be easy/difficult for girls and boys)
Address multiple sexual-psychosocial risk and protective factors (such as knowledge, perceived risks, values, attitudes, perceived norms, and self-efficacy)	To be informed by gender analysis of forms of risk and strategies to overcome this
Teaching methods	
Actions	**Enhancing the centrality of gender**
Create a safe social environment in which youths can participate	Undertake a gender analysis of how young men and young women use the learning environment and which processes encourage participation by all
Include multiple activities in which youths can participate	To be informed by gender analysis of activities
Use instructionally sound teaching methods that actively involve participants, that help participants personalise the information, and that are designed to change each group of risk and protective factors	To be informed by gender analysis of how learners engage with instructions
Use activities, instructional methods, and behavioural messages that are appropriate to the culture and sexual experience of the participants	To be informed by gender analysis of widely used approaches and how these can change
Cover topics in a logical sequence	Take care that attention is given to topics that address girls and boys
Implementation	
Actions	**Enhancing the centrality of gender**
Secure at least minimal support from appropriate authorities, such as ministries of health, school districts, or community organisations	Support to be sought from government and civil-society organisations that have an interest in promoting gender equality

Table 2: Actions for effective curriculum-based HIV education programmes
continued

Implementation	
Actions	**Enhancing the centrality of gender**
Select educators with desired characteristics, train them, and provide them with monitoring, supervision, and support	To be informed by gender analysis. Monitoring and evaluation to be gender-sensitive
If needed, implement activities to recruit and retain youths and overcome barriers to their involvement (e.g. publicise the programme, obtain consent from youths and parents)	To be informed by gender analysis of how information circulates and how parents consent to the participation of their sons and daughters
Implement virtually all activities as designed	To be evaluated from a gender perspective looking at gender-disaggregated data and what the impact has been on girls and boys

Little is known about how ministries of education are addressing issues of masculinity and femininity through the curriculum, and with what outcomes. Teaching and learning resources dealing with masculinity have been developed in a number of contexts, including India (UNESCO 2006), Brazil, and Mexico (Instituto Promundo 2002), but little is known about the use of such materials in school settings. There are promising programmes such as the Conscientising Male Adolescents Programme in secondary schools in Nigeria, which uses a process of dialogue and enquiry to question and challenge existing gender norms and practices (USAID 2007).

The importance of involving students and teachers in researching gender norms and practices preparatory to developing the HIV curriculum cannot be overstated. This is critical for evidence-based curriculum development. A multi-country study (UNICEF 2002a) undertaken in Africa investigating children's perspectives on gender, sexuality, and HIV education provided a wealth of information revealing how boys and girls construct gender differences, the presence of sexual double standards, conflict between tradition and modernity, boys' power over girls, the activities of sugar daddies and mommies, and problematic relations with adults. How this has been translated into curricular practice across the seven participating countries is unclear, however, and would require follow-up research.

Research on gender issues relating to HIV-prevention education curricula remains the exception rather than the rule. A rare example concerns the development of Primary School Action for Better health (PSABH) in Kenya (Maticka-Tyndale *et al.* 2004). Analysis of focus-group discussions with young people led to the articulation of a sexual script that makes playing sex appear necessary and inevitable for Kenyan young people. Importantly, however, girls do not appear to be as powerless, nor do boys appear as powerful, as portrayed in some research. Knowledge of the content of the sexual script and the points where alternative directions can be taken has provided insights into potential strategies for developing HIV-prevention programming. Placing such programming within the context of existing scripts may support young people in developing new normative patterns of sexual encounter which may reduce young people's vulnerability to HIV infection.

The fundamental importance of including gender at all stages of the curriculum-development process on HIV education is clear enough. The way forward is for ministries of education to invest more in building gender-related technical capacity to carry out some of the processes detailed below.

Complementary approaches to curriculum-based HIV-prevention programmes typically involve the co-curriculum. These include peer-education programmes, school anti-AIDS clubs, ministry of education information, education, and communication (IEC) strategies, and the promotion of youth-friendly health services for STI treatment, voluntary counselling and testing, and condom distribution. However, while a number of these activities are documented, little is said about their gendered dynamics.

Anti-AIDS clubs target youth and out-of-school activities. There is a lack of research on anti-AIDS clubs from a gender perspective. It is clearly much needed to ensure programme effectiveness. One multi-country study (UNICEF 2002a) in sub-Saharan Africa found that boys dominated activities in school anti-AIDS clubs, while in Zimbabwe and Zambia it was reported that girls who joined these clubs were often seen as 'bad' girls who were actually chasing boys.

Teacher training

Research points to the need to pay more attention to teachers, since they are the means by which HIV-education programmes reach students (Gallant and Maticka-Tyndale 2004). Effective HIV educators need to be developed through pre-service and in-service training to teach a skills-based approach to HIV prevention. This requires the adoption of participatory teaching methods and classroom management skills, a major challenge in education systems that retain didactic teacher-centred pedagogy and where class sizes are large. Enhancing teachers' content knowledge of HIV is an important facet of teacher training, as is developing confidence to handle sensitive and taboo topics with ease in the classroom. To bring about a more transformative approach, gender-awareness training specifically designed to help teachers examine and confront their own biases and stereotyping and promote gender equality is clearly needed in both pre- and in-service training (USAID 2007). Teacher motivation and commitment to the programme are critically important factors in programme success.

Guidelines for teachers on HIV in all education institutions need to be prepared, disseminated, and used. Teachers' guides prepared from a gender perspective should be available to support the implementation of the HIV curriculum. These need to include attention to developing awareness about HIV and gender, and developing pedagogic skills for use in the classroom. Teachers' unions should be involved in supporting gender equality and HIV education efforts.

In generalised HIV epidemics, ministries of education need to respond to the losses of human capital by taking measures to manage the impact of HIV and mobilise partners such as workers' organisations in this endeavour. In the case of education systems, teachers' unions are key organisations that can be mobilised to help address both the impact of HIV and also HIV prevention. It is important for ministries of education to ensure an appropriate gender balance and to monitor attrition rates of the teaching stock from a gender perspective. Gender-disaggregated data in this respect would be useful. Gender also needs to be taken into account in designing strategies for HIV prevention among teachers, and teacher recruitment.

The most noticeable impact on the system in high-impact contexts is the permanent loss of teachers through death, employment change, retirement, or chronic illness. HIV tends to exacerbate existing attrition rates. A less direct form of impact is temporary teacher loss through illness or occasional and compassionate leave to attend funerals of colleagues or family members. Temporary absences will be harder to measure than permanent loss, and since teacher-attendance records are often neglected, this form of impact may be underestimated (*ibid.*). These constitute dimensions of the impact of HIV on the supply of education that also include the losses of education managers, teacher educators, and other key staff. The gender dimensions of these need to kept under review.

The recent expansion of access to anti-retroviral therapy (ART) through initiatives such as the WHO Three by Five initiative and PEPFAR has important implications for the supply of teachers. Ensuring that teachers have access to treatment is an important area for policy development and capacity-building. ART can prolong life and productive service in the classroom. While costly, it will still be a cost-effective solution to teacher absenteeism through HIV illness and loss through early mortality. ART, if properly rolled out to all who require it (women and men alike), is likely to have a significant effect on the impact of HIV on the sector.

The impact of HIV and AIDS on children has been comprehensively described, including the ability of children orphaned or made vulnerable by AIDS to continue to access and benefit from education. There are a number of ways in which HIV and AIDS impact on educational opportunities for children. In school, children who are either infected with or affected by HIV face possible discrimination by fellow pupils and by teachers. There is the reduced ability of affected families to pay for school fees, uniforms, books, and shoes, and the increased demand for child work at home or in the workplace, as well as the need for children to provide care for sick members of the household. In AIDS-affected households there may be a lower expected return on the investment in children's schooling (Grainger *et al.* 2001). The learning capacity of children affected by HIV is negatively affected, by factors including poor nutrition, hunger, trauma, and emotional distress (Kelly 2005). Teachers often report that orphaned children are 'listless, excessively reserved and do not play or laugh as much as other children.'

It is of critical importance to make schools more responsive to the needs of orphans and vulnerable children (OVC) and to consider gender issues as part of this and enable these children to continue their education despite the challenges they face at home or in the community (USAID 2003). Human Rights Watch (2005) recommends the development of best practices for schools. Possible strategies identified include training teachers or guidance counsellors to address bereavement issues, supporting school-based peer-support groups, keeping schools open at night, liaising with community-based organisations to identify the most vulnerable children, and sensitising teachers to the needs of HIV-affected children. The World Bank OVC Toolkit for Sub-Saharan Africa advocates developing school-based psychosocial counselling services (World Bank 2004b), but gender as yet has not been highlighted.

The UNAIDS IATT on Education recommends (UNAIDS IATT on Education 2004) training and support of teachers and village committees to identify vulnerable children and support them to go to school; empowering teacher–parent–community associations to support schools to serve the needs of vulnerable children; establishing school–community campaigns to reduce discrimination related to HIV and AIDS; protection against sexual abuse and exploitation by focusing on safety and security in child-friendly schools; establishing and supporting clear codes of conduct and training for school staff; and developing comprehensive HIV and AIDS workplace policies compliant with the ILO Code of Practice on HIV/AIDS in the Workplace (International Labour Organization 2001). Gender is a key aspect of the context of HIV-affected vulnerable children and needs to be given a central place in developing appropriate interventions in response.

The stigma and discrimination that children infected and affected by HIV face in school settings has been widely documented, for example in India (Human Rights Watch 2004) and in sub-Saharan Africa (Human Rights Watch 2005). It leads to discriminatory acts that can culminate in exclusion from education. In Rwanda, for example, children from families living with HIV are reportedly prevented from associating with or playing with others at secondary school (Perkins and Mulyanga 2005). The practice of isolating such students is apparently common, though not sanctioned by the school authorities. Verbal abuse in various forms by other students is also reported. A study of HIV-infected and affected children in South Africa found that most of the stories of discrimination at school related to other learners rather than teachers (Save the Children 2001). Through such HIV-related stigmatisation at school, educational inequity and the vulnerability of the children targeted are exacerbated.

Strategies for success include tackling gender and racial stereotypes, and efforts should be made to counter prejudice against minorities that are discriminated against. Life-skills education and counselling to help HIV-infected and affected children cope with stigma should be promoted (Parker and Aggleton 2003). Workplace policies for the education sector should include zero tolerance for HIV-related stigma and discrimination.

The impact of stigma and discrimination against people living with HIV in the family and in the community can be profound and wide-ranging. It appears to be related to gender, class, and social status, with poor people generally most adversely affected. Associations of people living with HIV report the fear of revealing their HIV status because of the fear of being isolated and discriminated against by colleagues, humiliated by others, ousted from their jobs, and regarded as immoral.

Addressing the stigmatisation of children and adults living with HIV or affected by HIV and AIDS is an area where education and teachers in particular can make a significant contribution to the multi-sectoral approach that is required to tackle this particular social phenomenon. Teachers have a potentially powerful role in combating HIV-related stigma and discrimination among the children they teach, the community they serve, and the profession to which they belong. In settings where there is high HIV prevalence, teachers are likely to be in contact with children affected by HIV, and have a clear duty to ensure not only that their own actions are non-stigmatising and non-discriminatory towards them in the school environment, but also to ensure that they seek to shape the values and behaviours of others in the same direction. Teachers who are gender-aware will have enhanced capacity to support children and adults.

Some conclusions

The potential for highlighting gender in developing an effective response to HIV is, despite islands of good practice, not yet realised. Ministries of education need to prioritise the following in developing their education-sector responses to HIV:

- consider putting gender education at the heart of the sector response to HIV;

- develop a comprehensive sector policy for HIV that provides a clear vision of how gender will be addressed in the HIV response;

- establish institutional capacity for a policy-based approach to gender and HIV, including monitoring and evaluation;

- ensure that the gender dimensions of vulnerability and risk are appropriately and adequately addressed in the HIV-related curriculum;

- invest in gender training in pre-service and in-service teacher training;

- put aside funding for evaluation studies to develop an evidence base to identify what works in gender and HIV education.

There is an urgent need for governments to move along the intervention continuum towards more transformative approaches. Working along the WHO paradigm from policies that 'do no harm' to those that are 'gender-sensitive' is not technically difficult to arrange, but it does require political will and financial resources. There needs to be a concern with an evidence-based approach to curriculum development, informed by the views of the target population. Technical capacity and good administrative systems are critical to success. Robust gender-disaggregated monitoring and evaluation arrangements need to be put in place to verify whether policy objectives are met. Achieving and implementing gender-sensitive policy would be an enormous achievement and would likely make an important difference to the lives of young people. Beyond that, the move towards transformative initiatives would be of enormous significance. However, for the present, education ministries' greatest challenge is to move towards mainstreaming HIV and gender, and from rhetoric to reality.

Note

1   See FRESH (Focusing Resources on Effective School Health). FRESH resources are produced by WHO, UNICEF, UNESCO, and the World Bank. They are available from www.freshschools.org/

References

Barker, G. and C. Ricardo (2005) 'Young Men and the Construction of Masculinity in Sub-Saharan Africa: Implications for HIV/AIDS, Conflict and Violence', World Bank Social Development Paper No. 26, Washington DC: World Bank.

CfBT (2006) 'An Analysis of HIV/AIDS Policy Formulation and Implementation Structures, Mechanism and Processes in the Education Sector in Kenya', Nairobi: CfBT.

Clarke, D. (2005) 'Planning and Evaluation for Gender Equality in Education in the Context of HIV and AIDS', London: University of London Institute of Education.

Department for Children, Schools and Families (2006) 'Homophobic Bullying: Safe to Learn: Embedding Anti-Bullying Work in Schools', London: Department for Children, Schools and Families.

Department for International Development (2005) 'Girls' Education: Towards a Better Future for All', London: Department for International Development.

Department of Education (1999) 'National Policy on HIV/AIDS for Learners and Educators in Public Schools and Students and Educators in Further Education and Training Institutions', Pretoria.

Dillabough, J. (2006) 'Gender theory and research in education', in M. Arnot and M. Mac An Ghaill (eds.), *The RoutledgeFalmer Reader in Gender and Education*, Abingdon: Routledge.

Directorate General of Health Services, Ministry of Health and Family Welfare, and Government of Bangladesh (1996) 'National Policy on HIV/AIDS and STD Related Issues', Dhaka.

Gallant, M. and E. Maticka-Tyndale (2004) 'School-based HIV prevention programmes for African youth', *Social Science and Medicine* 58: 1337–51.

Government of Sierra Leone (2005) 'HIV/AIDS Policy for Education Sector', Freetown.

Grainger, C., D. Webb, and L. Elliott (2001) 'Children Affected by HIV/AIDS: Rights and Responses in the Developing World', London: Save the Children.

Human Rights Watch (2004) 'Futures Forsaken. Abuses Against Children Affected by HIV/AIDS', New York: Human Rights Watch.

Human Rights Watch (2005) 'Letting them Fail. Government Neglect and the Right to Education of Children Affected by AIDS', New York: Human Rights Watch.

Instituto PROMUNDO (2002) 'Program H', Rio de Janeiro.

International Labour Organization (2001) 'The ILO Code of Practice on HIV/AIDS in the Workplace', Geneva: International Labour Organization.

International Labour Organization and UNESCO (2006) 'Improving Responses to HIV/AIDS in Education Sector Workplaces', Joint ILO/UNESCO Southern Africa Subregional Workshop, 30 Nov–2 Dec, Maputo, Mozambique, Geneva: ILO.

Kelly, M. (2005) 'The response of the educational system to the needs of orphans and vulnerable children affected by HIV/AIDS', in G. Foster, C. Levine, and J. Williamson, *A Generation at Risk: The Global Impact of HIV/AIDS on Orphans And Vulnerable Children*, Cambridge: Cambridge University Press.

Kelly, M. and B. Bain (2005) *Education and HIV/AIDS in the Caribbean*, Kingston: Ian Randle Publishers.

Kenyway, J. and L. Fitzclarence (1997) 'Masculinity, violence and schooling: challenging poisonous pedagogies', *Gender and Education* 9(1): 117–34.

Kirby, D., A. Obasi, and B. Laris (2006) 'The effectiveness of sex education interventions in schools in developing countries', in *UNAIDS Task Team on Young People: Preventing HIV/AIDS in Young People*, New York: UNAIDS.

Kirby, D., L. Short, J. Collins, D. Rugg, L. Kolbe, M. Howard, B. Miller, F. Sonenstein, and L.S. Zabin (1994) 'School-Based Programs to Reduce Sexual Risk Behaviors: a Review of Effectiveness', Public Health Reports 109(3): 339–61.

Leach, F. (2004) 'School-Based Gender Violence in Africa: A Risk to Adolescent Sexual Health', in C. Coombe (ed.) *The HIV Challenge to Education. A Collection of Essays*, Paris: UNESCO, IIEP.

Leach, F., P. Machakanja, and J. Mandoga (2000) 'Preliminary Investigation of the Abuse of Girls in Zimbabwean Junior Secondary Schools', Education Research Serial Number 39, London: Department for International Development.

Leach, F., V. Fiscian, E. Kadzamira, E. Lemani, and P. Machakanja (2003) 'An Investigative Study of the Abuse of Girls in African Schools', Educational Paper: Researching the Issues, Number 54, London: Department for International Development.

Maticka-Tyndale, E., M. Gallant, C. Brouillard-Coyle, D. Holland, K. Metcalfe, J. Wildish, and M. Gichuru (2004) 'The Sexual Scripts of Young Kenyan people and HIV Prevention', *Culture, Health and Sexuality* 7(1):27–41.

Ministry of Basic Education, Sport and Culture and the Ministry of Higher Education, Training and Employment Creation (2003) 'National Policy on HIV/AIDS for the Education Sector', Windhoek.

Ministry of Education, Youth and Culture (2001) 'HIV/AIDS Management in Schools', Kingston: Ministry of Education, Youth and Culture.

National AIDS Control Organisation (2007) 'Policy Framework for Children and AIDS', New Delhi: National AIDS Control Organisation.

Office of the Co-ordinating Minister for People's Welfare and National AIDS Commission (2003) 'Indonesia National HIV/AIDS Strategy 2003–2007', Jakarta.

Parker R. and P. Aggleton (2003) 'HIV and AIDS-related stigma and discrimination: A conceptual framework and implications for action', *Social Science and Medicine*, 57(1):13–24

Perkins, N. and S. Mulyanga (2005) 'My Right to Belong. Stories of Stigma Reduction Efforts Across Africa', Nairobi: ActionAid International.

Pulerwitz, J., G. Barker, M. Segundo, and M. Nascimento (2006) 'Promoting More Gender Equitable Norms and Behaviours Among Young Men as an HIV/AIDS Prevention Strategy', Horizons Final Report, Washington DC: Population Council.

Republic of Kenya (2005) 'Education Sector Policy on HIV and AIDS', Nairobi.

Save the Children (2001) 'The Role of Stigma and Discrimination in Increasing the Vulnerability of Children and Youth Infected with and Affected by HIV/AIDS South Africa'.

Schneker, I. and J. Nyirenda (2002) 'Preventing HIV/AIDS in Schools', UNESCO IBE Educational Practices Series No 9, Geneva.

Stover, J. and A. Johnston (1999) 'The Art of Policy Formulation: Experiences from Africa in Developing National HIV/AIDS Policies', Washington DC: The Policy Project, Futures Group International.

UNAIDS (1998) 'Gender and HIV/AIDS: Technical Update', Geneva.

UNAIDS IATT on Education (2003) 'HIV/AIDS and Education: A Strategic Approach', Paris: UNESCO.

UNAIDS IATT on Education (2004) 'HIV/AIDS and Education: The Role of Education in the Protection, Care, Support of Orphans and Vulnerable Children Living in a World with HIV and AIDS', Paris: UNESCO.

UNAIDS IATT on Young People (2006) 'Preventing HIV/AIDS in Young People. A Systematic Review of the Evidence from Developing Countries', Geneva: WHO.

UNESCO (2005) 'Overview: Good Policy and Practice in HIV and AIDS and Education', Booklet 1, Paris: UNESCO.

UNESCO (2006) 'Masculinity for Boys: Resource Guide for Peer Educators', New Delhi: UNESCO.

UNICEF (2002a) 'Breaking Silence: Gendered and Sexual Identities in HIV/AIDS Education', Young Voices Series, Nairobi: UNICEF.

UNICEF (2002b) 'HIV/AIDS Education: A Gender Perspective: Tips and Tools', New York: UNICEF.

UNICEF (2005) 'Girls, HIV/AIDS and Education', New York: UNICEF.

UNICEF, UNFPA, and UNESCO (2007) 'Responding to the HIV Prevention Needs of Adolescents and Young People in Asia: Towards (Cost) Effective Policies and Programmes'.

USAID (2003) 'Increasing Learning Opportunities for Orphans and Vulnerable Children in Africa', Africa Bureau Brief No 3, Washington DC: USAID.

USAID (2004) 'Unsafe Schools: A Literature Review of Schools-Related Gender-Based Violence in Developing Countries', The Center for Research on Women at Wellesley College, Washington DC: USAID.

USAID (2007) 'EQUATE Technical Brief: Gender Education and HIV/AIDS', Washington DC: USAID.

WHO (2003) 'Integrating Gender into HIV/AIDS Programmes: A Review Paper', Geneva: WHO.

World Bank (2002) 'Education and HIV/AIDS: A Window of Hope', Washington DC.

World Bank (2004a) 'Sourcebook of HIV Prevention Programmes in Sub-Saharan Africa', Washington DC: World Bank.

World Bank (2004b) 'The OVC Toolkit for Sub-Saharan Africa', Washington DC: World Bank.

World Bank (2004c) 'Turning Bureaucrats into Warriors: Preparing and Implementing Multi-Sectoral HIV/AIDS Programs in Africa: A Generic Operations Manual', Washington DC: World Bank.

7 'One finger cannot kill a louse' – working with schools on gender, sexuality, and HIV in rural Zambia

Gill Gordon

Introduction

Countries in Southern Africa have the highest HIV prevalence in the world, and recent figures for Zambia show a prevalence rate among 15–49 year olds of 15.6 per cent (UNAIDS 2007a). However, the epidemic disproportionately affects women, with women making up 57 per cent of people aged 15 and above living with HIV (UNAIDS 2007b). Young women are particularly at risk of contracting HIV in Zambia. There are estimated to be more than twice the number of young women than young men living with HIV and AIDS in Zambia, while the HIV prevalence rate among young women aged 14–19 is between three and six times that of young men in the same age group (Kaiser Family Foundation 2005). HIV prevalence peaks in older men aged 35 to 39 years (UNAIDS/WHO 2006). In addition, 85,000 children in Zambia were estimated to be living with HIV, and there were an estimated 630,000 AIDS orphans (Kaiser Family Foundation 2005). There is significant variation in the epidemic's impact, with much higher HIV prevalence rates occurring in urban areas and, although prevalence rates appear to have stabilised somewhat in recent years, much work remains to be done in terms of developing an appropriate response (UNAIDS 2007a). Only 45 per cent of young people aged 15–24 years correctly identified ways of preventing sexual transmission of HIV and rejected major misconceptions about HIV transmission (UNAIDS 2007b).

Over 70 per cent of Zambians live in poverty, and social indicators show a decline, with life expectancy at about 33 years. Economic growth is insufficient to support population growth, and HIV and AIDS place a strain on government resources. HIV and AIDS will continue to ravage Zambian economic, political, cultural, and social development for the foreseeable future (US Department of State 2008). Poverty, migration, and urbanisation, combined with poor control of sexually transmitted infections, gender inequalities, and violence have all contributed to high prevalence. This situation calls for an urgent, integrated, expanded, and effective response to reduce HIV transmission and care for those living with HIV.

Many HIV-prevention programmes have limited impact because they focus on biomedical facts and individual behaviour change and fail to address the multiple and complex factors that make people vulnerable to high-risk sexual activity. However, taking behaviour-change models and their frameworks as starting points for analysing and responding to these factors results in interventions and programmes of a very different nature, which are concerned with individual and group empowerment, social support, and the creation of health-enabling environments. Bandura (1996) argues that a combination of confidence, skills, and ownership of information increases young people's ability to take control of their health, while the work of Freire (1993) emphasises the need for participatory educational approaches to enable young people to identify the factors that prevent them from adopting healthy behaviour, and to develop actions to overcome them. This includes actions which contribute to more enabling social environments such as the building of alliances with bodies or leaders who can contribute to a multi-sector response (Gillies 1998).

This chapter investigates the potential of primary schools to be focal points for co-ordinated interventions that support and empower young people and create enabling social environments. Schools are part of national education structures which have the potential to reach large numbers of children at an age when they are developing their identities and the majority are free from HIV and not yet sexually active. Evidence from other sub-Saharan African countries shows some success in increasing knowledge and changing attitudes (Kirby *et al.* 2005), while other research questions whether the school can adequately address broad social dimensions of change such as gender and sexuality (Campbell and Mzaidume 2002; Plummer *et al.* 2004).

This question is explored in this chapter through reflection on the experience of designing and implementing an HIV-prevention programme in rural Zambia. The International HIV/AIDS Alliance has been working with two NGOs, Planned Parenthood Association of Zambia and Young, Happy, Healthy and Safe (YHHS), and with the ministries of health and education in Chipata District in the Eastern Province of Zambia to improve young people's sexual and reproductive health and well-being since 2003. The programme is entitled 'Training Teachers to Teach Pupils aged 10–15 years about Sexuality and Life-skills in Zambia' and will be referred to as the Teaching Sexuality and Life-skills programme in this chapter. The author has provided direction and technical support to the programme from its inception. The information in this chapter was generated through participatory assessments, activities, and reflection with the stakeholders listed above, and the views expressed in the chapter reflect a common understanding of the experience with the programme. The Teaching Sexuality and Life-skills programme has been working with men and women of different ages in communities and schools, using participatory methodologies to explore gender and sexuality over a period of around eight years, which has generated rich context-specific information on issues considered important by young and older community members.

The chapter begins with a brief overview of the changing factors that influence male and female vulnerability to HIV in Zambia, and specifically rural Eastern Province, and their implications for interventions. This is followed by an introduction to the programme and discussion of some of the challenges experienced in its design and implementation. The chapter then considers the question of whether primary schools can provide an appropriate focal point for co-ordinated interventions to address HIV, and discusses some of the lessons learned and implications for policy. It argues that investing in primary schools and their communities can change some important social factors to support safer sexual behaviour.

HIV vulnerability of young men and women in Zambia

This section describes some of the factors that protect or put young people at risk of HIV infection in Zambia, with a focus on gender. While this section focuses on risk factors for women, this is not intended to imply that men are demons and women victims. Boys and men are also disadvantaged by some gender norms, and poverty disadvantages everyone.

According to UNAIDS, the main drivers of the HIV epidemic in Zambia are concurrent sexual partners, transactional intergenerational sex, gender inequalities, poverty, stigma, and discrimination. In addition, women and girls are overburdened with caring for the sick and other dependants. Deep inequalities based on gender and age have contributed to an increase in the incidence of domestic violence, and as a result exposure to HIV has been exacerbated (UNAIDS 2007b). So there is a broad recognition that not only are women, on the whole, more vulnerable to HIV, but that men and women are vulnerable in different ways.

Zambian society is essentially patriarchal, and culture and religion are male-dominated, in spite of some matrilineal groups. There is a clear difference in expectations and labour between men and women, and a number of norms and practices reinforce the inferior status of girls and women. These are reflected in derogatory language about women in songs, proverbs, and arts. Religious teaching in Zambia also reinforces the subordination of women, and submission to husbands is routinely taught by all religions (CEDAW 2004). The government of Zambia is promoting greater gender equality through its policies and programmes, and reports progress to CEDAW. Statutory laws which promote equality are gaining ground over those customary laws which lower the status of women.

Research has shown that married women are at higher risk of HIV infection than their single counterparts (Altman 2004). Young people face contradictory messages about gendered identities and sexuality as they grow up. In Zambia, long-held values and norms are being challenged through diverse means, including through formal and informal education. This is happening with particular speed in urban settings where young people operate in a cash economy and interact with mass media and global networks. They have different leisure activities from young people in rural communities, and opportunities outside the home to form new types of sexual relationships. In rural areas, young people have fewer options for leisure, marriage, or sexual partners and may face a different set of challenges, including seasonal poverty; the need to engage in risky sexual behaviour in exchange for basic necessities; early marriage; and harmful traditional practices.

Issues from Zambia's rural Eastern Province

The population of Eastern Province is predominantly Chewa. Chewa culture is the dominant cultural influence, Christianity to a lesser extent. In Chewa culture, lessons on sexuality and expectation of male and female behaviour are done in secret by *alangizi* and *nyau* puberty advisers during initiation courses. In this context, the correct way to perform sexually is taught very explicitly, using simulated sexual movements, songs, and dances. Boys and some girls are encouraged to practise for perfection in marriage. Discussing sexuality more openly outside this context with trained peers or in school is new and has been triggered by a recognised need to address the HIV epidemic. There has been some opposition to this openness, but the majority of community members, particularly younger ones, have appreciated this opportunity. Parents seem to be shy to talk about sex with their children the world over, and Zambia is no exception (Rasing 2003).

Young people in Zambia are 'caught between norms and values and the reality of life' in relation to sexual behaviour and relationships (Warenius *et al.* 2007). In rural Eastern Province, there are some contradictions between the norms and values of Chewa culture and state laws and religion, especially for males. For example, some aspects of Chewa culture encourage boys and girls to practise sex before marriage, and married men to have more than one wife, whereas Christianity promotes abstinence until marriage, and fidelity within it. Young men have tended to follow the Chewa culture because they find it more in tune with their preferences (Heslop 2007), but young and old alike are reluctant to talk about their sexual lives in their communities. In Chipata District, many organisations have received USAID funds to promote 'abstinence only' prevention programmes, which has stigmatised sexually active young people. This has made it more difficult for young people to obtain condoms and negotiate their use (Gordon and Mwale 2006). Thus, while young people may get basic information about sexually transmitted infections, HIV, and pregnancy, they do not have opportunities to apply it to the realities of their own lives.

Marriage and fertility are highly valued, and some of the norms related to being a responsible, respectful, and hard-working husband, wife, parent, and family member are protective against HIV. 'One finger cannot kill a louse' is the translation of a Chichewa proverb used to teach that a husband and wife need to co-operate to make a good marriage.

At marriage the husband's family pays *lobola* or bride price to the girl's family. Young unmarried men typically have a number of sexual partners before they can afford to marry, and typically they marry girls about six years younger than themselves. A newly married couple are likely to have frequent sex without condoms, putting the wife at risk. Women may find it hard to leave an abusive marriage, because the *lobola* must be repaid. They are expected to accept polygamy in and outside marriage. This lowers their status, solidarity, and commitment to the marriage. Adultery by women is a reason for divorce in customary law, but this does not apply to men. However, as elsewhere in Zambia, Chewa boys tend to be aggressive in pushing for sex, while girls tend to be passive (Rasing 2003). Simpson (2007) links this to ideologies of masculinity which value aggression. Rasing cites research by UNICEF which showed that half of the girls interviewed said they had been forced to have sex at least once, whereas 15 per cent of the boys admitted to having forced a girl to have sexual contact. In addition, girls and women tend to be blamed for the transmission of HIV (Abrahamsen 1997).

In participatory assessments carried out in Eastern Province, the following were highlighted as problems exacerbating women's vulnerability to HIV: poverty, sexual abuse, and costs of schooling. Economic poverty and inequitable sharing of resources in households may result in women and young people not having enough food or money to meet their needs. Everyone works on the farm, but men usually decide on the use of the food and income. Poverty and marginalisation of women and their families force women and girls into transactional sex – that is sex for money, food, household goods, or other necessities – often with men who are much older. Thirty-eight per cent of girls in Zambia had recently exchanged sex for gifts or money (Young, Happy, Healthy and Safe 2004; Murray *et al.* 2003). While research suggests that the longer girls stay at school the more likely they are to delay sex and protect themselves (Boler 2006), school is also seen as a risky environment because girls living in poverty may exchange sex to pay their fees or to buy food and goods to survive at school away from home (Gordon 2003).

Girls also feel at risk of sexual abuse as they go about their daily business; for example, when walking to school, selling in the market, fetching firewood or water, or simply being alone at home or in a teacher's office (Gordon 2005). The lack of accessible clinics, police posts, and victim-support units makes it difficult to take effective action after rape, and the legal system often reflects discrimination against women and blames the girl. This means that sexual abuse often goes unreported. Cases are often quietly settled with the payment of cattle to avoid the loss of resources to the man's family that would be incurred with a jail sentence.

The international community has coined the term 'the feminisation of the epidemic', and this is disseminated through the media and programmes in Zambia, which reinforce men's tendency to feel that they are immune to HIV and to see women as responsible for spreading HIV. While the estimated number of young women aged 15–24 years living with HIV is twice that of young men, the high prevalence of HIV infection in men aged 35–39 years is rarely discussed. A Chichewa proverb says that 'men are like children in relation to sex, they cannot be expected to control themselves'; and when questioned, some men will say 'I didn't use a condom because she didn't insist on it' (Gordon 2003).

Implications for HIV and education

The context described above indicates that multi-faceted strategies are needed to create environments which support young people's sexual health. It also demonstrates the importance of using participatory tools with community groups and stakeholders to analyse local contexts and enable the kind of critical reflection that can result in collective change and ownership. Young people need information about sex, and support to understand what this means in terms of their sexual relationships and their sexual behaviour. An HIV and AIDS education-programme response must be based on social analysis.

The Teaching Sexuality and Life-skills programme was established in 2003 in mainly rural, basic primary schools, grades 4–9 in Chipata District, Eastern Zambia. The programme aimed to reduce sexually transmitted infections (including HIV), pregnancy, gender inequality, and sexual violence towards and among young people. It identified a three-pronged approach to bringing about sustainable change: empowering young people, and those who affect and influence the well-being of these young people, through their active engagement with new knowledge and values, and skills and confidence in decision-making, communication, and the ability to assert their rights; comprehensive and accessible education services; and building enabling environments which protect young people from unwanted and unsafe sexual activity.

The programme was added to a broader community-based programme for young people, as a response to community requests to train teachers in primary schools in sexuality and life-skills. The ministry of education at district and headquarters level was involved in all aspects as a partner from the programme's inception; for example, in selecting schools, designing the curriculum, and training and monitoring. Experts from the curriculum-development centre attended all the curriculum- and materials-development workshops. The initial 13 schools were involved in developing and testing the materials, and a cadre of trainers was selected to train new schools. Five new schools were selected to implement the programme, using the training manual and materials.

Mobilising communities

In the past, in Zambia as elsewhere, much of the health education aimed at changing behaviour has taken the form of 'experts' passing on information to a passive audience. However, there is increasing evidence to suggest that change is more sustainable when promoted through peer groups who can motivate and develop the skills and confidence for others to take action. People are most likely to adopt healthy behaviours if they see liked and trusted peers practising these behaviours (Campbell 2004). However, mobilising communities is often seen as complex because of diverse agency or NGO agendas and because of constraints on time and resources needed to build trust. In addition, there is still limited understanding of how peer-education programmes bring health benefits (Campbell and Mzaidume 2002).

In the Teaching Sexuality and Life-skills programme, the Planned Parenthood Association of Zambia carried out awareness-raising sessions with communities on the sexual and reproductive health needs of young people. A group of adults and young people were trained to carry out a participatory needs-assessment and planning process. Groups of men and women of different ages and key stakeholders used a range of participatory learning and action tools to describe their vision of good sexual and reproductive health, analyse and solve problems, and plan actions to reach their goals. Through this process they also identified individuals who could influence and provide ongoing support to young people, from across the community, including traditional leaders and counsellors (*alangizi* and *nyau*), parents, teachers, health-centre staff, government officials, NGO workers, and religious leaders.

A steering group comprising leaders, sector workers, NGOs, and young people was established to co-ordinate accessible services for young people and other activities, including workshops to discuss gender and sexuality values and practices, how they are changing, and their impact on people's sexual and reproductive health, well-being, and rights. For example, the project held workshops with the *alangizi* and *nyau* to explore local practices relating to puberty and consider what changes were needed and what new information and skills young people required to grow up safely. Young people were trained as peer educators to facilitate interactive sexuality and life-skills training, and strong working relationships were established with the school and health centre. Peer-learning groups of different kinds were set up within which trust could be built and sensitive issues discussed and analysed. These included groups of out-of-school youth, traditional counsellors, and parents. They also included teachers.

Primary schools as the hub for formal and informal education

Links with schools led to the collective decision that the programme should train teachers to provide sexuality and life-skills education in primary schools, starting at the age of ten years. From this, schools themselves became recognised as important hubs or focal points for the programme's diverse range of teaching and learning activities about sexual and reproductive health and HIV and AIDS, which encompassed the surrounding community.

 Gradually more and more people participated in interactive sessions and found them helpful. They gained confidence from participation and learning new skills, and some groups even developed proposals for funding for livelihood projects with the ministry of agriculture. Over time, the majority of community members appreciated the teaching because they learned more about the topics and found them helpful themselves. Collective pressure for change built as more groups and individuals participated in the interactive sessions and found them beneficial.

A curriculum and learning materials for sexuality and life-skills education in the primary school were developed, drawing on the results of the assessment and research into the impact of sexuality and HIV-prevention curricula, and characteristics of successful programmes. These include creating a safe environment for pupils; focusing on clear goals for preventing pregnancy, sexually transmitted infections, and HIV; emphasising healthy and non-risky behaviours; and using instructionally sound teaching methods that employ appropriate activities and messages related to culture, age, and experience, and actively involve participants and help them to personalise the information (Kirby *et al.* 2005). The curriculum was developed by a diverse team, drawing on different backgrounds, which designed activities and material consistent with community values and available resources. After initial training in sexuality, gender, and sexual and reproductive health awareness, the teachers conducted an in-depth participatory needs assessment with their pupils. Teachers, ministry of education officials, curriculum development specialists, and NGO staff then used the findings to develop the curriculum and pupils' materials, using questions, stories, and situations from the pupils. Topics and content were matched to the questions and issues that the pupils had brought up. These have been arranged through the grades in a spiral curriculum, building successively on previous learning, based on the developmental needs of the pupils.

The training of teachers was integrated with the development of the curriculum and learning materials, and two training and reference manuals entitled 'Preparing to Teach Sexuality and Life-skills' and 'Teaching Sexuality and Life-skills' were developed to enable the trained teachers to train others. Learners' books entitled 'Our Future: Sexuality and Life-skills' for grades 4–5, 6–7, and 8–9 were developed with the teachers and learners and tested in the classroom. Feedback from the pupils after lessons and workshops was incorporated into the materials. Male and female teachers and pupils were equally involved throughout the whole process.

The 'Our Future' pupils' books provide factual information about puberty, friendship, marriage, rights, gender, sexuality, reproduction, sexually transmitted infections, HIV and AIDS, and drug use. They contain interactive learning activities and illustrations, which engage young people in reflecting on and practising the values and skills needed to develop caring and loving relationships, make good decisions, solve problems, and seek help. All the materials have an explicit commitment to developing positive values such as co-operation, kindness, politeness, trustworthiness, courage, respect, and confidentiality. The three elements of internalising values (or 'virtues'), understanding facts, and developing life-skills make a holistic package.

In response to pupils' fears about sexuality education, an initial set of lessons was developed, entitled 'Learning about Sexuality and Life-skills Safely'; this included guiding rules, rights, trust, talking about sexuality safely, interaction between boys and girls and teachers, and where to seek help if abused or harassed. Stories and role plays allowed pupils to practise skills and rehearse how they would deal with difficult situations.

Importantly, the topics and stories designed to trigger discussion are authentic to the pupils' lived experience and based on their context and needs. As a Zambian curriculum specialist commented, 'The materials are very strong because they include topics suggested by learners, teachers, parents and other stakeholders. The materials are tailored to the needs in the actual environment' (Anson Banda personal communication 2006).

Integration is a hallmark of the programme. The activities build on skills taught in the core curriculum, such as writing stories or poems, acting in drama, analysing local culture and language, and using maths or science. Homework activities aim to actively link the school with parents/carers and the community, through activities that contribute to the well-being of others and provide the opportunity to participate in community life, which in turn can become a protective environment.

Box 1: Examples of gender topics introduced into key curriculum areas

Knowledge: information about the Convention Against all Forms of Discrimination Against Women (CEDAW), which the government of Zambia has signed.

Critical-thinking skills: activities to describe gender norms and practices, explore their positive and negative effects, and identify aspects that pupils would like to change, using drama to rehearse new behaviours.

Virtues: exploring concepts of justice and courage in improving gender equality and relations.

Sexuality lessons are monitored using an adapted ministry of education format, which involves observation of classes and feedback by pupils and teachers. The parent–teacher associations are involved in the monitoring, and parents are invited to learn about sexuality and life-skills, attend pupils' lessons and give feedback, and get involved in homework and community activities such as drama with sexuality messages. Schools developed a policy for sexuality and HIV and AIDS.

Are schools the best place to teach sexuality and life-skills?

This section examines the success of the Teaching Sexuality and Life-skills approach, in which the primary school is the focal point for co-ordinated interventions on gender, sexuality, and HIV. As primary enrolment is high and over-age enrolment still a major feature of Zambian schools, schools have the potential to reach large numbers of young people. Also, as statistics from other sub-Saharan countries (e.g. Tanzania; see Plummer *et al.* 2007) indicate, a large percentage of pupils in the upper grades of primary schooling are aged between 15 and 17 years and likely to be sexually active.

Campbell (2004) identifies a number of challenges in schools-based peer education in South Africa, including the regulated nature of the school environment, rigid teacher control, didactic teaching methods, and a focus on biomedical aspects rather than social issues. Male-dominated activities and negative, stigmatising learner attitudes towards HIV undermined the learning (*ibid.*). Plummer *et al.* (2007) note that large-scale, innovative, integrated, and multi-faceted adolescent sexual and reproductive health interventions are urgently needed in sub-Saharan Africa. But Plummer recognises that while using schools and health facilities 'may maximise intervention coverage and sustainability…the impact of the use of these structures on intervention content and delivery is not well documented' (*ibid.*). However, there are examples of school-focused interventions that use the school curriculum to address HIV and AIDS and tackle issues of sexual harassment, as documented by Mirembe (2006), but this is not on the scale envisaged by Plummer. Mirembe in his work in Uganda stresses the importance of teachers using democratic practices to challenge injustices, and of students, through their active participation, working out for themselves possible and manageable solutions (*ibid.* 225).

In the Teaching Sexuality and Life-skills programme, teachers and pupils acknowledge that sexual activity, gender-based abuse and harassment, and HIV transmission occur in and around their schools because of factors including lack of parental supervision of young adolescents, and teachers posted without their spouses who have power to attract pupils and reward sexual favours. While relationships and behaviour within the school reflect those in the wider social environment, there are ways in which the school environment can become a place that respects rights and protects students.

Pre-service and in-service teacher training now includes topics such as communicating, protection, ethics, and rights. But this training needs also to challenge the culture of authority, hierarchy, and social control in the majority of schools so that teachers not only learn about gender equality and rights but practise it in their lives (Aikman and Unterhalter 2007). Working with the whole school and community is necessary in order to create a climate that promotes child protection and does not accept abuse. Robust school and ministry policies are also needed, which encourage pupils to report abuse and take sufficient action on cases to deter teachers from abuse.

There are positive signs of change in Zambia. For example, when elders carry out their puberty teaching, it no longer entails boys and girls leaving school for a month and being expected to carry out practices which put them at risk of HIV infection (Young, Happy, Healthy and Safe 2006). There are also examples of teachers being instrumental in preventing early marriage and enforcing the policy that allows girls to return to school after a pregnancy (*ibid.*).

Teachers can be change agents in the school and community through acting as positive role models and teaching important information, values, and skills on sexuality in a way that mirrors their own behaviour and challenges negative norms and behaviours. Sexual abuse of students by teachers is increasingly being documented (Dreyer 2004) and discussed (Leach, this volume). Teachers, especially young female teachers, may themselves be exploited and abused by staff of ministries or training colleges who have the power to exploit institutional practices (see Teni-Atinga 2006).

In the Teaching Sexuality and Life-skills programme, teachers participated in a five-day workshop using experiential learning activities to share their own experiences of gender and sexuality as they were growing up, and in their personal and professional lives. They drew maps and acted role plays to generate discussion on why schools are a high-risk environment for HIV transmission for pupils and teachers. Acknowledging their own contribution to this situation, they used a problem-solving carousel to identify their roles and actions to make the school a safer place for everyone (see Box 2).

Box 2: Some examples of workshop activities

Teachers acted a role play showing a girl pupil who had sexual relationships with a sugar-daddy who bought her essentials, a boyfriend who helped with homework, and a teacher who gave her good grades. Using a technique called 'hot-seating', participants asked the characters questions to understand why they behaved as they did. This revealed the sources of power that males exercise over girls. However, the girl also had some agency in selecting partners who met her needs for progress with a possibility of pleasure. The actor-teacher was not able to resist the beauty and offer of undemanding love. Teachers acknowledged that this situation is not uncommon and can have negative consequences for pupils and teachers.

In the 'fishbowl' activity, male and female teachers asked each other 'all the questions they always wanted to ask the opposite sex about gender and sexuality but were afraid to ask'. This revealed a lot of mutual concerns and misunderstandings, which increased empathy and motivation for gender change.

In contexts such as Eastern Province, Zambia, many teachers do not know much about the reality of their students' lives, and therefore their concerns, questions, and experiences. Training sessions indicated that teachers were invariably surprised at the extent of young people's sexual knowledge and experience, the sophistication of their questions and concerns, and their level of risk of HIV infection.

The evidence from the Teaching Sexuality and Life-skills programme and its carefully constructed training programmes indicates that the school can be an appropriate, enabling, and safe environment for sexuality education. It requires, however, the active involvement of students in designing the content and approach to the lessons. And it calls for a child-protection policy for the school to which all staff, students, and community sign up. And the programme reinforces the conclusion of Plummer *et al.* (2007), from work on adolescent sexual health in Tanzania, that given the right training and ongoing support, opportunities for self-reflection and interrogation of their own attitudes and experiences relating to gender and sexuality, teachers can be the right people to facilitate sexuality education.

Some outcomes of the programme

The programme has encouraged teachers to reflect on changes in their own lives, and those of their pupils and communities, through teachers' support meetings and workshops since its inception. A mid-term review of the programme was carried out in 2006, after three years of programme activity in the initial 13 schools (Carnegie 2006). The reflections and the mid-term review showed that there have been very positive outcomes in cognitive and affective dimensions for teachers, students, and community members.

Knowledgeable and skilled teachers

The project helped teachers to bring together their personal and professional lives and to think in terms of 'we' rather than 'them and us' about their pupils and the members of the community, including those living with HIV. They were changed in an affective as well as cognitive way by the project activities. Many teachers and their supervisors appreciated their increased skills in using the interactive learning activities and felt able to talk more comfortably about sexuality with teachers, pupils, and family members. Teachers also reported that the training was very relevant to their own lives and had brought about positive changes. Seven months after the gender and sexuality training, a male teacher reported:

> *The course has brought a great change. I have changed in empathy, sexually, how to avoid HIV, how to live positively, avoidance of stigma, and equity between myself and my wife.*
> (International HIV/AIDS Alliance 2004)

The teachers reported how the experience of carrying out the participatory needs assessment with their pupils profoundly shifted or deepened their understanding of young people's lives. Their relationships with their pupils have changed from authoritarian and judgemental to more caring relationships. In school settings formerly characterised by hierarchical relationships and rote learning, teachers were more willing to listen to young people and respond to their views. One female teacher said:

> *I have learnt to respect my pupils' rights and discuss sexual and reproductive health topics with them without being shy.*
> (*ibid.*)

The pupils also noted changes in their teachers. One Grade 7 pupil said:

> *Before the project, teachers used to be uncomfortable teaching about sexuality, but now they feel free and we no longer feel shy. We used to be afraid to talk to teachers when we had a personal problem, like one of us was pregnant, but now we are free to talk with them.*
> (*ibid.*)

The training process aimed to develop suitable teachers into a cadre of trainers who could be engaged as facilitators for school or college-based training. A group of nine teachers now have skills that are being recognised by other NGOs, schools, and colleges, which has created a demand for them to train in other initiatives.

More confident, knowledgeable, virtuous, and skilful pupils

Teachers reported changes that they had observed in their pupils after teaching the sexuality and life-skills classes for six months or a year. Some teachers who were transferred to new schools not involved in the project noticed a marked difference in pupils' confidence, ability to talk about sexuality, relationships with their classmates, and use of life-skills such as communication and assertiveness. This motivated them to start the Sexuality and Life-skills programme in their new school.

There is a marked improvement in the school environment in terms of the way in which students are co-operative, friendly, and care for and support each other. Students support each other in small groups, and bullying and sexual harassment have reduced. Sexual-abuse cases are being reported, and schools and communities report a reduction in early marriages, pregnancies, sexually transmitted infections, rape cases, and absenteeism. Students are also able and willing to share sexuality and life-skills information with other pupils in other schools.

> *The project has helped us to live in a proper way, taking proper decisions. We have learnt our rights and how to react to people who want to infringe our rights.*

> *We show our Sexuality Education book to our friends who don't go to school. We even show our parents our books. At first our parents were against the project. They said it was not appropriate. But after the project meetings, our parents now accept it.*

> *We used not to understand about puberty changes. Before the boys would touch the girls' breasts and hips, but now they don't try.*

> *When a girl was pregnant we used to laugh at her, but we no longer do that. We used to laugh at physical changes in our friends, but now we don't. We encourage others to enjoy growing up. We are able to respect each other more.*
> (Class 7–9 pupils in focus-group discussions at Chiwoko and Changkhanga Basic Schools)

A safer school and local environment

The parent–teacher associations strongly support the programme and have requested that sexuality and life-skills education is extended to the whole community. Parents report more friendliness and respect in the home, and they are more accepting of the reality of young people's sexuality. This has led to more relaxed relationships between parents and children and more co-operation between parents/guardians over problems such as early pregnancy. Parents in particular identified the impact of the project in achieving more equal gender attitudes and a reduction in early marriages.

> *The project helps children to know what is good and what is wrong. It helps them to know the consequences and avoid risks. It helps modern children to grow up with knowledge and self-control.*
>
> *Traditionally women cannot say 'no'. This project is changing that through sensitisation. Girls are now able to say 'no'. Gender relations are changing.*
>
> *Early marriage was previously so common. Now the chief is advising head teachers not to allow parents to give their children in early marriage.*
> (Parents and community leaders, focus-group discussion, Changkhanga Basic School)
>
> *Parents used to say that talk about sex was an abomination and insulting. They used to hide information about sex and they would beat us if we talked about it. But now they support us. We are allowed to talk about sexuality. Parents no longer think it is a taboo.*
> (Class 7–9 pupils, focus-group discussion, Changkhanga Basic School)

Changes in the community

> *We go to our teachers for help, especially our sexuality education teachers.*
>
> *We go to the health centre for help. It has a youth friendly corner. They do peer education and drama. Particularly the nurses are helpful.*
> (Class 7–9 pupils, focus-group discussion, Changkhanga Basic School)

Mobilising the community and working with those individuals who have an influence on the lives of young people has played a major role in building a safe and supportive environment. Now only a minority oppose the teaching of sexual and reproductive health to young people. Some of the practices harmful to young people are changing, as described below, but the scale of the challenge should not be underestimated.

One of the big successes has been the careful and sensitive work with the *alangizi* and *nyau* who have been responsive and willing to reflect on social change. They came together and agreed on how they needed to adapt their teaching to protect young people. They not only questioned cultural practices but considered new information, practices, and teaching methods. They have been very active and developed a picture book with key facts and songs on different topics. *Alangizi* who had been through training then trained their colleagues and presented their new practices to community leaders and stakeholders. Many *alangizi* now teach their new curriculum and have adapted their ceremonies so that young people stay in school and are not exposed to pressures to start sexual activity early. The chiefs, elders, and churches reinforce these changes. Regular meetings with the community have been important for responding to any emerging concerns about the project. The *alangizi* now work closely with the peer educators, schools, and community drama groups.

The potential and challenges for expanding the programme nationally

Ministry of education staff and teachers in the project district, and the minister for education, would like to see the initiative scaled up. However, moving from a successful programme at a relatively small scale to a national programme presents a series of challenges that need to be carefully addressed if 'scaling up' is to be successful. These challenges are not new, and many a small-scale project has faltered at this stage. The Teaching Sexuality and Life-skills programme is showing considerable success, and further evaluations are expected over the coming year, but clearly this is a complex programme addressing complex issues. This section reflects on challenges at different levels and of different kinds for expanding the programme.

Challenges at the policy level

As this chapter has discussed, this programme is ambitious and multi-dimensional. Part of the challenge has been to engage the community and young people themselves from the very beginning, and to ensure their commitment and ownership of the programme. This approach is key to the success of the programme and to achieving changes in attitudes and behaviour. Changes in attitudes and beliefs, and changes in people's sexual behaviour and practices, take time. Collecting valid data on sexual behaviour is difficult. This means that it will take time and careful nurturing for the programme to produce key impact data that can be used for advocacy for changes at the national policy level.

While there is strong support for the programme, there is also competition for funding for HIV and AIDS and education programmes, most of which comes from international donors who have their own interests and strategies. In Zambia there are a number of initiatives working with schools producing curricula and learning materials and carrying out teacher training. NGOs, donors, and publishing houses are in competition for endorsement of their learning materials by the Curriculum Development Centre. Members of parliament have a major influence on what is acceptable in terms of curriculum content. With the Teaching Sexuality and Life-skills programme, the materials are more comprehensive and potentially controversial than other available sex-education materials, suggesting that there is a bigger task of awareness raising and advocacy to be done at the national level. The Curriculum Development Centre has strongly recommended the 'Our Future' books for national use, subject to some adjustments to controversial topics and explicit language.

Challenges at the programme level

This programme has set out to work with schools, aware that they have many competing demands on their time and resources. Schools are struggling to carry out their core business adequately, because of sickness or absence of teachers, and struggling to meet parents' expectations of good examination results. Then there are demands on schools from NGOs with different projects and material incentives for schools to become involved. It is important to understand this context from the start and recognise the constraints on head teachers, teachers, and community members who may be ambivalent or opposed to another new intervention.

Integrating sexuality and life-skills into the core curriculum has been challenging because of the packed curriculum and concern with examination results. Integration will become easier when the new Zambian syllabus is rolled out across all schools in the next few years. This allocates 20 per cent of curriculum time to 'community studies', which teachers are expected to design with community members to address their priority issues. Some communities have already requested that the sexuality and life-skills teaching is included in community studies.

Working with the government and government structures and agencies from the start is essential for the bigger impact of this programme. The NGO (YHHS) and government have brought different skills and resources to work together under a shared sense of ownership and responsibility. The school heads and ministry of education officials believe YHHS has been important in maintaining motivation and quality and in bringing additional funding for community work in the intervention. In any expansion of the programme to new districts, a shared commitment to the concept and values of the programme by an NGO, the schools, and the ministry at district, zonal, and national levels will be crucial for its sustained success.

For primary schools to become thriving hubs, community mobilisation and engagement is also essential. Parent–teacher associations are government structures that form the link between community and school. Their members are important players in the programme. A key strength of this programme is its implementation through a strong, functional partnership between a civil-society organisation and government, with the NGOs playing a key role in mobilising the community. Communities have requested that the 'Our Future' books are translated into Chichewa, and a small group of parents and leaders trained to loan the books and teach others about sexual and reproductive health.

Training is a major challenge to sustaining and expanding the programme. With constant turnover of teachers there is a need for ongoing training, particularly because of the high levels of transfers of teachers each year. Importantly, all stakeholders have recommended that the programme is included in pre-service teacher training to sensitise all teachers to sexuality and gender and mitigate the problem of teacher transfers. The quality, depth, and continuity of training will need to be maintained if the programme is expanded, in order to achieve the same results. A process that aims to change gender norms and behaviour, and relationships between teachers and pupils, and enhance the quality of the teaching/learning process will require investment in training and support for teachers. The programme in new locations will still be resource-intensive if the same good results are to be achieved. What the programme has achieved to aid this process is a group of skilled school-based core trainers who train others, not only in their own schools but in new schools as they come on board with the programme. As the programme grows, a network of trainers of trainers, mentors, model schools, and exchanges will provide a mesh of support across the country.

These are big challenges for the Teaching Sexuality and Life-skills programme, but important because, as this chapter reminds us, 'one finger cannot kill a louse'.

Conclusion

Engaging young people, teachers, and communities in the analysis of the complex and specific social factors that either protect them or put them at risk of unsafe sex is essential for the design of effective HIV-prevention programmes. An approach based on developing critical thinking through participatory methods enables young people to develop their analysis and empowers them to take more control of their lives. Sexual and reproductive health education in the context of HIV needs to start from analysis of social issues, including gender and sexuality, and integrate new knowledge and skills and develop new values. Schools and their teachers are in a unique position to work not only with their students, but to become focal points and hubs where the surrounding community engage with the same range of issues and learning opportunities, and create safe and health-enabling environments.

The success of this complex programme to change individual and collective behaviour that makes people vulnerable to high-risk sexual activity rests on the ownership, commitment, and motivation of the local school staff, the authorities, and the community. The Teaching Sexuality and Life-skills programme has shown that this kind of change can happen but that it takes time. Intensive community mobilisation with good resources, skills, and leadership has brought rewards; there has been active participation and support from community elders and teachers (*alangizi* and *nyau*). It also shows that the primary school can be a site for positive change in knowledge, norms, and behaviour at personal and societal levels.

However, there are some major challenges in expanding, institutionalising, and sustaining this model of working. It has to be built through a strong partnership between government and civil society to ensure sustainability; and with and through existing government structures, strategies, and objectives. Through partnerships such as this at local and national levels, and through real synergies between practice and policy, commitment to children's rights, democracy, and gender equality will be realised and consolidated, thus bringing Zambia closer to realising its aim of protecting all young people from HIV infection and re-infection, and caring for those living with HIV.

Resources

The following materials developed on the programme are downloadable from www.aidsalliance.org

Our Future: Sexuality and Life Skills Education for Young People. Books for pupils, Grades 4–5, 6–7, and 8–9.

Our Future: Preparing to Teach Sexuality and Life Skills. An awareness-training manual for teachers and community workers.

Our Future: Teaching Sexuality and Life Skills. A guide for teachers using Our Future pupils books, grades 4–5, 6–7, and 8–9.

References

Abrahamsen, R. (1997) 'Gender dimensions of AIDS in Zambia', *Journal of Gender Studies* 6(2).

Aikman, S. and E. Unterhalter (2007) *Practising Gender Equality in Education*, Oxford: Oxfam GB.

Altman, L. (2004) 'HIV Risk Greater for Young African Bride', *The New York Times*, February 29.

Bandura, A. (1996) *Self-efficacy in Changing Societies*, Cambridge: Cambridge University Press.

Boler, T. (2006) 'Girl Power: Girls' Education, Sexual Behaviour and AIDS in Africa,' London: ActionAid.

Campbell, C. (2004) 'Creating environments that support peer education: experiences from HIV/AIDS prevention in South Africa', *Health Education*, 104(4): 197–200.

Campbell, C. and Y. Mzaidume (2002) 'How can HIV be prevented in South Africa? A social perspective', *British Medical Journal* 324(7331): 229–32.

Carnegie, R. (2006) 'Mid-term Review of Initiative on Training Teachers to Teach Sexuality and Life-skills to Pupils aged 10–15 years in Zambia', unpublished report, International HIV/AIDS Alliance.

CEDAW (2004) 'Report from Zambia on Progress in Achieving CEDAW Objectives'.

Dreyer, A. (2004) 'Working with teachers – how can we challenge gender violence?' *Gender Violence in Schools Newsletters*, available from Centre for International Education, University of Sussex.

Freire, P. (1973/1993) *Education for Critical Consciousness*, New York: Continuum.

Gillies, P. (1998) 'The effectiveness of alliances and partnerships for health promotion', *Health Promotion International*, 13: 1–21.

Gordon, G. (2003) 'Training Teachers to Teach Sexuality and Life Skills Education to Pupils aged 10–15 years in Zambia. Report on workshop on sexuality, gender and HIV/AIDS awareness, 6–13 August, 2003', unpublished report, International HIV/AIDS Alliance.

Gordon, G. (2005) 'Comic Relief - Project Number CR1220: Working with Young People in Zambia to Improve their Sexual and Reproductive Health - end of project report', unpublished report, International HIV/AIDS Alliance.

Gordon, G. and V. Mwale (2006) 'Preventing HIV with young people: a case study from Zambia', *Reproductive Health Matters* 14 (28): 68–79.

Heslop, J. (2007) 'Feedback on Fieldwork with HAPPY Project, Zambia', presentation to discussion group 'Revisiting men's engagement in HIV, gender, and sexuality', Institute of Development Studies, University of Sussex, 30 November.

International HIV/AIDS Alliance (2004) 'Annual Report on Training Teachers to Teach Sexuality and Life-skills to Pupils aged 10–15 years in Zambia'.

Kaiser Family Foundation (2005) 'The HIV/AIDS Epidemic in Zambia', www.kff.org/hivaids/upload/7369.pdf (last accessed January 2008).

Kirby, D., B.A. Laris, and L. Rolleri (2005) 'Impact of Sex and HIV Education Programs on Sexual Behaviours of Youth in Developing and Developed Countries', FHI Youth Research Working Paper No. 2.

Mirembe, R. (2006) 'Gender, AIDS and schooling in Uganda: a curriculum intervention', in F. Leach and C. Mitchell (eds.) *Combating Gender Violence in and Around Schools*, Stoke on Trent: Trentham Books, pp. 217–26.

Murray, N., M. Chatterji, D. London, and P. Anglewicz (2003) 'The Factors Influencing Transactional Sex Among Young Men and Women in Twelve Sub-Saharan African Countries', Washington DC: USAID Policy Project.

Plummer, M., D.A. Ross, D. Wight, J. Changalucha, G. Mshana, J. Wamoyi, J. Todd, A. Anemona, F.F. Mosha, A.I.N. Obasi, and R.J. Hayes (2004) '"A bit more truthful": the validity of adolescent sexual behaviour data collected in rural Northern Tanzania using five methods', *Sexually Transmitted Infection* 80: ii49–ii56.

Plummer, M.L., D. Wight, J. Wamoyi, K. Nyalali, T. Ingall, G. Mshana, Z.S. Shigongo, A.I.N. Obasi, and D.A. Ross (2007) 'Are schools a good setting for adolescent sexual health promotion in rural Africa? A qualitative assessment from Tanzania', *Health Education Research* 22(4): 483–99.

Rasing, T. (2003) 'HIV/AIDS and Sex Education among the Youth in Zambia: Towards Behavioural Change', http://asc.leidenuniv.nl/pdf/paper09102003.pdf (last accessed January 2008).

Simpson, A. (2007) 'Learning sex and gender in Zambia: masculinities and HIV/AIDS risk', *Sexualities*, 10(2) 173–88.

Teni-Atinga, G. (2006) 'Ghanaian trainee teachers' narrative of sexual harassment: a study of institutional practices', in F. Leach and C. Mitchell (eds.) *Combating Gender Violence in and Around Schools*, Stoke on Trent: Trentham Books, pp. 199–206.

UNAIDS (2007a) '2007 AIDS Epidemic Update', Geneva: UNAIDS.

UNAIDS (2007b) 'Zambia Country Profile', www.unaids.org/en/CountryResponses/Countries/zambia.asp (last accessed January 2008).

UNAIDS/WHO AIDS (2006) 'Epidemic Update', December.

US Department of State (2008) 'Background note: Zambia', www.state.gov/r/pa/ei/bgn/2359.htm (last accessed April 2008).

Warenius, L., K.O. Pettersson, E. Nissen, B. Höjer, P. Chishimba, and E. Faxelid (2007) 'Vulnerability and sexual and reproductive health among Zambian secondary school students', *Culture, Health & Sexuality*, 9(5): 533–44.

WHO/UNICEF/UNAIDS (2006) 'Epidemiological Fact Sheets on HIV/AIDS and Sexually Transmitted Infections, Zambia 2006', www.who.int/GlobalAtlas/predefinedReports/EFS2006/EFS_PDFs/EFS2006_ZM.pdf (last accessed April 2008).

Young, Happy, Healthy and Safe (2004) 'Participatory Assessment Report', Chipata: Young, Happy, Healthy and Safe.

Young, Happy, Healthy and Safe (2006) 'Annual Report', unpublished programme report, International HIV/AIDS Alliance.

8   Mobilising care: accounts of gender equality, schooling, and the HIV epidemic in Durban, South Africa[1]

Elaine Unterhalter, Amy North, Robert Morrell, Deevia Bhana, Debbie Epstein, and Lebo Moletsane

The AIDS epidemic in South Africa is one of the most severe in the world. By the end of 2005, 5.5 million people were living with HIV in South Africa, and almost 1000 AIDS deaths occurred every day (Avert *et al.* 2006). The effects of the pandemic are highly gendered: women are estimated to comprise approximately 56 per cent of those infected with HIV, with the single largest group of women being those aged 15–34 (Whiteside and Sunter 2000). In KwaZulu-Natal province it was estimated in 2000 (on the basis of survey data) that among 15–19-year-olds, the vast majority of whom are in school, 15.64 per cent of African girls were likely to be HIV-positive, compared with 2.58 per cent of African boys (Morrell *et al.* 2001: 51). The impact of the epidemic on education has been devastating. Schools have had to deal with the effects of both teachers and learners being infected with or affected by HIV, while at the same time finding ways to enable learners to protect themselves from infection. This chapter examines the different ways in which two township schools in South Africa responded to the HIV epidemic over a six-year period (2000–2006). Central to its analysis is a concern with the extent to which the two schools have incorporated an understanding of gender into their responses to the epidemic, and the way in which the gender regimes within the schools have influenced and been affected by these responses.

The chapter traces a shift from a reluctance to acknowledge the importance of gender equity in addressing HIV to more active and proactive engagement with gender and the impact of the epidemic. In doing so, it explores the way in which teachers and learners in both schools have responded creatively to ill health, bereavements, and poverty. The emergence of a strong ethos of care is documented, while at the same time the frequency of sanctioned gender-based violence is noted. Poverty and poor resourcing have limited the transformative impact of interventions among learners and teachers, as have the continuing taken-for-granted gender inequalities in decision-making within the school.

About the research

Over six years (2000–2006) researchers from universities in South Africa and the UK conducted a study in two township schools in the Durban area to explore the ways in which they were affected by and responded to the HIV epidemic, violence, and gender inequality. The team used a number of qualitative methods to develop a 'thick description' (Geertz 1983) of the schools in relation to gender, violence, and HIV. Initial exploration of the extent of existing HIV-prevention initiatives and anti-violence work in KwaZulu-Natal schools was accompanied by a review of research literature on HIV and AIDS, gender, and/or violence internationally. Two schools were selected for in-depth case-study research because of their location in working-class townships in Durban with high levels of poverty. To protect the anonymity of the schools and the teachers and learners referred to in this chapter, they have all been given pseudonyms. The schools were suitable for in-depth case study because in 2000–2001 they were functional, compared with others in the same townships that scarcely operated at this time because of crime and poor management. The principals and teachers in both schools agreed to take part in the study, and good working relations were established.

A range of methods were used. In 2000–2001 two surveys were conducted in both schools to try to establish the extent of sexual activity among young people, and learners' knowledge of HIV and AIDS. In the same period, a series of discussions with single-sex groups of learners in grades 9 and 10 took place to explore themes relating to understandings of violence and schooling. Subsequently, discussions were held with six to eight learners in each of the two schools. Teacher researchers (teachers who worked at the school and in addition gathered qualitative data) began to document aspects of each school's history, organisation, and day-to-day events, particularly with regard to violence and education about HIV and AIDS. Interactive methodologies were used to explore teacher and student responses to these issues and to encourage reflection on them.

In 2001 the research team commissioned DramAIDE (Drama-in-AIDS Education), an HIV, AIDS, and sexuality education NGO based at the Universities of Natal and Zululand, to develop, implement, and evaluate an HIV, AIDS, and gender education project in the two schools. DramAIDE used drama to teach about life skills, gender, and AIDS-related themes, to learners and a group of teachers in each school. This intervention in the schools comprised 15 workshops spread over a month. These were adapted from the pilot programme 'Mobilising Young Men to Care' and took on a wider gender-equity scope. In the workshops, participatory methods were used to enable students and staff to challenge assumptions, and work towards gender-equity and explore the issues raised by the HIV epidemic for themselves (Thorpe 2005). Thirty volunteer learners in each school were selected to participate. A researcher worked with DramAIDE to evaluate the processes and procedures in the intervention. The workshops at Dingiswayo School involved grade 8 learners, while those at Lillian Ngoyi School involved grades 9, 10, and 11. Teacher workshops on the same themes were also conducted, using similar drama methodologies. Six months later a further set of single-sex focus-group discussions and interviews were held with learners who had taken part in the DramAIDE project. These explored participants' lives, reactions, and actions in relation to the DramAIDE project both within the schools and beyond, from their own perspectives.

The following year, follow-up interviews and in-depth ethnographic observations took place at Lillian Ngoyi in April and May 2002 (Kent 2002; Kent 2004). Additional material from learners relating to understandings of gender, poverty, and sexuality was collected in 2003 in the form of a writing exercise on the theme of letters to and from a well-known 'agony aunt' in a magazine (Unterhalter *et al.* 2004). In 2004 the research team returned to the schools to conduct a further series of interviews and assess the changes that had occurred. Discussions were held with teachers involved in taking 'Life Orientation' classes, and with those who had specific responsibilities for counselling. This involved reading out a prepared scenario (of a boy who has difficulties at home and who needs assistance) and asking the teachers to respond (Bhana *et al.* 2006). Group interviews were also conducted with some of the students. In Lillian Ngoyi, the students interviewed were peer educators: that is students who provide support to other students in the school on HIV and related issues. A last round of interviews and observations took place in both schools in 2005.

About the schools

Lillian Ngoyi and Dingiswayo High are located in the two largest townships in the Greater Durban Area. KwaMashu, where Lillian Ngoyi is located, is the older of the two, established in the wake of the Cato Manor removals from 1958 to 1965 (Moller *et al.* 1978: 3). Umlazi, where Dingiswayo High is situated, was constructed a few years later (in the late 1960s). Initially there was little to distinguish one township from the other. Both attracted residents looking for job opportunities in the city; both were over-crowded, with household sizes of seven to eight people per tiny two-bedroom abode (Moller *et al.* 1978: 6; May 1986: 119); both initially were poorly resourced. From the start, both sprawling townships had high levels of crime that remain a feature to this day (Moller *et al.* 1978: 19; Ndabandaba 1987).[2] Yet, relative to squatter camps, both townships were places where the better-resourced, frequently employed lived (May 1986: 31; Freund 1996: 131).

The two schools share many similar features beyond that of their township locations. Both are coeducational. They are poorly resourced compared with middle-class, former white, suburban schools, though by national standards they have reasonably good facilities. Both are headed by African, Zulu-speaking male teachers who have been in office for over a decade. Both are considered to be among the better-run in their respective areas. They have good matriculation results, and thus attract more pupils than they can accommodate: both have well over one thousand learners.

However, the ways in which they have interacted and dealt with their surroundings differ. At Dingiswayo, discipline and efficiency have been emphasised, and the school has little relationship with the surrounding community, operating 'rather like an island or a fort' (Moletsane *et al.* 2002). Throughout the research period, corporal punishment continued to be practised, even though its use was prohibited by law in 1996. There was a zero-tolerance approach towards lateness, drug usage, and gangster entry into the school grounds (*ibid.*: 42). In contrast, at Lillian Ngoyi, corporal punishment has been resisted by learners, and outside organisations have an influence on the school, particularly through teacher membership of SADTU (South African Democratic Teachers Union) and through community organisations. Reflecting the legacies of the anti-apartheid struggles, which are still seen in the KwaMashu township, teachers in interviews with the research team often drew on discourses of democracy, liberty, and equality. The school environment appeared much freer than that in Dingiwayo, and teachers less authoritarian, and more able to talk informally and joke with learners. Nonetheless, efforts to ensure that the school was a 'safe place' into which the violence of the surrounding township could not filter meant that strict codes of conduct were used to ensure that the students abided by the school's rules and regulations and not those from outside (Kent 2004: 62).

The impacts of HIV and AIDS have been profound in the two townships. KwaZulu-Natal is the province with the highest HIV prevalence in South Africa. In 2000 this was estimated to be 36.2 per cent.[3] High prevalence rates have not prevented those affected suffering from the harmful effects of stigma. This is tragically illustrated by the case of Gugu Dlamini, who was brutally murdered in KwaMashu township on 12 December 1999. It is believed that she was stoned to death by members of her community two weeks after publicly speaking about her HIV-positive status at a World AIDS Day event (Wright 2000 cited in Kent 2002).

Violence is a daily reality for those living and working in KwaMashu and Umlazi. Kent (2002) describes KwaMashu as 'a dangerous place', noting that during her stay of 25 days one teacher witnessed a fellow teacher being raped and murdered close to his home. Teachers reported two cases of female students being physically abused. Between January and April 2002, three female students were raped (*ibid.*: 61). Such violence has a very clear gender dimension. In interviews with teachers and students throughout the period, many instances of rape, encounters with armed men, and accounts of violent incidents were reported (Morrell *et al.* 2001; Unterhalter *et al.* 2004).

Distancing the epidemic

During the initial phases of research in the two schools, it was clear that while general awareness of HIV was high among both teachers and learners, the HIV pandemic was, to some extent, seen as being external to the schools. It was perceived as being something that occurred outside the school gates, rather than affecting and being affected by practices within them. In early interviews at Dingiswayo the head teacher spoke about a child who had left school and may have had AIDS in her family. His tone was impersonal and official. He implied she was now somewhere both physically and socially very far from the life of the school. AIDS education, according to the guidance teachers at Dingiswayo, in these early interviews, was a distant 'scientific' topic on which they requested technical assistance. At Lillian Ngoyi in this early phase there was sometimes a frisson when we spoke about AIDS, but action on this for a number of teachers was part of a wider community activism. General awareness of HIV within the schools was framed using narrow medical terms. It was not linked with any discussion of gender equity. The role played by gender inequalities in the HIV pandemic was unacknowledged.

The disconnect in understandings of HIV and gender equality was demonstrated in the responses of teachers in both schools to the DramAIDE intervention. On the one hand, by and large, in both schools, the teachers' understanding of the HIV messages from the DramAIDE intervention was astute. On the other, unless specifically probed, teachers' responses were generally devoid of any engagement with gender-equity issues. The following comments by two Dingiswayo teachers illustrate their perceptions of what the intervention was about:

> *It went very well because it was dealing with the issues, which the students are familiar with. AIDS, abuse, and things like that. After the training the students became enabled to talk about it to their peers.*
> (Norma)

> *And also it highlighted some of the issues in terms of how the teachers are supposed to get involved in terms of this killer disease. So it was sort of a reinforcement. It made us to be aware of the fact that we are like an integral part…I think the teachers have more time with the kids. I think they are the ones who are supposed to teach the kids on how to, like to prevent this killer disease.*
> (Bongi)

Significantly, AIDS rather than gender equity was seen as the major point of the intervention. This limited understanding of the epidemic and its links with gender relations was also a feature of teaching. When teaching about HIV and AIDS after the intervention, teachers did not seem to be clearly addressing gender equality, although this had been a major focus of the intervention. Talking about her guidance lessons, a teacher at Lillian Ngoyi illustrated this as follows:

> *I talked to the grade 10s...about AIDS in guidance [lessons]. I asked them, 'If you found out you are positive what would you do?'. One boy said, 'No, I'd go on with my partner because I know that she is positive as well'. 'Will you use a condom?' He said, 'No, I won't...because I know that I have AIDS so what's the use?'. But other boys, you know said, 'No, it's wrong if you don't use a condom even if you know that you are positive. You have to use it to prevent re-infection.' So I saw that [the intervention] had an impact on both boys and girls...*
> (Thuli)

While Thuli showed a sophisticated understanding of HIV and AIDS, she said very little, for example, about the importance of gender equity and the use of condoms. The strategy was advocated mainly for self-preservation, rather than respect for the other person's dignity and equality in a relationship. By not questioning the learners' stance, she displayed a level of ignorance regarding the importance of gender equity in relationships and its significance for the epidemic.

The DramAIDE intervention exposed different practices by male and female teachers. In discussion some male teachers responded positively to the intervention; however, in later actions they actively undermined the gender-equity and HIV messages of the workshops. Mark Thorpe observed: 'In a Durban staffroom I watched a female teacher attempt to chastise a male colleague. He had passed her class – whose students he knew on fairly familiar terms – and commented: "Oh, I am sorry for you all...you will not know the pleasures of flesh to flesh like our generation!"' (2005: 203).

The female teacher had attempted to explain to her male colleague that while such remarks were intended to be humorous they served to undermine HIV education. However, this was brushed aside. Kent (2002) also heard similar remarks made jocularly by male teachers, which revealed considerable ambiguity and even hostility.

Kent's work in Lillian Ngoyi revealed other worrying ways in which teacher behaviour in the school not only undermined messages regarding HIV risk and safe behaviour, but also had damaging implications for gender equality within the school. Her analysis of space in the school explored the ways in which sexualities were performed by learners and teachers, exposing the ways in which masculinities and femininities were maintained and policed within the school and, as a result, how gender inequalities were reinforced (Kent 2002: 78). She shows how gender inequalities in the school are reproduced through the hierarchical school structure, where positions of power were given to men. Places where only men congregated were spaces where socially useful knowledge was exchanged, and these served 'to police subordinate females', as girls and female teachers were excluded (*ibid.*: 51). She noted that while teachers expected girls to be more mature and responsible than the boys, and blamed girls' truancy on 'their involvement with boys, risk-taking and sexual activity' (*ibid.*), activities and displays of hegemonic masculinity among boys were expected and accepted (*ibid.*: 50). Such double standards in terms of expectations sent out strong – and dangerous – messages to learners regarding appropriate forms of masculinity and femininity and their implications for behaviour and gender relations.

The comments of many of the learners – both boys and girls – in both the DramAIDE intervention and the subsequent group discussions echoed these dominant assumptions about masculinity and femininity. In the sexualised environments of the schools, where sexual flirtation and flaunting were publicly sanctioned ways of expressing masculinity, many male learners appropriated – either publicly in group discussions or privately in writing for research teams – a discourse of rampant, uncontrollable, and often violent male sexuality.

The research team found that while most of the learners in the schools knew about HIV and AIDS, and 70 per cent were able to identify unprotected sex as a cause, this knowledge was not associated with more particular understandings concerning the body, oneself, and relationships with others. In discussion groups with boys, while some appropriated AIDS knowledge, using it as a basis for enhancing their own power and status in the school, others found it difficult to express their feelings in what was for them a difficult and sensitive topic. Some ignored their vulnerability to the virus and continued to express their masculinity through exaggerated displays of heterosexuality, including the perception that it was normal, and expected to have lots of girlfriends.

Similarly, Thorpe notes that gender-identity issues were a common concern in the DramAIDE workshops and that these often centred on adolescent assumptions about femininity and masculinity, including the attitude among boys that it was desirable to have several sexual partners. Young men expected to be told in detail about their girlfriends' movements, but were very secretive about their own affairs. They regarded violence as an appropriate 'punishment' for the 'bad behaviour' of their girlfriends, and this attitude had been internalised by many girls too. There was a sense of risk inherent in male lifestyles, and an expectation that women could and should accept or tolerate this kind of behaviour (Thorpe 2005: 201).

Such understandings of what it means to be male and female had a direct and visible impact on the relationships between girls and boys within the schools. Kent writes of the normalisation of sexual harassment in Lillian Ngoyi, which was 'rarely acknowledged as anything other than students having "fun"' (Kent

2002: 58–9). She recounts how, when about to conduct an interview with a female student, she witnessed a boy run past and grab her groin before smiling and running on. When she asked the student council why the boy behaved in such a way, a male student claimed: 'It's ok to touch a woman like that, or touch her breasts. It's like a style to represent that you've grown, that you see her…it's a way of touching a lady' (*ibid.*: 59).

In such a context, and as a result of their own direct and personal experiences of violence and abuse, many of the girls interviewed by the research team viewed their knowledge of HIV as disabling, given their own vulnerability to rape and other forms of violence linked to their sexuality. They felt they lived under a constant threat of rape and felt pressure to have sex with their boyfriends, regardless of their knowledge about the links between unprotected sex and HIV and the use of condoms, explaining that a demand to use a condom was seen as a mark of mistrust.

Up close and personal

However, despite the overriding acceptance of the dominant models of masculinity and femininity within the schools, manifested through the discourse and behaviour of many teachers and learners, the picture that emerged was complex, and often contradictory. Gender identities and behaviours changed over the course of our research project. In a survey conducted by Morrell in 2001, for example, nearly 80 per cent of 450 students interviewed said that the DramAIDE intervention had caused them to change their behaviour. Teacher and learner responses varied both within and between schools. Thus not all teachers or learners, male or female, conformed to gender stereotypes or expected norms of masculinity or femininity. The discussions with girls revealed that despite their fears and concerns about rape and being pressurised into unprotected sex, girls were not simply passive respondents to male demands. Some girls acknowledged that having unprotected sex was not always the result of boys putting pressure on them: often girls demanded the same from their boyfriends, telling them 'if you trust me you won't use a condom'. Girls described choosing to exchange sex for money, or having sex with someone to achieve a certain status. In the focus-group discussions and in personal writing, many girls refused aspirations to simply marry, viewing themselves as agents able to achieve an education, pursue successful careers, and make a productive social contribution (Morrell *et al.* 2001; Unterhalter *et al.* 2004). Meanwhile, the focus-group discussions with boys and the personal writing revealed that, although some boys were keen to boast of their sexual exploits, others, while not abandoning heterosexuality, sought to give it emotional content and to abandon notions of unbridled entitlement to the female body. Not all those interviewed felt that sex, or having multiple girlfriends, was obligatory. Boys' letters to 'Dear Dolly' spoke about anxiety and peer pressure in relation to hyper-masculinity (Unterhalter *et al.* 2004).

For some, the DramAIDE intervention opened up new spaces for them to express and develop their voices of resistance, which were often silenced, subordinated, and marginalised elsewhere. However, the prevalence and strength of such voices varied considerably between the two schools. In Dingiswayo, the workshops reflected the rather disciplined atmosphere of the school itself: participants did not speak out of turn (Thorpe 2001: 39), and some learners – particularly the girls – did not answer any questions in a group context. Significantly even the most dominant girl in the school did not challenge the boys in their views (*ibid.*: 12). When they did speak out, the girls indicated a wish to preserve a 'good girl image', and to mirror their teachers' concern with teaching them morally acceptable behaviour (Moletsane *et al.* 2002). However, in contrast, at Lillian Ngoyi, Thorpe noted the willingness of some of the female learners to express opinions and challenge the views of boys: 'I was struck by the lack of the "victim" image from some of the girls, such as one saying she went for "status" in a relationship, which was followed by a "whooping" like on an Oprah Winfrey show' (2001: 18).

Following the intervention, Lillian Ngoyi girls spoke enthusiastically about the way in which they had found it empowering. One of the girls asserted: 'I've learned that if you like you've been abused, like raped don't…ahhh break the silence, you have to talk about it. Stand up and talk about and tell everybody that this and this and this and that people have abused me…' (Moletsane *et al.* 2002). Boys also responded positively to the intervention, talking about improved relationships with and respect for their girlfriends. As one explained: 'I'm [now] speaking to my girlfriend. Last time I was not using a condom [when having] sex with her, but now I know that it is not good not to use a condom. Now I use a condom if I do it.'

Similarly, while among the staff at Dingiswayo there appeared to be a level of acceptance of gender inequality, at Lillian Ngoyi following the DramAIDE interventions more profound changes in gender discourses among some of the staff members seemed to have occurred. Male and female teachers spoke positively about girls' enhanced confidence after the intervention, and expressed their eagerness to support girls and boys within the school. One male teacher explained: 'When you talk about HIV and AIDS all of us are willing to support no matter whether it's male and female' (*ibid.*).

Such comments provided evidence of a willingness to engage with the issues, challenge accepted norms of behaviour, and move towards a deeper and more equitable understanding of HIV, gender, and relationships. The voices of resistance suggested that, despite the pervasive gender inequality within the schools, alternative views were possible, at least within the relatively safe spaces of the DramAIDE workshops and focus-group discussions and private writing. At the mid point of the study, these attitudes seemed to represent the seeds of change, the possibility of building more equitable and caring models of masculinity and femininity, and models of relationships. However, in the context of the continued practices of exaggerated displays of masculinity, sexual harassment, and the subordination and exclusion of women and girls from male spaces of power within the school, the extent to which these ideas would find the space to grow and bring about wider-reaching and more profound changes in both discourse and behaviour was not clear.

An ethos of care

In 2005, when the researchers returned to the schools, it was clear that the epidemic was no longer linguistically or conceptually distant. Some children and their parents and neighbours were ill or had died. Teachers and learners had found ways to deal and cope with the continued onslaught of the HIV epidemic. Both groups had adapted and changed aspects of their own attitudes and behaviour. Most striking was the way in which in both schools, an ethos of care was being increasingly adopted and valued. This was the most direct acknowledgment of the epidemic.

As the toll that the pandemic was taking on members of the school communities increased, in the absence of trained counsellors within schools, increasingly teachers found themselves taking on roles of providing care and support to students. Teachers found themselves being called upon to 'provide logistical support for homeless and hungry learners, to intervene in cases of serious domestic assault, to deal with rape cases and to provide support to HIV infected and affected learners' (Bhana *et al.* 2006: 13). In the under-resourced schools, where teachers were already overstretched by their regular teaching duties, providing such care and support was not always easy. However, despite a lack of training, support, and rewards, many of the teachers interviewed were performing vital care work, often making considerable personal sacrifices in order to do so.

In many cases such care work involved supporting children affected by HIV. Teachers interviewed readily acknowledged HIV as a real problem within the schools. They saw it as a situation that was all around them, that could no longer be ignored, or viewed as something external to the school. One teacher at Lillian Ngoyi claimed: 'there are a lot of kids who are affected by HIV in this school'. She explained:

> *So I could see it now that in the class that there are cases, because you will find that certain individuals are absent, and when you ask them 'Why are you not coming to school?', they say 'My mother is sick; my father is sick'. 'How sick is he/she?' 'Sir she couldn't stand up on his own; she couldn't wash; she couldn't walk'.*

Sometimes students themselves have been infected with the virus. Despite continued stigma which makes it difficult for those infected by the HIV virus to be open about their status, the teachers explained that often students find the confidence to confide in a teacher they trust. The same teacher explained how she helped a boy who had confided in her to learn to live with his HIV-positive status:

> *And I stayed with him, I talked to him, I tried to counsel him…And I remember it was before June last year when he said he doesn't feel that he would be able to write the exams. And I told him I called him and I even told him you know who will die first between the two of us? Because it was just the two of us. And I said 'Who will die first between the two of us? Is it you or me?' And he said he doesn't know… And I became very much more happy [because the boy thought he might live a long life]…And when I encouraged that boy, he did very well, because we talked about the food, we talked about the behaviour, we talked about everything.*

Another teacher described the satisfaction she felt in helping a girl find the confidence to tell her mother about her status:

> *And that girl was happy about it. She came back to me and she has told her mother. So, the battle of trying to make her accept the situation and to try and break it out she told her mother. She came to me and she hugged me, and she told me thank you.*

Teachers in both schools have learnt to find ways to ensure that children who are suffering from abuse, sometime at the hands of relatives, feel able to confide in them. Sometimes this involves using their formal lessons as prompts for 'excavating the silences' (Brink 1998, cited in Stein 1999: 6) among the learners concerning embarrassing or traumatic issues that confront them (Bhana *et al.* 2006). One male teacher from Dingiswayo explained: 'But it does happen that when you are presenting your lesson it is really about abuse, then they tend to have that confidence in you and they come and they confide in you their problems, the problems that they are experiencing in their homes.'

Ensuring that they provide emotional and material support to those who need it has required teachers in the schools to develop the skill to read the signs and identify those children who were having problems, even if they didn't come forward themselves. The same teacher described identifying a girl in need of support:

> *So there was one student there eh a female student with a very you know pale shirt. It's like you can see you know that she is having a problem. So I had to take her out of the classroom and have a talk with her. So I ask her and it eventually came up that she doesn't have parents and she is living with an auntie who is not working. So, I talked to her. Then there were some other problems, which I identified…in my mind I have to do something about this child. I'll have to get a shirt for her…So some problems…you just identify children, because they don't come up themselves and tell you even if they do have problems. So in most cases we are the people who see that there is a problem here.*

Providing material support is another important dimension of care work for the teachers in the two schools. As the HIV epidemic has worsened, there has been a deepening of the poverty experienced by the poorest learners. In both schools, teachers recognised this poverty and its harmful effects and tried to help learners with uniforms or 'old clothing' and tried to raise funds for learners' most basic needs. Poverty, often combined with sickness or death in the family due to HIV, means that the teachers in both schools found that children were often coming to school hungry. They responded by starting a feeding scheme, providing the children with bread, peanut butter, and other food. HIV-affected learners have few social-support systems, and teachers increasingly filled the gaps. Teachers even described finding themselves helping with funeral costs and providing the finance to help learners go to see social workers.

Teachers explained that in situations of great need they could not but respond. They saw their caring and support work as something they simply had to carry out, given the needs around them. As one explained:

> *When the child has been hurt. When the child has been abused physically by whoever. When the child has just found out that she is HIV or he is HIV whatever you've got to he's crying he's desperate, thinks the whole world is falling, and you've got to be there.*

Providing care came with challenges and sacrifices. Teachers expressed their frustration at the obstacles they encountered when trying to help the pupils in their care. Some felt exasperated by the difficulty of obtaining outside help and treatment for those infected by HIV or affected by abuse. Others described the stress of having to deal with caring for learners on top of worrying about their own families: 'You end up working so hard – but having to attend to so many things including your own family and your relatives and also going under the same thing.'

Some of the teachers interviewed acknowledged that they simply were not able to provide all the care that was required of them (Bhana *et al.* 2006). And a clear sense of frustration at the lack of support and training to help them deal with the range of situations they encountered in the school was common to almost all the teachers. As one explained: 'Well it's a bit difficult because we as you put it we have not been trained to confront this but we do our ultimate best.'

Implications for gender relations

The importance given to caring in the two schools has some important implications for gender relations. Care work, and the skills associated with it, have historically been understood as women's work. As such this has often been an undervalued, unrecognised, and invisible aspect of teachers' – especially female teachers' – work. However, in the two schools, the crisis precipitated by HIV, as well as the poverty and violence experienced by the students, has resulted in increased value being placed by the school management, not only on care work itself, but also on the 'feminine' skills and characteristics associated with it. In both schools the femininities concerned with mothering and care have come to be validated, demanded, and creatively implemented with extraordinary vigour and a feeling of community connection.

Moreover, as the demands for care have increased, many of the teachers interviewed, including the male teachers, have come to see care as being integral to their work (Bhana *et al.* 2006). In both schools, men's involvement in care work has increased. Male teachers' engagement with emotional support has been acknowledged by pupils. Increasingly, male teachers have been providing significant levels of care by listening, advising, and actively assisting. Such involvement has required men to extend their emotional repertoires to include caring for the self and others. Thus there has been an emergence of some new forms of masculinity that include the ability to express emotion and offer care, in contrast to forms in which emotion and affect are eschewed.

These responses of both male and female teachers suggest that a more holistic understanding of some aspects of the HIV epidemic is emerging. Teachers spoke explicitly about the links between poverty and HIV, and about the impact of violence and abuse. Although they failed to explore the links between gender inequality and HIV directly, many of the teachers appeared willing to engage with the some of gendered issues arising from the epidemic in the schools.

However, the picture that emerges is not always a straightforward one. Contradictions in both the discourse and behaviour of some of the teachers were clear. Some, including those identified by pupils and staff as being particularly caring and supportive and leading the way in providing advice on HIV and related issues, expressed frustration at no longer being able to use corporal punishment to discipline the children. Others argued that the number of rights now held by children in the schools, and their awareness of them, was undermining what were seen as positive cultural practices, such as virginity testing: 'some of the kids they say, virginity testing it infringes their rights. They talk about their rights of not wanting to be tested, and yet that belief was a good one.'

The high levels of pregnancy among schoolgirls was another issue much discussed by staff members. While some teachers demonstrated great sympathy for girls who become pregnant, others were less certain that such girls should be allowed to attend school at all. Questions regarding sexual harassment or abusive relationships within the school also elicited a diversity of – sometimes contradictory – responses. On the whole there seemed to be a continued reluctance to acknowledge the existence of abusive relationships or sexual harassment *within* the schools.

In addition, the teachers' frustrations regarding the lack of support they received for their care work was an indication that although the 'feminine' traits of care – and concern for pupils in relation to issues such as HIV – have become more valued within both schools, this is not necessarily reflected in the official structures and hierarchies. The continued low status of Life Orientation within both schools would appear to confirm this. Although teachers felt that its status was likely to improve, as it became compulsory in 2006, teachers explained that 'Life Orientation is looked down upon' in comparison with more traditional subjects, particularly those that affect matriculation results. The low status of and lack of support for Life Orientation teachers, and other teachers taking on care responsibilities within both schools, raised questions about the sustainability of some of the changes that have occurred. As long as their care role is not officially recognised, rewarded, and supported, it is not realistic to expect teachers to continue to go beyond the call of duty and dedicate time and energy indefinitely to the multiple problems with which they are confronted.

Despite the emerging concern with care and the increased recognition of the need to engage with the gendered issues arising from the HIV pandemic and its ramifications within the schools, gender hierarchies in both schools persist. Women were still the minority in management positions, and thus largely excluded from the structures of power and decision-making in both schools. There were some indications from teachers that this might be changing, albeit slowly. However, others seemed to accept the situation as normal, with one teacher describing the lack of women in management as something 'indigenous'.

Student involvement

The way in which some of the teachers were using care as a response to the epidemic did not go unnoticed or unappreciated by students. In Lillian Ngoyi, the peer educators interviewed spoke warmly about their teachers and the way in which as well as teaching they have tried to understand, respect, and support them. They confirmed that both female and male teachers have provided support in the school, mentioning in particular two teachers who were particularly supportive, and who they felt really made an effort to understand teenagers like themselves. One of these teachers is a woman, and the other is a man. Referring to the male teacher, one of the girls explains: 'It's like he's a man…And in the meantime you see him as a teenager, girl. I don't understand this, but like he can talk like he can talk; he can advise us as like girls.'

In Lillian Ngoyi, the students themselves also clearly articulated the same ethos of care seen in the interviews with teachers. They spoke with pride of their role as peer educators, and the way in which this had enabled them both to raise awareness of issues around HIV and AIDS and to help and support other students. As one explained:

> *Like I'm proud of what we've achieved. Firstly we gained the respect and the trust of the learners. Ja. They like changed they like trusted us they were able like to tell us problems as I have said and uh we were not only looking at an aspect of HIV and AIDS, we also were like we looked at the aspect of poverty. Like we said that one of the things that I'm proud of…we were able us learners to sit down with the governing body and tell them look at the problem we have got. Learners coming from poor backgrounds, they come to school with empty stomachs and then to go back to school with empty stomachs. So we need you guys to help us. We need to start a feeding scheme or something. It has been successful and it has helped quite a lot a number of people. And uh another thing it's like I'm proud of, it's like we've made a lot, although some of them do not come back and tell us like say, 'hey you've changed my life' and everything, but I see that it has made a lot of people aware of the fact of HIV and AIDS.*

Other students spoke about how they had learned to empathise with others, and explained how they had helped students with relationship problems or provided support and advice to students with sick relatives. One girl described the pride she felt in helping a girl from Tanzania feel welcome in the school.

In Lillian Ngoyi, the peer-education programme has clearly provided those involved with an invaluable space in which to develop, nurture, and value a collective concern with caring for and about others. As a mixed programme, which brings together boys and girls, it has also provided boys with a space to challenge and think beyond traditional expectations of masculinity and explore models of behaviour centred on care and respect for others, to show feelings of sympathy, even to cry. The interviews in 2005 revealed that many traditional preconceptions about HIV, masculinity, femininity, and the expected behaviour of and relationship between boys and girls persisted on the part of both sexes.

However, the animated debates that took place between boys and girls within the group on such issues as virginity testing and the treatment of girls who are pregnant suggested an increased awareness of and ability to articulate and listen to alternative views.

For girls and boys alike, the experience of being peer educators has clearly been an empowering one, and one which has enabled them to develop their own and others' understandings of HIV and the way in which it is related to issues such as gender and relationships, and to the students' own lives and behaviours. Yet despite their increased awareness of issues concerning gender and HIV, and the confidence with which they spoke about this, the confusion and preoccupations that girls and boys felt about their own lives and relationships were also clear. They spoke about their frustration that so many girls in the school were still falling pregnant, and about their despondency at how little they could help each other. One girl explained the continued pressure that girls were under to have unprotected sex:

> *Ja, what I was going to add, and to their point, it is because the girls today just lack the self-confidence, they don't have the confidence. They don't believe to their selves, because if a boy promised a girl that if you don't want to do the sex with me, I will run away from you, and then the girl said oh okay let's do it.*

In Dingiswayo, where the peer-education programme had not been directly encouraged by the school principal and had ceased to function, the problems of peer pressure, the need to conform to expectations, and the difficulties of saying no came through even more strongly in the responses of the learners, in this case particularly those of the boys. One boy explained that there's a feeling that 'if you've never had sex you're not a man, you're not going to exist as a man'. Another elaborated:

> *Our friends say stuff we do not want to do, and we end up doing it. Like let's say ja Phumlani is one of my best friends, so if he says if he says Khumlani go and have sex it's the right thing to do. I would say hai man. You lie, it's not true. You know in a group of friends I will end up being pressurised because I want to do the coolest thing to do, and I'll end sleeping with a girl.*

Teachers from both schools reaffirmed the view that, despite their increased knowledge about HIV, girls and boys still felt under pressure to practise behaviour that they knew to be unsafe. At Dingiswayo, when a member of the research team commented on the articulate nature of the female learners interviewed, one teacher replied, 'I don't know how to put this, but they wouldn't be this assertive when they are with their boyfriends'. At Lillian Ngoyi a teacher described her frustration at being told by girls that they could never have sex with a condom because 'If you feel you don't have money to buy clothes or whatever you like, you have got to enter into a relationship with an adult or a person who is working. Therefore you can't do it with a condom because he's got to give something back to you.'

These comments suggest that the ongoing impact of poverty and the persistence of generalised expectations concerning masculinity and femininity and how these must be performed mean that, despite their ability to articulate messages regarding empowerment, safe sex, and equality, the ability of many students to modify their own behaviour in a way that protects themselves and others may be limited.

Conclusion

During the time span of the research project, it is clear that there have been important changes in the way in which the two schools have understood and responded to the AIDS epidemic, and the way in which they have drawn on ideas about gender equality in these responses. As the epidemic has progressed, and its effects in the schools have begun to be felt more keenly by both learners and staff, an initial reluctance to fully engage with the epidemic, and in particular its gendered dimensions, was replaced by a recognition of the need to creatively and proactively engage with the epidemic and related issues within the schools. In getting close to the epidemic, teachers and learners alike developed a strong ethos of care and support for those affected. As the importance of care came to be recognised and valued within the school, the femininities associated with care were increasingly validated and demanded by both men and women. Such changes opened space for the development of alternative visions of masculinity and femininity. Over time, these voices of resistance – representing a questioning of the dominant forms of masculinity and femininity which were based on hyper-displays of masculine heterosexuality and the subordination and exclusion of women and girls from male spaces of power – grew a little more pronounced.

These changes represent a small step forward in understanding and responding to the epidemic and engaging with approaches to gender equality. However, at the same time, despite this articulation of alternative views concerning HIV and gender, in both schools more traditional visions continued to play a role in the formation of identities and social relations. Gender inequalities continue to be accepted and normalised in power structures within the schools. Both teachers and learners suggest that the ways in which gender identities are performed means gender-based harassment and discrimination have not yet been eliminated. The existence of multiple discourses and their contradictory nature allows for individuals to take up different positions at different times. This means that somebody can talk about gender equity while still engaging in abusive behaviour, or they can use the language of gender equity to articulate a position that points to trying to live differently. Examining such persistent inequalities further, and finding ways to address them, will be critical to ensuring that the emergent changes witnessed so far in the two schools can be built on and sustained, and their transformative potential realised.

Notes

1   This chapter synthesises research reported in a number of published studies (Morrell *et al.* 2001; Moletsane *et al.* 2002; Unterhalter *et al.* 2004; Epstein *et al.* 2004) and presents additional material. Morrell *et al.* 2008 is a full report on this study.

2   This evaluation was undertaken by Mark Thorpe. A report on his observations was written up as a working paper for the project (Thorpe 2001).

3   www.saps.gov.za/statistics/reports/crimestats/2006/_pdf/provinces/kwazulu_natal/ durban_south/umlazi.pdf (last accessed September 2007).

4   www.ukzn.ac.za/heard/resources/Stats/WEB%20stats_July04.pdf (last accessed May 2008)

References

Avert/ UNAIDS/WHO (2006) 'Annex 2: HIV/AIDS estimates and data, 2005', in 'UNAIDS 2006 Report on the Global AIDS Epidemic'.

Bhana, D., R. Morrell, D. Epstein, and R. Moletsane (2006) 'The hidden work of caring: teachers and the maturing AIDS epidemic in diverse secondary schools in Durban', *Journal of Education* 28: 5–24.

Epstein, D., R.Morrell, R. Moletsane, and E. Unterhalter (2004) 'Gender and HIV/AIDS in Africa south of the Sahara: interventions, activism, identities', *Transformation* 54, 1–16.

Freund, B. (1996) 'Confrontation and social change: Natal and the forging ahead of Apartheid 1949–72', in R. Morrell (ed.), *Political Economy and Identities in KwaZulu-Natal: Historical and Social Perspectives*, Durban: Indicator Press.

Geertz, C. (1983) *Local Knowledge: Further Essays in Interpretive Anthropology*, New York: Basic Books.

Kent, A. (2002) '"Let's Talk About Sex, Baby!" Negotiating Space, Performance and Sexualities within a Compulsory Heterosexual School Regime in South Africa, in the Context of the HIV/AIDS Epidemic', unpublished dissertation, MA in Gender, Education and International Development, Institute of Education, University of London.

Kent, A. (2004) 'Living life on the edge: examining space and sexualities within a township high school in greater Durban, in the context of the HIV epidemic', *Transformation: Critical Perspectives on Southern Africa* 54: 59–75.

May, J.D. (1986) 'A Study of Income and Expenditure and Other Socio-economic Structures in Urban KwaZulu: Umlazi', Durban: KwaZulu Finance and Investment Corporation.

Mbali, M. (2004) 'AIDS discourses and the South African state: government denialism and post-apartheid AIDS policy-making', *Transformation* 54: 104–22.

Moletsane, R., R. Morrell, E. Unterhalter, and D. Epstein (2002) 'Instituting gender equality in schools: working in an HIV/AIDS environment', in *Perspectives in Education* 20(2): 37–53.

Moller, V., L. Schlemmer, J. Kuzwayo, and B. Mbanda (1978) 'A Black Township in Durban: A Study of Needs and Problems', unpublished paper, Durban: University of Natal, Centre for Applied Social Sciences.

Morrell, R., E. Unterhalter, R. Moletsane, and D. Epstein (2001) 'Missing the message: HIV interventions and learners in South African schools', *Canadian Women Studies* 21(2): 90–5.

Morrell, R., D. Epstein, E. Unterhalter, D. Bhana, and R. Moletsane (2008) *Towards Equality? Gender in South African Schools During the HIV and AIDS Pandemic*, Durban: University of KwaZulu-Natal Press.

Ndabandaba, G.L. (1987) *Crimes of Violence in Black Townships*, Durban: Butterworth.

Stein, P. (1999) 'Drawing the unsayable: cannibals, sexuality and multimodality in a Johannesburg classroom', *Perspectives in Education* 18(2): 61–83.

Thorpe, M. (2001) 'An Evaluation of the Intervention of DramAIDE's Programme: "Mobilising Young Men to Care", in Two Township Schools in Durban', commissioned research, Durban, University of Natal.

Thorpe, M. (2005) 'Learning about HIV/AIDS in schools: does a gender-equality approach make a difference?' in S. Aikman and E.Unterhalter (eds.), *Beyond Access: Transforming Policy and Practice for Gender Equality in Education*, Oxford: Oxfam GB.

Unterhalter, E., D. Epstein, R. Morrell, and R. Moletsane (2004) 'Be yourself: class, race, gender and sexuality in South African schoolchildren's accounts of social relations', *Pedagogy, Culture and Society* 12(1): 53–72.

Whiteside, A. and C. Sunter (2000) *AIDS: The Challenge for South Africa*, Johannesburg: Human and Rosseau.

9 Development, gender, HIV and AIDS, and adult education: challenges in Thailand

Usa Duongsaa

Introduction

Since the beginning of the HIV and AIDS epidemic in Thailand it is estimated that more than one million people have been infected with the virus (UNDP 2004). Concerted efforts to tackle the epidemic have meant that, after reaching their peak in the early 1990s, infection rates have fallen over the last decade. However, despite this, the prevalence of HIV in the country remains significant: more than one in every one hundred adults is currently infected (UNAIDS 2006). Such statistics highlight the scale of the epidemic in Thailand. However, HIV and AIDS is not only about statistics and how many people are infected, how many have access to treatment and care, how many pass away, or how many have access to learning about prevention. It is about people and how they are part of their communities and how they relate to each other, support each other and learn from each other. HIV and AIDS have a human face, and touch people personally.

This chapter examines the HIV and AIDS epidemic in Thailand through the personal story of Pimjai, a woman living with HIV and AIDS in a rural northern community. Through an exploration of how Pimjai became infected, how she has dealt with her HIV-positive status, and how she worked to support those in her community infected and affected by HIV, it examines the linkages that exist between development issues, gender, and HIV and AIDS. It considers the way in which adult education can be used to curb the transmission of HIV and AIDS and to mitigate the impact of HIV and AIDS on the lives of the women and men affected by it.

Thailand – a shining success?

Thailand is often held up as a shining example of success in the global battle against HIV and AIDS. It is one of few developing countries in which public policy has had a real impact on preventing the spread of HIV on a national scale (www.avert.org/adisthai.htm). In the early 1990s a massive public awareness campaign on HIV and AIDS was launched, which took advantage of the country's strong public communication infrastructure (UNDP 2004). Anti-AIDS messages were aired hourly on the six television networks and 488 radio networks across the country, and all schools were required to teach AIDS-education classes. Meanwhile the '100 per cent condom programme' was initiated, targeting commercial sex establishments. Condoms were distributed free to brothels and massage parlours, and their use was made compulsory for sex workers and their clients. If brothels failed to comply, they could be closed down (www.avert.org./aidsthai.htm).

These national efforts to control HIV have had impressive results. Commercial visits to sex workers were reduced by half, condom use was increased, and the number of new cases of HIV decreased, dropping from 143,000 in 1991 to 19,000 in 2003 (www.avert.org/aidsthai.htm). Since the 1990s, declining levels of HIV and other sexually transmitted diseases have been recorded in the country (UNAIDS 2006). However, Thailand's relative success in HIV and AIDS prevention and care must also be attributed to efforts made by non-government organisations, the Positive People Group and Network for people living with HIV and AIDS, and local responses from communities (UNAIDS 2001).

Thailand's record on providing treatment to those living with HIV and AIDS is also impressive. Since 2000, anti-retroviral drugs have been used in Thailand, and in 2003 the government made an official commitment to ensuring adequate treatment for all people living with HIV and AIDS. Most recently, the decision by the Thai government to use generic anti-retroviral drugs has reduced the cost of treatment for those infected with HIV, which has meant that treatment is increasingly reaching those who need it. According to the World Health Organisation, by the end of 2006 around 88 per cent of those who required treatment with anti-retroviral drugs in Thailand were receiving them (WHO 2007). Thailand has also had considerable success in scaling up prevention of mother-to-child transmission (UNAIDS 2006).

Yet despite these successes, there is no room for complacency; the HIV epidemic in Thailand has never eased off in particular regions and among certain groups, and in recent years it is clear that prevention efforts have not kept pace with the changing face of the epidemic. Currently the majority of investments in HIV-related activities are for treatment, care, and support, with only around ten per cent being invested in prevention programming. According to UNAIDS, the Thai government has reduced its HIV-prevention budget by two-thirds in recent years (UNAIDS n.d.).

Meanwhile, current trends suggest that infection rates could be on the rise, particularly among certain groups at high risk. Men who have sex with men accounted for approximately 20 per cent of HIV infections in 2003 and 45 per cent in 2005; infection rates among injecting drug users remain extremely high at around 35–50 per cent and are thought to be increasing in some areas (www.avert.org). Other groups with high prevalence rates include migrant workers in the construction, agriculture, and fishing industries.

In 2003 over ten per cent of brothel-based sex workers were living with HIV. Despite this, condom use during paid sex is decreasing: a study among female sex workers in Chang Mai, Bangkok, and Mae Hong Son found that condoms were used in only 51 per cent of commercial sex encounters (UNAIDS 2006). Although the 100 per cent condom programme is still officially in place, it appears no longer to be applied as strictly as it once was. Moreover, sex work has become increasingly common, and the number of establishments has risen. Many of these are not brothels and so are not covered by the 100 per cent programme, and it is thought that women who solicit sex in 'unofficial' venues such as restaurants or bars often do not use condoms (www.avert.org).

Young people are also increasingly affected by HIV, and AIDS is now the leading cause of death among young adults (UNDP 2004). Yet, due to unfortunate complacency and the resulting neglect of HIV and AIDS prevention during the Thaksin Shinawatra administration from 2001 to 2006, the lack of mass public information campaigns led to a decrease in awareness among young people. Pre-marital sex has become more common among young Thais, and this is often unprotected. Only 20–30 per cent of sexually active young people use condoms (www.avert.org).

The high levels of infection among identifiable high-risk groups are particularly alarming, and point to the need for targeted interventions addressing particular segments of the population. However, it is clear that as the epidemic has progressed, the spread of HIV in Thailand has become more varied. As Pimjai's story shows, it affects diverse sections of the population, including those who do not engage in obviously high-risk behaviour, such as housewives. According to the Ministry of Health, more than one-third of infections in 2005 were among women who had been infected by their long-term partner (UNAIDS 2006).

Pimjai's story[1]

Pimjai is a woman who has been living with HIV and AIDS for more than 15 years. She has been open about her sero-status and working on HIV and AIDS issues for almost as long. In many ways Pimjai's case is typical of that of an infected woman. She was born into a poor family in a rural community in Mae Rim District in northern Thailand. Her family's poverty meant that she had to leave her education early, and was able to complete only grade 4 at the local school. She did odd jobs to earn money as she grew up, including helping her father with welding work and building houses.

When she was 22 years old, Pimjai fell in love and married a young man. Some time after marriage, her husband left to work in Bangkok, hoping to get a better job with better pay that would enable him to build a better life for his family. However, life and work in the capital did not turn out to be as easy as he expected, and he returned home. Pimjai and her husband continued to work with her father until her husband became sick with a series of illnesses that prompted a doctor to recommend a blood test for HIV. The blood-test result was positive. Pimjai, who was pregnant at the time, decided to have a blood test as well, and later learned that she was also HIV-positive. It was believed that her husband had picked up the HIV virus from sex workers that he had occasionally frequented while working away in Bangkok. On his return home, through unprotected sex, he had unintentionally infected Pimjai and possibly the unborn baby. Pimjai later miscarried.

It wasn't easy for Pimjai to come to terms with being HIV-positive. At the time, HIV and AIDS was branded as a fearful and incurable disease. Posters and television and radio spots that continuously bombarded the public with messages such as 'AIDS kills' and 'AIDS is incurable: you will die!' resulted in widespread fear, stigmatisation, and discrimination against people living with HIV and AIDS. Pimjai had her share of dark periods and she attempted suicide on several occasions. However, daily meditation, combined with good counselling, helped Pimjai to learn to come to terms with her HIV-positive status and to live with the virus. Although it took her some time before she could muster enough courage to tell her parents and siblings about her sero-status, when she did so, her disclosure was accepted by her loving family, which brought her great relief and inspired her to live positively.

However, despite acceptance in the family, Pimjai faced severe discrimination in the community after disclosing her status. For example, when she went to the local food shop she had to buy her own bowl and spoon, and after she left the shopkeeper would 'sterilise' the table and the chair where she had sat with hot water. Whenever she participated in community events, others isolated her from the group. At that time it was very rare for HIV-infected people to disclose their sero-status to the public, and Pimjai was the first one in the community to do so. She and her family felt left to face the situation alone (Duongsaa 2004).

Supporting others: the Community Health Project

As Pimjai learned to take care of herself and her husband – who died peacefully in her arms – she decided to form a small peer-support group to help other positive people in the community. The inspiration came from various sources:

the loving acceptance and support from her own family; the comfort from meeting other people living with HIV in Chiangmai; and her experience of serving as volunteer with the Chiangmai Red Cross Centre and the Orchid Clinic, which taught her the joy of helping others. Thus the Community Health Project was born. Pimjai's house in Mae Rim District of Chiangmai was used as the project office, with Pimjai herself serving as the project co-ordinator. Her father (who was the chair of local health volunteers in the village) served as the chair of the project committee, which consisted of representatives from the government and NGO sectors, as well as local community leaders.

The Community Health Project received support from the AIDS Network Development Foundation, which provided a small grant to cover project activities and conducted workshops to train Pimjai and other HIV-positive people in proposal development, project-cycle management, basic accounting and book-keeping, evaluation, and report writing. It also conducted regular seminars which allowed Pimjai and other AIDS activists to meet and share experiences about HIV and AIDS-related issues. Through these activities Pimjai became increasingly competent at managing her group and providing assistance to her peers. After participating in a study visit to see savings groups and to see income-generating activities in southern Thailand, Pimjai was inspired to expand her project from health-focused activities and moral support to include economic assistance, networking, and advocacy.

At present the Community Health Project is actively engaged in HIV and AIDS prevention, and care and support activities. This includes health services run by the group: doctors carry out weekly health checks, free milk for infants is provided daily, and throughout the year counselling, home visits, and career support are provided. While people living with HIV and AIDS remain the major group of clients, the project has reached out to other groups and is also working with community leaders, housewives, children infected with and affected by HIV and AIDS, people with disabilities, the elderly, and other marginalised groups. The project co-ordinates its work with the local schools, the health centres, the local government, NGOs, and other communities.

The project's savings groups and income-generating activities, involving both people living with HIV and AIDS and other community members, are thriving and expanding to include neighbouring communities. Training is another key element of Community Health Project's work, and various monthly training workshops are held for different groups. These workshops concern issues relating to HIV and AIDS, but also other issues relating to problems emerging within the community. For example, workshops for the youth group have addressed issues relating to the natural environment as well as the role of peer education in HIV prevention. Adult group workshops have included workshops for housewives and their husbands, focusing on HIV prevention and condom use. Monthly community forums and other regular training sessions provide additional opportunities for community members to discuss and learn more about issues of concern to them.

As it has expanded its focus and its membership base, the Community Health Project has become a well-known group, benefiting a wide range of community members. It has brought about improvements in the quality of life for people within the community, and it has also changed attitudes towards HIV and those infected and affected by it. There is now greater acceptance and understanding in the community, and virtually no stigmatisation or discrimination against people living with HIV and AIDS. The project has received financial and technical support from several agencies, but has also made efforts to raise local resources. It has been showcased as an effective initiative by people living with HIV and AIDS, and is regularly visited by AIDS activists not only from Thailand but from around the world.

Living positively

Pimjai continues to learn and develop her own skills and knowledge through reading and sharing experiences with others. She keeps busy managing the project, providing counselling to peers and the public, co-ordinating support for those who need it, helping dying friends to pass away in peace and dignity, comforting grieving families, giving talks to schools and communities, and organising seminars to promote a better understanding of HIV and greater recognition of the capacities of people who live with the virus. She has also become active in the people's movement at the national level, advocating for health for all and for people's rights to participate in social and governance issues.

Pimjai has often publicly and proudly said 'I'm thankful for being HIV-positive'. She explains:

> *If I had not had HIV I would have remained an ordinary housewife who was concerned only about how to make money and take care of my family. I would have continued to do welding in the community and would not have learned anything else. But, because of HIV, I have learned the real meaning of life. Life is not about being wealthy; it is about being useful. I have taken care of many HIV-positive friends. I have worked for many other people. I have travelled to many places, attended many meetings, met many interesting people, even shaken hands with the prime minister, given many presentations, welcomed many visitors, and had many opportunities for learning.*

Understanding risk: a participatory gender analysis

During the past few years, the AIDS Education Programme (AEP) of Chiangmai University has been collaborating with the Asian–South Pacific Bureau of Adult Education (ASPBAE) in developing and trying out a set of participatory tools for gender-orientated analysis of HIV risks and responses, which can be used to promote awareness of HIV and AIDS and gender in the community. These participatory techniques have been designed to help people, both men and women, to analyse the links between gender, development, and HIV and AIDS, and how these issues relate to themselves in their own contexts.

The techniques used include the analysis of gender values and the way in which marriage partners are selected; an analysis of the time spent on men's work and women's work; the analysis of risky behaviours and connections between different groups in the community; gender roles and values in HIV and AIDS prevention and care; and gender differences in control of and access to resources in HIV and AIDS prevention and care. The tools have been used in workshops with small mixed groups of men and women in five countries in South Asia, seven countries in South-East Asia, and three countries in East Asia. For example, a workshop held in Chiangmai, Thailand, involved participants from Thailand, Viet Nam, Malaysia, China, and Indonesia. It sought to provide participants with skills in using participatory gender analysis to promote HIV and AIDS awareness in their areas of work. In doing so, it helped the participants explore their own perceptions and understandings of the links between HIV and gender.

In each case the workshops have yielded startlingly similar results in terms of gender values and roles, women's burdens and vulnerabilities, misconceptions about risks, and differential access to and control over resources. They suggest that very similar patterns to those seen in Pimjai's story may be observed in other Asian countries.

Gender norms and values

The workshops included exercises in which participants were asked to identify qualities or characteristics that were considered important in a marriage partner. In all workshops this revealed the persistence of traditional gender norms and expectations. Men's expectations about their spouse focused on virginity, beauty, patience, good cooking and house-keeping skills, fidelity, as well as their ability to take care of children. In contrast, women's expectations about their spouse included honesty, sincerity, creative thinking, being healthy (including sexual performance), good education, bravery, economic stability, and social status.

When asked to list the qualities associated with being male, participants included being responsible, non-smoking, polite, highly educated, gallant, leaders, active, faithful, sympathetic, understanding, brave, healthy, emotional, vulnerable, money earners, sharing housework, having a stable occupation, enjoying a high position in society, and fathering children. Qualities associated with being female included being gentle, beautiful, nice, talkative, patient, responsible, good at house-keeping, hard-working, non-complaining, caring and understanding, being a mother, doing the cooking, and giving birth.

This list of 'male qualities' contains some characteristics – vulnerability and being emotional – that would seem to challenge traditional conceptions of masculinity. Overall, however, it is clear that men were perceived as being active and in the leading roles, whereas women were perceived as being passive and in the caring roles (Hallacy 1999). Identifying and reflecting upon these gendered expectations enabled participants to reflect on their own preconceptions regarding what it means to be a male or female, how this affects their own behaviour and relationships with others, and what this means for gendered relations and behaviour more broadly.

Risk analysis

The gender norms and values identified in these first exercises were reflected in the analysis of the time involved in men's work and women's work, where the patterns from different countries were almost the same. Participants agreed that men's work and women's work are different and that women spend more time working: generally women rise earlier than men to start housework, and go to bed later than men do. They recognised that women's roles are dictated by traditional cultural norms, that women do more domestic work and perform more time-consuming, repetitive work, and that even women who work outside the home like their spouse have an additional burden of household work that men do not have. Men on the other hand were perceived to engage in heavier work and more dangerous work, and to do more technologically demanding work that requires more skills and brings in more pay than women's work.

Analysis of the ways in which men and women do different work and use their time differently enabled participants not only to understand how gender norms and values determine what work men and women are able to engage in, and how it is valued and rewarded differentially by gender, but it also permitted an exploration of how this affected men's and women's vulnerabilities to HIV infection.

When asked to analyse the links between gendered patterns of time use and HIV risk, participants noted that men earn more money than women and retain part of their income for drinking and visiting sex workers, and that it was more acceptable for men than women to travel in relation to their work, thus experiencing increased opportunities to engage in risky behaviours. It was also agreed that men have more time for social activities and recreation, and that men and women would not engage in the same recreational activities. Whereas men would go out of the house and have more time to visit friends, play sports and so on, women's recreation would usually take place in the home. Men's recreational activities outside the home present more opportunities to engage in behaviours that put them at risk of HIV transmission than the female recreational activities taking place within the home (*ibid.*).

Initially, women participating in the workshop considered themselves and other 'ordinary women' to be at low risk of HIV infection, even if they knew their spouse had frequented sex workers and they could identify sex workers as being at high risk of HIV infection. However, a participatory activity that involved making connections between different groups with different levels of HIV risk, followed by participatory reflection and discussion, revealed the way in which even those who were not engaged in any risky behaviours directly were not risk-free. The links which were made between the different groups – from those viewed as high-risk by the participants, including drug users and prostitutes, to 'ordinary' men and women – showed how the housewives and young women could contract the HIV virus from their roaming husbands and boyfriends and would then be likely to pass it on to their babies.

The exercise would typically end with the startled realisation of each of the participants that practically everybody was at risk, and that everybody could be affected by AIDS, including themselves (Duangsa and Duongsaa 1994). Rather than simply giving information about HIV and AIDS and risky behaviour, the activity enabled participants to situate themselves – and their own actions and behaviour – within the HIV problematic. It clearly demonstrated the importance of enabling people to relate to the issue of HIV by making it tangible, visible, and directly relevant to their lives, in order to build the kind of deeper awareness needed as a precursor to behaviour change. In addition, by exposing the links between groups, and revealing the extent to which HIV cuts across groups and communities, the exercise helped reveal the extent to which HIV is not just the problem of infected individuals but is rather a problem for the community more broadly.

Gendered roles in prevention and care

The participatory exercises revealed that in every country, men and women have different values and roles, and different information relating to HIV and AIDS prevention and care. Through the discussion of prepared statements regarding 'male' or 'female' behaviour and a list of the different resources linked to HIV prevention and care, and who controls and has access to them, participants were able to analyse how gendered patterns of behaviour and resource access affect men's and women's vulnerability to HIV differently, and how they are affected by infection.

Participants agreed that men have more knowledge about HIV and AIDS, are aware of how to put on a condom properly, and have more opportunities to have multiple sexual partners, to have sex with sex workers, and to buy and carry condoms. Women meanwhile have an unequal role in negotiating sexual issues, including condom use. They feel less comfortable discussing sex, sexuality, sexually transmitted diseases, and HIV risks and protection, and are more vulnerable to sexual harassment and/or rape. They are normally expected to keep virginity until marriage (while men are expected to have sexual experiences before marriage) and are more likely than men to contract HIV from their spouse. In addition, women are the primary caretakers of people with AIDS in the family. Such different values and roles among men and women clearly reflect the influences of prevailing social and cultural values and norms already governing the usual gender roles and expectations of the two sexes in everyday life, and in all social interactions and relationships (Hallacy 1999). They have clear implications for HIV risk, and also result in the burden of caring for those infected and affected by HIV falling most heavily on women.

The workshop enabled participants to develop an understanding of the way in which HIV and AIDS are related to sex, sexuality, education, economic status, and social status, and how all of these factors are connected to gender. It revealed how men and women are vulnerable to HIV transmission in different ways, because of different traditional gender norms and values which have been socialised through social expectations and attitudes which shape men's and women's roles in prevention and care.

Understanding these gendered dimensions of the epidemic challenges us to find new approaches to HIV and AIDS education, and interventions that are more gender-sensitive and include gender messages that will challenge the prevailing traditional stereotypical gender norms and values.

Learning from Pimjai

Pimjai's story is an extremely inspiring one. It demonstrates the enormous impact that grassroots initiatives can have, and also how dedicated and dynamic individuals such as Pimjai can play a significant role in improving the lives of those affected by HIV and in protecting others from infection. It shows us that everybody has the capacity to respond to the epidemic, and that this capacity can be nurtured and mobilised so that everybody can make a difference. It is also important in that it draws attention to the complex interplay between development, gender, and HIV and AIDS in Thailand, and the crucial importance of understanding and addressing these interconnections if HIV-prevention efforts are to be successful.

Poverty and gender inequality, risk and vulnerability

Pimjai's infection with the HIV virus was intrinsically linked to her status as a poor, rural woman. In Thailand a process of uneven development and the unequal distribution of wealth and resources has placed increasing pressure on the environment and resulted in the loss of agriculture-based livelihoods. With few job opportunities, and faced by the prospect of continued poverty in their own communities, many young men like Pimjai's husband (and young women too) migrate to work in the big cities.

Pimjai's family is typical. The husband was understood to be the head of the family, the one expected to migrate to the big cities to earn money to provide for family members. As a man, his relatively greater education and vocational skills made it possible for him to go looking for better job prospects in Bangkok. Meanwhile women in rural Thailand are more likely to be poor, to have less education, and less access to land, credit, cash, and social services. The fact that many women are dependent on men for their economic security means that they also have limited space for negotiating the terms of desirable relationships with their partners, including negotiating safe sex or no sex.

Like most of the many women to have been infected by their husbands, Pimjai never thought she might be at risk of contracting HIV. She was faithful to her husband and she thought her husband would be faithful to her. Her husband, on the other hand, had been socialised into believing that it is fine for a man to be unfaithful to his wife. In fact it is seen as manly to patronise sex workers or to have multiple partners and not to use protection. And for migrant men alone in an alien city, the absence of community restrictions and sanctions, and the existence of peer pressure, make them more likely to indulge in drinking, using drugs, and frequenting sex workers.

The sex workers with whom men like Pimjai's husband engage in unprotected sex – putting themselves and their partners at risk of HIV infection – tend to be used as convenient scapegoats and branded as the cause of HIV transmission. However, they too are the victims of the same poverty and gender norms and values which make them vulnerable to infection in the first place. Most sex workers enter the trade because of poverty, and many are migrants. Some are trafficked, others are lured into the trade by promises of good work with good pay.

The sex work that they carry out is itself an outcome of gender values that perceive women as objects to cater for the desires of men, a view that is reinforced by the continual portrayal of women as sex objects in the mass media.

The portrayal of sex workers as 'bad women' is contrasted with 'good women' – that is young women and housewives. This dichotomy is degrading to women and puts many women at risk of HIV. While it is considered normal for 'bad women' to talk about sex, it is taboo for 'good women' to know about or talk about sex and sexuality, especially young women. This limits many women's access to information and counselling related to sexuality. It also limits their desire or ability to negotiate with their partners about condom use, for fear of being regarded as having had previous sexual experiences, which would put them in the category of 'bad women'.

Early AIDS campaigns, which advised Thai men to use condoms when they had sex with sex workers, have resulted in many people seeing condoms as something to be used with 'bad women' only: many men would not use condoms with their girlfriends or wives, and these 'good women' would feel slighted if their boyfriends or husband used condoms with them. Paradoxically, although they were very successful at reducing transmission between sex workers and their clients in the short term, the failure of campaigns such as the 100 per cent condom programme to integrate a broader gender analysis may have in fact contributed to increasing women's vulnerability, limiting their ability to protect themselves effectively against HIV and AIDS.

Poverty, gender inequality, and experiences of HIV

As well as increasing their vulnerability to HIV, poverty prevents people who live with HIV and AIDS from having a good quality of life, by affecting access to information, treatment, facilities, and services, and general care and support. HIV and AIDS in turn often impact on poverty and the lives of poor people in an alarming way. The costs of health care can place an enormous burden on affected families, which is often compounded by decreases in income due to illness or loss of work; the depletion of family savings leads to loss of economic security; and earnings are forgone due to the deaths of relatively young family members at the height of their earning years. Increased economic hardship often results in reduced resources to meet the needs of women, children, and the elderly in the family. In many cases orphaned children become the economic burden of their grandparents, other relatives, or community.

And when HIV hits, the burden of dealing with it tends to fall more heavily on women. In Thailand, traditional gender norms and values that portray women as nurturers and care-providers have resulted in women being expected to shoulder more responsibilities in caring for those infected with HIV in the family. As Pimjai's story illustrates, the wife of a person living with HIV and AIDS usually goes to great lengths to earn money to provide treatment and care for the husband, often sacrificing her own as well as her children's quality of life in the process. Unfortunately, when women themselves get infected, the reverse does not often occur.

Providing information and building awareness

Like Pimjai and her husband, many poor people in Thailand, particularly women, and especially those living in remote rural and ethnic communities, have little or no education. Despite national prevention campaigns, information regarding HIV and AIDS – how to protect themselves from it, where to obtain free condoms, and where they can go for information, counselling, testing, and care – does not always reach them. Ensuring that this information is made available and accessible to men and women is clearly essential to helping protect them from HIV and AIDS. However, Pimjai's story shows that simply providing this information is not enough. Even when they are aware of HIV and the way in which it is transmitted, many women like Pimjai are unlikely to use protection with their partner. Pimjai simply did not expect her husband to be infected, and was not aware of the closeness of the links that existed between herself and the high-risk sex workers in the city. Moreover, the gender expectations within Thai society meant that, even if she had wanted to insist on the use of protection, her ability to negotiate the use of a condom is likely to have been limited.

It is clear that education and HIV-prevention programmes must seek to build a deeper awareness of HIV that reveals the interplay between HIV, gender, and poverty and enables a more profound understanding of the way in which this affects the vulnerability of different groups – including women like Pimjai – to infection. In doing so, such programmes must challenge the gender inequalities and the associated behavioural expectations that place women – as well as men – at increased risk of contracting HIV.

Conclusion

Pimjai is just one of a large number of women living with HIV and AIDS in Thailand and other countries in Asia. However, in many ways her story exemplifies the growing young and female face of the epidemic. Highlighting the interconnectedness of HIV and AIDS with development and gender issues, her story serves as a reminder of the urgent need to tackle the underlying causes of poverty and gender inequality if the struggle against the epidemic is to be won. Her story also functions as an inspiration for what can be done.

Pimjai's story demonstrates the crucial role that initiatives such as the Community Health Project can play in helping to protect men and women from infection and to improve lives of those living with HIV and AIDS through raising awareness and understanding of HIV, and providing men and women in poor communities with skills and training. Education for children, young people, and adults – women and men – is a basic need and a basic right that provides the foundation for seeking, processing, and applying knowledge and information throughout life. Conversely, lack of, or inadequate education and training opportunities for women and girls are intrinsically linked to their lack of empowerment and increased vulnerability to HIV and AIDS. It is essential therefore that more intensive and extensive efforts, with appropriate budgetary allocation, are made to empower women through equal access to education and vocational skills training.

However, we must ask what kind of education is available, and whether this is literacy education, post-literacy education, basic education, or vocational skills training. Having facts and information alone is not sufficient to make men and women change behaviours, and knowledge alone does not necessarily lead to action. The participatory exercises outlined above were structured to help men and women to become aware of problems and to be able to relate themselves directly to them. Only then will people be willing to start to make real changes in their behaviours. To be truly useful, education, particularly adult education, needs to enable men and women not just to recite what HIV and AIDS is, what it does to the body, and what the main ways to prevent it are, but also to enable them to analyse their own personal risks and their own possible responses to these risks. They need to be able to personalise and localise the problem of HIV and AIDS before they become committed to taking action and finding solutions. Gender-sensitivity training must be a central part of this. We need to raise both men's and women's awareness of gender inequalities and how this affects our lives. In this way we can build an understanding of the way in which gender bias and behaviours can make us and those around us more vulnerable to HIV and AIDS.

It is essential that we continue to work to develop wide-reaching participatory programmes which are grounded in the understanding that knowledge alone does not lead to action. These must be linked to advocacy and structural change and developed in partnership with other sectors, in close collaboration with poverty-alleviation measures focused on reducing migration, prostitution, drug use, and peddling, and also with concrete initiatives that promote women's empowerment and equality in economic, social, cultural, political, and legal sectors. In doing this we need to become more open and more accepting, with the focus on learning.

Most importantly, we need to understand and accept our own limitations and, following Pimjai's example, continue to educate ourselves and reach out to others.

Note

1   The information for this case study comes from: Community Health Project (2005) 'Case Study of Community Health Project (CHP) Part 1: Leading The Way For Marginalized People With HIV/AIDS', and Community Health Project (2005) 'Case Study of Community Health Project (CHP) Part 2'.

References

AVERT HIV and AIDS in Thailand (n.d.) www.avert.org/aidsthai.htm, (last checked February 2008).

Duangsa, D. and U. Duongsaa (1994) 'Using PRA to Promote AIDS Awareness', paper presented at the International Workshop on Socio-Cultural Dimensions of HIV/AIDS Control and Care in Thailand, Chiangmai, Thailand.

Duongsaa, U. (2004) 'Development, Gender, HIV/AIDS and Adult Education: Linkages, Lessons Learned and Challenges', paper prepared for Beyond Access seminar, University of East Anglia, www.ioe.ac.uk/schools/efps/GenderEducDev/Usa%20Duongsaa%20paper.pdf (last accessed May 2008).

Hallacy, J. (1999) 'Report on the Mekhong Sub-Regional Training Workshop on Using Gender-Oriented PRA to Promote HIV/AIDS Awareness', Hua Hin, Thailand.

UNAIDS (2001) 'Development of and Lessons Learned from Positive People Groups and Network, Study Report: The Case of the Upper North, Thailand'.

UNAIDS (2006) 'Report on the Global AIDS Epidemic', available online at: www.unaids.org/en/HIV_data/2006GlobalReport/default.asp (last checked February 2008).

UNAIDS (n.d.) www.unaids.org/en/Regions_Countries/Countries/thailand.asp (last checked February 2008).

UNDP (2004) 'Thailand's Response to HIV/AIDS: Progress and Challenges', Bangkok, available at www.undp.org/hiv/pubs.htm (last checked February 2008).

WHO (2007) 'Progress Report: Towards Universal Access: Scaling up Priority HIV/AIDS interventions in the Health Sector', available at www.searo.who.int/en/Section10/Section18/Section2008_13202.htm (last checked February 2008).

10 Engaging the community to promote gender equity among young men: experiences from 'Yari Dosti' in Mumbai

Sujata Khandekar, Mahendra Rokade, Vilas Sarmalkar, Ravi K. Verma, Vaishali Mahendra, and Julie Pulerwitz

Introduction

This chapter describes experiences of community mobilisation in a research-based intervention programme called *Yari Dosti* (meaning 'bonding among men'). *Yari Dosti* was initiated in 2003 to promote gender equity as a strategy to reduce behaviour that was putting young men at risk of HIV, and to reduce violence against women in low-income communities in Mumbai, India.

Gender attitudes and behaviours are largely the reflections of social norms and practices that support and sustain them. Many of these gender norms lead young men to attach great value to sexual prowess, multiple sexual partners, authority, and aggression, thus increasing the risk of HIV and violence against women. *Yari Dosti* was developed out of the belief that risky sexual attitudes and behaviours among men can be changed by first understanding how men construct masculinity and gender attitudes, and then by working with young men and their community to highlight which aspects of their gendered attitudes and behaviour lead to risk for them and their partners, and helping them redefine 'appropriate' social roles for men and women (i.e. gender roles). This approach, therefore, sees community engagement and mobilisation as integral to challenging and changing inequitable gender attitudes and behaviours.

This chapter examines the design and process of research, exploring the links between gender and masculinity, sexuality, and risk behaviour. It then considers the approach, design, and implementation of the intervention based on the research findings. It examines the evaluation and monitoring framework using the Gender Equitable Men Scale (GEMS) and discusses scale-up strategies of this extensively evaluated and validated intervention. It ends with conclusions and lessons learned from the programme.

Why is *Yari Dosti* significant?

The *Yari Dosti* programme is significant and distinct in more ways than one. The significance of the research lies in both its concept and its methodology. In terms of the concept, its focus on construction of masculinity was its distinct feature. HIV and AIDS-related programmes have in the past predominantly focused on safe sex and condom use as a preventive strategy, whereas *Yari Dosti* focused on attitudes which lead to decisions related to (un)safe sex and condom (non)use. In terms of methodology, the involvement of grassroots activists in every stage of the research and intervention, especially as researchers, makes this a distinctive programme. This methodology has helped to reduce the gap between the researcher and the researched, and has facilitated an easy and natural transfer of ownership of the programme from the research organisation (which conceptualised the pro- gramme) to the implementing organisation. The distinctiveness of the programme also lies in the research questions which revolved around issues of gender, masculinity, and sexuality, without trivialising them. Questions related to HIV and AIDS were subtly embedded in a broader mesh of questions on gender and sexuality. This helped ensure that *Yari Dosti* was not seen as a potentially 'stigmatised' HIV and AIDS programme.

Working with men on issues of gender and sexuality is a challenge. Achieving the balance between positions of men as 'victims of masculinity' and 'perpetrators of violence' is a tightrope walk. The *Yari Dosti* programme has clearly indicated that it is possible to work with young men on issues of gender and sexuality, and that change in deep-rooted gender attitudes is possible. The research also explicitly indicates that involving grassroots activists and peers is a successful strategy for such research and intervention programmes.

Young men's knowledge about sexuality

It is estimated that there are 5.1 million people living with HIV in India (National AIDS Control Organisation 2006). Almost half of new HIV infections are believed to occur among young men below the age of 30 (NACO 2005). Most evidence suggests that knowledge about HIV and AIDS is low among youth (Apte 2004; Bhende 1994; Abraham and Deshpande 2001), and very few young men see themselves as vulnerable (UNAIDS 2000). Jejeebhoy (1998), in her study with Indian adolescents on sexual and reproductive behaviour, has concluded that whatever knowledge adolescents have is incomplete and confused.

An important factor influencing young men's HIV risk in India is that from very early in their lives they learn notions of masculinity that promote inequitable gender-related attitudes and behaviours. In addition, women learn to tolerate and also to reinforce these notions of masculinity and inequitable gender-related attitudes, which further increases women's vulnerability to HIV infections and violence. It is therefore argued that challenging prevailing social norms of masculinity (and femininity) is essential in promoting sexual health and reducing vulnerabilities for both young men and young women. As Bhende (2000) notes, very few interventions in India have attempted to influence or change norms and risky behaviour. Interventions dealing with issues related to sexuality are a challenge in the Indian context. Notions of immorality and taboos associated with sex and sexuality complicate and stigmatise issues relating to young people's sexual health. As a rule, parents do not speak about sex-related matters with their children. Sex-education programmes in schools are often received with hostility by parents and also by teachers, which resulted in the imposition of a ban on sex education in schools by many states in India in 2007.

It is only since the rise of HIV and AIDS that sexuality has been extensively discussed in the public domain, yet much of these discussions revolve only around condom use and safe sex. Any intervention encompassing gender and sexuality in relation to the HIV and AIDS epidemic is a challenging task in terms of both design and implementation. An intervention with out-of-school youth in a community context is particularly challenging, owing to the diverse nature of communities, survival issues, time availability, and many other reasons. However, in order to reach out to young men who are outside of any formal structures (education, employment etc.), community-based interventions become crucial. And the success of community-based interventions depends a great deal on the transfer of 'ownership' of the programme to the community.

The partnership and the researched communities

The *Yari Dosti* programme is an example of meaningful partnership between CORO for Literacy (hereafter referred to as CORO), an organisation with a strong community presence in Mumbai; Vishwas Sanskruti Kala Manch (VSKM), a community-based organisation of young men and women using performing arts as a tool for change; the Population Council (Horizons Program), an international research organisation; and Instituto Promundo, a Brazil-based NGO. This partnership largely grew out of individual initiatives (for example, proactive communication and feedback on issues of common concern such as violence against women), similar organisational philosophies (seeing men as partners and not as obstacles in the fight against HIV and AIDS and violence against women; and generating programme ownership from within communities), and the felt need to learn and draw from each other's strengths and resources.

Community mobilisation

CORO was part of all the research and intervention activities and was solely responsible for community-based mobilisation and the implementation of the *Yari Dosti* programme. CORO was established in 1989, when it was led by middle-class, upper-caste, well-educated activists in good employment. Subsequently it was transformed into an organisation led by young men and women from the communities where it operated, predominantly the *Dalit* (scheduled caste) and the minority communities. CORO provided the impetus to create VSKM, which, having worked on social issues and on issues relating to community women, was seen by the communities as going against the norm or comprising 'positive deviants'. The *Yari Dosti* research team consisted of nine married and unmarried young male VSKM activists who were slightly older than the participants in the intervention.

The researched communities

The *Yari Dosti* intervention site included three large slum pockets in north-east Mumbai, covering a population of about 300,000. A large majority of the population are migrant workers from various parts of India, particularly the northern states and rural Maharashtra, and are a mix of Muslims, Hindus, and Buddhists. The slums are characterised by congested shanties with marginal employment or unemployment, low literacy rates, an absence of minimum basic amenities, a high prevalence of violence against women, and intense criminal activities. These communities were selected because their ethnic and religious mix represented a typical Mumbai slum. Young men who participated in the research are mostly second-generation migrants. Participants' occupations ranged from being 'students' to 'unemployed' to 'marginally employed' (engaged in marginal jobs as daily wagers). Participants' groups were a mix of married and unmarried young men.

Research on the lifestyle of young men

The first step of the *Yari Dosti* programme was to conduct research with young men between the ages of 16 and 24, exploring links between gender and masculinity, sexuality, and risk behaviour. This research aimed to understand the lifestyle of young men in these communities. The data collected during the in-depth interviews and key-informant interviews provided information about young men's perception of masculinity, their upbringing, social networks, social habits, passions, daily activities, attitudes and behaviour related to sex, and their knowledge of and attitudes to HIV and AIDS.

Training the research team

The research began with training the research team and building their capacity to undertake qualitative research on gender and sexuality. It consisted of two components: deepening members' understanding of gender and sexuality issues, and building skills in qualitative research methods. Individual research team members drawn from VSKM had varied levels of understanding about gender and sexuality issues. Most had worked on women-centred issues in a humanitarian framework, which had implications for their understandings of gender and sexuality. A humanitarian framework takes its opposition to violence against women from a welfare approach, and draws on attitudes suffused with well-meaning sympathy and kindness. *Yari Dosti*, however, is based on a human-rights framework, drawing on individuals' right to dignity and right to freedom, which significantly broadens the scope of gender and sexuality issues.

Deep-rooted unequal gender construction and its prominent reflection in the realm of sexuality made training processes extensive and elaborate, as well as a challenge for the trainers. The research team members had come with their own assumptions, beliefs, and normalised perceptions relating to gender and sexuality, which had never been challenged as directly as they were during the formative research training. They expressed popular justifications for gender inequality, and equitable views on gender relations only in limited domains (e.g. accepting a proposition to educate girls, but rejecting a proposition of a woman having the right to deny sex to her husband/partner). The training aimed to promote a space where team members could engage in self-reflection in order to look at issues of sex and sexuality in a more objective and non-judgemental way, which is a prerequisite in order to undertake research on gender and sexuality.

The training was in the form of participatory, interactive discussions, and became a continuous and evolving process for all those involved in the research. Trainers observed a lot of giggling among team members when terms related to sexual organs, sexual acts, and same-sex behaviour were mentioned. To address this, one exercise consisted of asking team members to write down all the words related to sexual organs and sexual acts in local languages on a piece of paper, and then getting them to read each of these words aloud. This was followed by discussions about the local meaning and origin of each word, which helped team members to overcome their inhibitions and to view sex and sexuality as an important and serious aspect of human life. Intensive short-term training was later carried out on various relevant issues as and when they arose.

Training on qualitative research methods was a relatively easy process, compared with the training on issues of gender and sexuality (probably owing to its emphasis on skills rather than perceptions). Team members' familiarity with

various communications strategies such as street theatre, interviewing, facilitating meetings, and so on was useful when deploying qualitative research tools.
Training sessions on qualitative methods were followed by field practice, and this
experience was shared and approaches refined.

Talking about sex

The research data were collected mainly through 45 in-depth interviews with
young men in the researched communities. The interviewees were identified
through a 'social mapping' (where different types of young men were approached)
and then by using 'snowball' techniques (where acquaintances of the original
young men were then approached). Systems were put in place to check, re-check,
and cross-check the collected data. Upbringing, lifestyles, hobbies, social networks,
peer groups, perceptions of gender, violence, sexuality, sexual behaviour, and
sexual experiences, knowledge and attitudes about HIV and AIDS were all
explored during interviews.

The research team members who carried out the interviews were initially
sceptical about the willingness of respondents to divulge information about
intimate behaviour and sexual experiences, but to their surprise they found
young men to be quite eager to talk. 'Spicy discussions' and gossip about sex were
very common among young men. More non-judgemental, dispassionate, and
serious discussions which addressed anxieties and misconceptions among young
men were new to them. However, young men talked profusely about their
anxieties and concerns related to sexual performance and sexual health, such as
masturbation and 'night falls' (wet dreams).

The research team found that two major factors were helpful in getting
respondents to open up about sex and sexuality. The first was that the interviewers
were from a similar socio-economic background to the respondents. This helped
to establish rapport quickly (instantly in many cases) between the interviewer and
the interviewee, and it helped to reduce the degree of 'exaggeration' by
respondents in narrations, because the interviewers were familiar with the
community situation. The second helpful factor was that the interviewers talked
about their own dilemmas relating to sex and sexuality at the beginning of the
interview, and described their own search for some reliable space to voice their
concerns. With interviewers who were only slightly older than respondents, the
former were seen by respondents as peers in whom they could confide, as well as
individuals whom they could respect.

Nevertheless, the data-collection phase was stressful for both interviewers and
respondents. For some of the interviewers, stories gathered during data
collection reminded them of their own past, while some respondents later

reported having been anxious because they had disclosed very private and personal information to the interviewers. Ways of debriefing were created for interviewers and respondents which helped to reduce stress and also to strengthen bonding among the research team members.

What does it mean to be a 'real man'?

'Who do you think is a "real man" (*asli mard*)?' was the question used as an entry point by the interviewers. This led to unpacking 'bundles' of perceptions, beliefs, norms, and practices concerning gender and sexuality among young men in the researched area. This section looks at the findings which informed the design of the intervention.

'Real men': traits, attributes, and behaviour

The data indicated that the respondents have no single construct of masculinity, but rather there is a continuum of masculinities ranging from 'feminine men' to 'macho men', with the latter generally being preferred. Respondents described 'real men' in terms of traits and physical attributes: 'real men should have good physique, be physically strong, able to have sex many times, and able to entertain woman sexually…'; attitudinal attributes: 'in a crisis situation one can prove his masculinity…You may come forward and take a lead in resolving it and prove your masculinity'; and behavioural attributes: 'a real man must take responsibility for all his family members. Most important is that he should look after his parents well'. The respondents ridiculed men with feminine characteristics and also men who have sex with men. But some of them also reported same-sex activity as their sexual debut. Some interviewees reported pleasurable experiences of having sex with men: '…one can't derive such a pleasure [in having sex with a man] from a sexual intercourse [with women]…'.

Sexual prowess and using force to control women

Aggression towards women and coercive sex were observed to be attributes of masculinity. This was seen as an expression of 'proving' one's masculinity:

> *…one day my girlfriend and I were returning from roaming in the evening and the road was quite empty. I put my hand on her shoulder and then over her body and pulled her to the corner of the road and started kissing her. She was not ready and tried to avoid it…I caught her hard, kept kissing her, removed her clothes and had sex with her…she kept refusing.*

Women were viewed as sex objects, and violence against women (physical and sexual) was perceived as the norm. Forms of sexual coercion ranged across a continuum, starting with non-physical tactics to try to have sexual contact with women such as teasing, jostling, and whistling, to youths who said that in a crowded area they would touch any part of a young woman's body. Sexually coercive behaviour (verbal or physical) was seen as demonstrating sexual power, and was directed towards women who appeared to challenge men's masculinity. Young men categorised girls into 'good and hence marriageable' (those who do not challenge their masculinity) and 'bad and hence deserving of coercion' (those who challenge their masculinity). They also presupposed a woman's refusal of sex to be consent ('she wanted it but said no…all say no but don't mean no').

Findings indicated that young men prove their masculinity through sexual power and coercion:

> *'unless a woman cries during sex…your masculinity is not proved.'*

> *'My friends challenged me. They said if you are a real man then engage that girl within eight days.'*

> *'When she said no to me, I said I have to show her I am the man and teach her a lesson.'*

Risk-taking as a masculine trait?

Lots of individual, group, or self-inflicted violence was reported. Risk-taking was equated with being masculine. Sexual activity was reported as one means of dealing with stress and frustration for young men. However, young men did not see themselves as being at risk or vulnerable to HIV and AIDS. The only risky sexual activity was perceived to be that with female sex workers, but not with men, *hijras* (transsexuals), casual partners, or wives. Young men reported that they used condoms, sometime two condoms, during sex with sex workers. Young men's low-risk perception is reflected in some of these quotes:

> *'…why should I use condoms during sexual relations with my own wife or girlfriend? It is not needed.'*

> *'…When somebody is sexually excited why would he spend time taking out a condom and putting it on his penis?'*

> *'…condom reduces sexual pleasure…'*

Peer influence

Peers were found to have the strongest influence on the young men. Other sources of information included doctors, gym trainers, pornographic films (popularly known as English films), media (TV and print media), voyeurism (watching live sex), community programmes, and school programmes. Many of the respondents reported that they had watched their parents having sex. This is common in slum communities, owing to the tiny sizes of houses. Groups of young men reported watching couples having sex during the night, and then narrating the details to their friends.

From knowledge to action: developing the intervention

Translating qualitative research findings into an intervention is a challenging task. The team of grassroots researchers was actively involved in this process, which ensured that the intervention would be relevant to and rooted in community realities in terms of content, methodology, and language. The intervention adapted 'Program H' activities (developed by Instituto Promundo and partners), which had been successfully tested in low-income communities in Brazil (Pulerwitz *et al.* 2006).

The research had indicated that the intervention needed to address the following areas: viewing women as mere sex objects, aggression towards women and coercive sex, low self-perception of risk, sexual anxieties, and substance abuse. Since peer pressure had emerged as the strongest influence on young men, it was decided that the intervention should be peer-led, and so it was designed to foster self-reflection on gender attitudes as well as offering alternative peer groups for young men who volunteered to be part of the programme. Working definitions of key concepts were developed. A 'gender-equitable man' was defined in much the same way as Program H defined the concept – as someone who: (1) supports relationships based on equality, respect, and intimacy rather than sexual conquest; (2) seeks to be involved as a domestic partner and father both in terms of child-care and household activities; (3) shares with his partner responsibility for reproductive health and disease prevention; (4) does not practise violence, and opposes violence in intimate relationships; and (5) questions homophobic tendencies and attitudes. It was at this point that the name *Yari Dosti* – which means 'friendship [or bonding] among men' – was agreed upon.

The intervention programme had two main components: group educational activities and a 'life style' social-marketing campaign that reinforced the gender-equitable and HIV-prevention messages forming the basis of the group education activities.

The *Yari Dosti* group educational component adopted a participatory format, and sessions were held once a week in a closed room in a community setting. These activities and exercises lasted two to three hours and continued over a period of six months. Here young men had the space to discuss issues of concern to them around gender, body, and sexuality. Exercises were planned to avoid 'preaching' at young men about behaving well, and instead allowed interactions that could lead participants to self-reflection on gender attitudes. Men were understood as partners in change and not as obstacles to change, and were also seen to be complex beings rather than homogeneous members of a 'monolithic' category.

Formation of participants' groups

The team which had carried out the formative research then became the facilitators of the education groups. They set up pilot intervention groups, attracting participants through a pamphlet that described the programme and stated that the facilitators wanted to share both their own experiences and formative study findings (with young men in the community) on issues related to sexuality. In addition to a variety of community members, the intervention team sought to include participants from certain 'types' of youth identified in the research: '*chamdinad*' (womaniser), '*bevada*' (alcoholic), '*tapori*' (vagabond), and others, as they often reported risky behaviours. Finally, 126 young men were enrolled to take part in the pilot intervention and divided into four different groups, each including a mix of religions, ethnicities, occupations, and educational and marital status.

Selected group exercises

Working with the issue of violence, story lines depicting realities from communities were developed:

> *Rahul liked his neighbour, a girl called Sunita, with whom he sometimes exchanged glances. One day, they went into an abandoned house and began to kiss. Rahul convinced her to take off her salwar-kamiz (local attire) and she agreed. She then got nervous and said she wanted to leave. Rahul told her that she had come this far, so they should go further. He continued trying to convince her to have sex, telling her that she was beautiful and that he really cared for her, but he did not physically force her. Is this violence?*

The stories were intentionally kept a little ambiguous or open-ended so that participants could reflect and debate, with the opportunity to change their positions if convinced by others' arguments. Deliberations covered a range of issues, including consent, forced consent, respect in relationships, the right to refuse sex, assumptions made by partners in intimate relationships, socialisation of girls and boys, peer pressures, and emotional blackmailing as a form of violence. Participants invariably brought issues of violence against their mother or sister into the discussion. Towards the end of a session, the facilitators would help participants to arrive at a common understanding about what constitutes violence, and especially violence against women. Such exercises, instead of labelling young men as perpetrators, created spaces for self-reflection and helped them open up windows for change, however narrow they may be.

Another exercise which generated meaningful and efficacious discussions was about sexual desire or excitement. The research had indicated that young men understood sex only as penetrative sex, with or without consent. Foreplay was described by young men as a 'waste of time'. To address this, a session on the 'erotic body' was utilised. Through participatory discussions and exercises, participants were able to reflect on how various parts of the body can give sexual pleasure and why respect for sexual partners and communication in intimate relationships is important. This session also explored stages of sexual pleasure, understanding your partner's sexual desires and needs, and safe(r) sex.

From reticence to free and open communication

It is significant that, without any monetary incentive, participation remained high throughout the intervention. Participants did report that they were initially attracted simply because of the notion of talking about sex, but such attitudes gradually changed as the intervention progressed. Initial scepticism and wariness of the need to speak in a 'politically correct' fashion were replaced by frank discussions of personal experiences (even intimate experiences). Most participants said that these group discussions stimulated them to question their attitudes and behaviours. Some of them even expressed an interest in extending the sessions to their friends, and volunteered to form groups to carry out more exercises. The programme illustrates a successful approach to engaging young men in self-reflection about deep-rooted attitudes about sexuality and gender.

The education groups were never described as being about HIV and AIDS prevention. Initial sessions focused on gender, the body, sexuality, and violence-related issues. As HIV and AIDS-related exercises were considered particularly taboo in the community, they were only introduced later at a point when the group had become receptive to discussions of these topics. Many participants, in fact, said that if exercises on HIV and AIDS had been part of the initial sessions, they might not have continued with the group, because of the stigma attached to the topic. However, eventually, HIV risk and violence against women became an integral part of group discussion. The approach taken by group facilitators was to illustrate links between inequitable gender attitudes, behaviour that increased risk of HIV infection, and violence against women. The interactions during these sessions indicated that discussing HIV prevention by focusing on high-risk/low-risk behaviours (the focus of many HIV and AIDS programmes) was not a particularly useful frame when approached from the perspective of intimate relationships, gender equality, and sexuality.

It was observed that participants were very receptive to sessions involving scientific information (e.g. sessions on the body, diseases and related treatments, knowledge about HIV and AIDS, etc.). Facilitators always made efforts to broaden the scope of discussions, and exercises involving certain types of attitudes (e.g. sessions on gender, violence, sexual diversity, etc.) often generated quite heated discussions. Facilitators' skills in communication and their field-work experience helped them to cope with such situations, as group discussions were marked not only by lively participation but also by major arguments. Facilitators also used their own techniques to develop strong group cohesion and sustain the motivation of participants. Theatrical performances, celebrations of personal events, home visits, and creative recap sessions were some of the strategies used.

Life Style Social Marketing Campaign

It emerged that participants were concerned about the stark difference between the environment during the classroom sessions (where the group had open discussions, and support for gender equity was developed among the whole group), and the external environment. Many participants expressed distress over the total absence of a supportive environment (i.e. supportive of their changing attitudes) outside the classroom. Therefore, the programme also attempted to encourage a supportive environment outside of the group sessions by implementing a 'Life Style' Social Marketing Campaign. As with the group education component, the campaign was adapted from Program H by young men (in collaboration with the larger project team), and then implemented by the young men themselves. The campaign included interactive street plays, with audience discussions after the plays, and the distribution and discussion of IEC (information, education, and communication) materials, such as posters and comic strips. The formats promoted positive gender-equitable images of 'real men' as possible alternatives to the prevailing ideas about what characteristics a 'real man' should have. For example, textual messages on two posters designed for the campaign read: 'Sanju never hits his wife – it does happen' or 'Rahul never forces himself on his partner – because he knows "no" from his partner really means NO'. The slogan of the campaign was *Soch sahi mard vahi* ('A real man *thinks* right').

Street plays took up issues related to gender and sexuality that emerged from the research. Violence, respect for your partner, the gendered division of labour, and safe(r) sex were four major themes. Community perceptions of gender and sexuality were portrayed through various characters and were forcefully contested by an 'equitable and gender-sensitive' male character. After each street performance, a group of CORO and VSKM activists interviewed viewers and assessed how well the message had got across.

Outcomes: from denial of gender equality to challenging norms

Impact on peer leaders

The new roles as researchers and facilitators, in general, enhanced the prestige and status of the young men. However, in addition, they travelled long personal journeys of introspection, self-confrontation, and struggle to become gender-sensitised individuals. These journeys were not easy, and they mentioned difficult times when their friends isolated them, believing that they had changed. Their new realisations about gender and sexuality also changed the nature of their own intimate relationships:

> *'I have lost intimacy with friends (because of the change in my attitudes)... Losing friends makes me unhappy.'*

> *'In my relationship with my girlfriend the question "Am I dominating?" is always at the top of my mind now. This is very irritating sometimes. Admittedly, however, the quality of our relationship has improved.'*

> *'...The intervention sessions have helped me become a listening person, a responsible person, and a thinking person. All this helped to better my performance in relating with people and attending to their issues.'*

> *'...my participation helped me to look at things in its related context...'*

The Gender Equitable Men Scale

There was a rigorous monitoring and evaluation system put in place for the programme. The Gender Equitable Men Scale (GEM Scale) was used to measure changes in the support for (in)equitable gender norms of the participants, and questions were asked about key additional outcomes, including violence and safer sex. External evaluators conducted interviews with participants and their close relatives. Pre-tests and post-tests were conducted with participants.

Almost all the young men who had joined education groups consistently participated in the intervention. Some of the original participants who had dropped out were interviewed, in order to find out why they had dropped out. Findings indicate that those who had dropped out had done so because of pressures of job-hunting and other time constraints.

The GEM Scale consists of 24 statements in five domains: (1) domestic life; (2) sexual relationships; (3) sexual and reproductive health; (4) violence; and (5) homophobia and relations with other men. The GEM Scale was originally developed and tested in Brazil (Pulerwitz and Barker 2008) and was again tested for its validity and utility for the Indian context before using it for evaluation of the pilot intervention. Some of the items in the GEM Scale (items were scored as *agree/partially agree/do not agree*) were the following:

- In my opinion, a woman can suggest using condoms just like a man can.

- If a guy gets a woman pregnant, the child is the responsibility of both.

- There are times when a woman deserves to be beaten.

- Men are always ready to have sex.

- A woman's most important role is to take care of her home and cook for her family.

- I would never have a gay friend.

Some pre- and post-test data using the GEM Scale are included in Table 1 to indicate positive change in support for gender equity. For example, the percentage of young men who said 'it is ok for a man to hit his wife if she refuses sex with him' dropped from 28 per cent to 3 per cent after the intervention.

Table 1: Proportion of participants who agree with GEM Scale statements

Statements	Pre-test data (%)	Post-test data (%)
A woman can suggest using a condom just like a man	58	89
I would be outraged if my wife asked me to use a condom	35	17
Women who carry condoms are easy	54	19
A man can hit a woman if she cheats on him	36	33
A man can hit a woman if she refuses sex	28	3
A woman should tolerate violence to keep family together	33	9
There are times when women deserve to be beaten	31	14

When the items were combined into the GEM Scale, there was an overall positive shift in support for gender-equitable norms ($p < .05$). There was also a significant reduction in harassment against women over the past three months reported by participants (80 per cent to 43 per cent; $p < .05$). Further, there were positive trends towards an increase in condom use, but these changes were not significant. For additional detail about this evaluation, see Verma *et al.* (2006).

In-depth interviews with participants and their friends and relatives also demonstrated change among the young men. A participant's mother reported that her son had started communicating with her and others in the family: 'My son was a very introverted type of person and rarely talked to us. But now he shares a lot of things with us'. Many young men reported improved relationships with their girlfriends or partners: 'I was about to divorce my wife due to misunderstanding. These sessions restrained me from doing that.'

There was a variety of changes in attitudes and behaviours reported by the participants:

> '...boys tease girls because they think it's natural and rightful. I know this because I was one of them...'

> 'After the session on erotic body, my views about sex have changed…I don't think many of us in this community ever thought like this.'

> 'Those who think that condom use reduces sexual pleasure are wrong. I also used to think so. But now I know each part of our body can give sexual pleasure. What is important is the understanding between the partners.'

It is very challenging to change deep-rooted gender attitudes in a short period of six months. Change in gender attitudes is a process, and facilitators found that the change process often started with denial of gender-inequitable attitudes and then moved from a justification of gender-based inequality to acceptance of the existence of gender-inequitable norms and practices. This acceptance further pushed participants to reflect on their attitudes and to explore ways to challenge these norms and behaviour.

Conclusions

The *Yari Dosti* programme addressed gender attitudes of young men that commonly lead to sexually risky behaviour. The evaluation of the programme indicated a significant reduction in young men's support for inequitable gender norms related to safe sex and violence, and some change in related behaviours. Thus, addressing gender attitudes and norms can be important components of HIV and violence prevention strategies. Further, this programme, which utilised interactive group education and community-based behaviour-change communication, and included significant involvement from the community, was successful in meeting its main goals. It should be considered a useful HIV and violence prevention tool.

The programme implementers feel that the programme's ability to address and change these gender attitudes was largely due to the importance given to the research component of *Yari Dosti*. It was crucial for understanding the construction of masculinities and the nature of unequal gender relations in these culturally mixed slum areas, and provided the basis for the development and adaptation of the intervention programme itself. The research indicated that there was no single construct of masculinity, but rather a continuum which ranged from constructions of 'feminine' men at one end of the scale to 'macho' men at the other – and the latter being the preferred construct of young men in the community. For these young men, their peer groups were the strongest influence on their construction of masculinity, which was infused by support for coercive heterosexual sex and violence against women. The research indicated the need to work with young men to help them analyse their sexuality and construct a more positive masculinity and more positive gender attitudes. Only by tackling deep-seated inequalities of gender attitudes and practices will young people be able to protect themselves against HIV and AIDS. While this is a big task which takes time and commitment, experiences from the community-based intervention *Yari Dosti* suggest that it *is* possible to change young men's attitudes to and relationships with sexual partners and prospective sexual partners.

Having well-trained researchers/facilitators was a crucial factor in *Yari Dosti*. Complex and taboo issues related to sexuality and gender were challenging for even the most well-trained facilitator to tackle, and changing their own deep-rooted gender attitudes was an evolving process. Hence continuous training and dialogue about dilemmas and issues that emerged in both their training and their facilitating was essential. Facilitators' communication skills, their understanding of group dynamics, and adequate clarity about and internalisation of gender and sexuality-related issues were fundamental. Counselling was available to support facilitators throughout the intervention, because of stress felt by the facilitators when exploring these sensitive topics. What the *Yari Dosti* programme has also shown, however, is that young men without former professional research training can acquire skills and perspectives that serve as a foundation for roles as effective change agents related to gender and HIV/violence prevention.

One of the key lessons from *Yari Dosti* is that ownership of the programme should rest with the community. Changing deep-rooted attitudes is a long process and needs to be supported from within the community. In this study local young men were involved from an early stage, which helped to make the transfer of 'ownership' of the programme from the research organisation to the implementing organisation easy and natural. CORO has been engaged with community-based activities for the last 18 years, and CORO's experience of grassroots work proved to be of immense importance to the programme.

Encouraged by the results of the pilot intervention described in this chapter, *Yari Dosti* was expanded in 2005 to include 750 young men in the slum communities of Mumbai, and 750 young men from the rural communities of Gorakhpur, Uttar Pradesh. The intervention has now been adapted and tested in urban as well as rural contexts and is ready for further scale-up. A *Yari Dosti* manual is being adapted to work with school-going boys (aged 12–18) in the public-school system. Further, based on feedback from the community, it was determined that there was a need to work also with young women to address inequitable gender practices and help reduce their vulnerability to violence and to HIV and AIDS. *Sakhi-Saheli* (meaning 'female friends'), a research-based intervention, is currently being implemented by CORO in Mumbai slums with 549 married and unmarried young women (aged 16–25).

Acknowledgements

The study team included Sujata Khandekar, Mahendra Rokade, and Vilas Sarmalkar, all from CORO; Dr Ravi Verma, formerly of Horizons/Population Council, and Vaishali Mahendra, Horizons/Population Council, New Delhi; Dr Julie Pulerwitz, formerly of Horizons/PATH, Washington DC; and Dr Gary Barker, Instituto PROMUNDO, Brazil.

For more details on this chapter, contact Sujata55@hotmail.com or rverma@icrw.org. Additional details about the study can be found at www.popcouncil.org.

References

Abraham, L. and B. Deshapande (2001) 'Youth Sexuality: A Guide to Recent Literature', Mumbai: Tata Institute of Social Sciences.

Apte, H. (2004) 'College men, sexual knowledge and pornography in Pune', in R. Verma *et al.* (eds.) *Sexuality in the Times of AIDS: Contemporary Perspectives from Communities*, New Delhi: Sage Publications.

Bhende, A. (1994) 'A study of sexuality of adolescent girls and boys in underprivileged groups in Mumbai', *Indian Journal of Social Work* 55(4 SI): 557–71.

Bhende, A. (2000) 'Evolving a Model of AIDS Prevention Education among Under Privileged Adolescent Girls In Urban India', paper presented at a workshop on Adolescent Sexual and Reproductive Health: Issues and Challenges, at the International Institute of Population Studies.

Jejeebhoy, S. (1998) 'Adolescent sexual and reproductive behaviour: a review of the evidence from India', *Social Science and Medicine* 46(10): 1275–90.

National AIDS Control Organisation (NACO) (2005) www.nacoonline.org/vasco/indianscene/overv.htm (last checked July 2007).

National AIDS Control Organisation (NACO) (2006) 'HIV/AIDS Epidemiological Surveillance and Estimation Report for the Year 2005', New Delhi: NACO.

Pulerwitz, J. and G. Barker (2008) 'Measuring attitudes toward gender norms among young men in Brazil: development and psychometric evaluation of the GEM Scale', *Men and Masculinities* 10: 322–38.

Pulerwitz, J., G. Barker, M. Segundo, and M. Nascimento (2006) 'Promoting More Gender-equitable Norms and Behaviors Among Young Men as an HIV/AIDS Prevention Strategy', Horizons Final Report, Washington DC: Population Council.

UNAIDS (2000) 'Report on the Global HIV/AIDS Epidemic'.

Verma, R., J. Pulerwitz, V. Mahendra, S. Khandekar, G. Barker, G. Fulpagare, and S.K. Singh (2006) 'Challenging and changing gender attitudes among young men in Mumbai, India', *Reproductive Health Matters* 14(28): 1–10.

11　Building multi-sectoral partnerships to deliver gendered HIV education in schools: the Nigerian experience

Omokhudu Idogho

Introduction

'Partnership' is one of those words that has had a central place in the development lexicon over the last two decades. The term is somewhat ambiguous, meaning different things to different people, depending on their operating context. Adams *et al.* (1995: 1) define partnership as a group of '... people (institutions) working together and maintaining equal power', while ActionAid International (2007) describes partnership as 'an arena of collective power in which people, organizations and networks come together with their knowledge, experiences, perspectives and resources in order to achieve commonly agreed objectives'. Underlying most definitions is the recognition that partnership is a process of collective inputs from diverse groups in the quest to achieve shared goals. Partnership can also be seen as a political, social, and economic process. It is central to constructing, socialising, and negotiating the knowledge, ideologies, ideas, approaches, and perspectives needed to work jointly for a common purpose (Zewdie 2007).

Partnership is a form of power in and of itself, but it is also a means to increase power, since a partnership provides the space and the structure for people, organisations, networks, and movements with similar views, beliefs, and commitment to come together to generate greater collective power and legitimacy (*ibid.*). This chapter views partnership as a group of people and institutions working together and pooling their knowledge, experiences, perspectives and resources in order to increase their collective power and achieve commonly agreed objectives. This kind of partnership can range from a continuum of collaboration to formal alliances. While collaboration implies co-operation at some stage, a formal alliance implies co-operation in all stages of the partnership. Partnerships to respond to HIV and AIDS have evolved over the last 25 years, from a single sector (health) to multi-sectoral partnership approaches such as that adopted in Nigeria.

Considering that the HIV pandemic is now understood to be a gendered health, development, and human-rights issue (UNIFEM 2001), it is vital that partnerships responding to HIV and AIDS create synergies with existing partnerships and coalitions campaigning for women rights, education rights, and social rights. The chapter explores the evolution of the partnership approach, focusing particularly on joint working between the women's rights, education, and HIV sectors, using Nigeria as a case study. It looks at attempts to provide gendered HIV and AIDS education programmes in schools. A strong gendered approach to HIV and AIDS education requires programmes that recognise and prioritise the practical and strategic needs of girls and boys. Lessons learned from emerging practice should be used to strengthen advocacy by education coalitions for good-quality gender-equitable policies that inform and promote HIV and AIDS education.

The chapter is presented in three sections. The first section explores the historical shift from a health-sector-based AIDS response to a health-sector-led approach, and finally to the new multi-sectoral AIDS-response paradigm. A central critique of the health-sector response was the weak prioritisation of the strategic and practical needs of women in their programming. The second section looks at the practical experiences of various partnerships aimed at strengthening school-based HIV and AIDS response which recognise the differing realities of the epidemic for girls and boys. This section attempts to analyse how the socio-cultural constructs of gender, patriarchy, and power relations were brought to bear in the working of the partnerships and their objectives. The final section distils key lessons about the approaches and challenges that these partnerships faced in including a women's-rights perspective in their work. The chapter ends by examining what is needed to ensure that a gendered analysis of AIDS is integral to future advocacy and networking.

The history of the partnership approach in the response to HIV and AIDS

International context

National responses to HIV and AIDS were launched in Nigeria in the 1980s and were driven and led by the health sector (Nigeria Federal Ministry of Health 1999). This health-sector-led response was drawn from a traditional public-health approach and was characterised by a strong focus on the technical aspects of the problem and epidemic. It did not focus on the social aspects of the drivers of the epidemic, such as the limited decision-making power of women in many sexual relationships.

In the early 1990s there was an increasing realisation that in order to prevent and respond effectively to HIV and AIDS, governments needed the support of civil society. The response was still led by the health sector but was expanded to include a limited range of new actors from other sectors, such as civil-society organisations (CSOs) (*ibid.*). The CSOs were limited to the priority areas identified by the health sector – often those programmatic areas which the Ministry of Health found difficult to implement. Typical areas of collaboration with CSOs included working with young people, especially girls in schools, or with female sex workers who were seen as engaged in an illegal occupation, making it impossible for the Ministry of Health to intervene directly.

Although the AIDS response now included a wide group of partners, most of the civil-society partners at this stage still operated from within a public-health para-digm. Few of these early partners had the capacity to organise a gendered response to the epidemic. The limited success achieved with this mono-sector approach led to a deeper political and policy understanding of the wider socio-cultural drivers underpinning vulnerability to HIV infection, and the need for a broader response. While the health-sector-led response focused on dealing with the visible elements of the determinants of the epidemic, the social constructions that underpin women's sexuality and relational power were being ignored. In addition, the prevailing silence associated with sex and sexuality, as well as the stigma associated with 'inappropriate' sexual behaviour, made it difficult for communities to engage in discussions and debates on the more social aspects of the HIV epidemic.

As these more complex social and gendered dimensions of HIV were realised, it became reconceptualised as a developmental issue. In turn, this led to a slow but definite broadening of the types and ranges of partners involved in responding to HIV and AIDS. But despite an increasing number of development NGOs becom-ing involved, there was a distinct lack of engagement with groups championing women's-rights issues (Msimang 2003). This absence seems to be found in other regions of the world too; in 2005, women's rights and HIV and AIDS organisations working in central and eastern Europe concluded that they were still not collaborating at a meaningful level.[1]

But in some countries, organisations have managed to work together in partnership to develop broad gendered and community-based AIDS responses (including in Uganda, Senegal, and Thailand) (Allen and Heald 2004). The lessons gleaned from these success stories highlight the multiple benefits of basing the response to HIV and AIDS firmly in the context of women's-rights issues. These partnerships were driven by a wide range of highly mobilised and motivated actors from across civil society, government, and the private sector. In Uganda this led to extensive promotion of 'zero grazing' (faithfulness and partner reduction) (Green *et al.* 2006). Innovative work by ActionAid Uganda on improving communication and relationship skills at the community level contributed to overcoming the silence surrounding the epidemic and its drivers (ActionAid Uganda 2000).

This increased openness in Ugandan communities and willingness to talk about sex, sexuality, and the AIDS epidemic soon found its way into more formal spaces, including at the highest political levels – as evidenced by open discussion about HIV and AIDS in both written policy documents and verbal statements. Open and more transparent communication enabled the examination of many of the social constructions which were simultaneously undermining women's rights and fuelling the epidemic. The open dialogue also led to the development of local strategies to transform the negative gender relationship between women and men (*ibid.*).

Another key factor in the success of the approaches in Uganda, Senegal, and Thailand was the inclusion of a wide range of ministries, departments, and agencies within government which were involved in designing, implementing, and evaluating the response to HIV and AIDS. Each sector brought different strengths and it was recognised that the education system had a crucial role to play in educating young people about HIV prevention, care, and support, as well as a potential to transform gender stereotypes. Given this situation, in 2000, UNAIDS started promoting the concept of multi-sectoral broad-based partnerships for the design and operation of national AIDS responses within the framework of the three 'Ones': One strategy; One institutional arrangement; and One monitoring and evaluation framework.

The Nigerian context

In Nigeria, the original health-sector-led approach was initiated and driven by the Department of Public Health of the Federal Ministry of Health (FMOH). Over time, it became the National AIDS and STD Control Programme (NASCP), which involved a range of civil-society actors but was still under the leadership of the health sector. Civil-society partners at this time were mostly health-related organisations and included the Society for Family Health (SFH), the Society for Women and AIDS in Africa Nigeria Chapter (SWAAN), and the Association for Reproductive Health (ARFH) (Nigeria Federal Ministry of Health 1999). As the FMOH (at that time) had no mandate to intervene in schools, civil-society organisations started independently carrying out HIV and AIDS education programmes in schools. While these initiatives succeeded in increasing levels of knowledge about HIV and AIDS in schools, they lacked a social-support component to help young people to overcome the many blocks to talking openly about sex and sexuality, and learn skills to enable them to practise safer sex.

With no reference to the social and gender dimensions to HIV it was therefore not surprising that HIV-prevalence rates continued to rise, increasing from 1.8 per cent in 1991 to peak at 5.8 per cent by 2001 (see Figure 1). Given this continued rise, the Nigerian government looked to Uganda's experience and transformed the National

AIDS Programme (NASCP) into a National Action Committee on AIDS (NACA), which included a broad-based membership drawn from civil society, and the private and public sectors. Partners included the Federal Ministry of Women Affairs (FMOWA), and ministries of Health, Education, Agriculture, Defence, Labour, and Internal Affairs, including paramilitary services (National Action Committee on AIDS 2000). The newly formed NACA led the production of the first national multi-sectoral strategic plan – the HIV and AIDS Emergency Action Plan (HEAP).

Figure 1: HIV-prevalence rates in Nigeria, 1991–2005

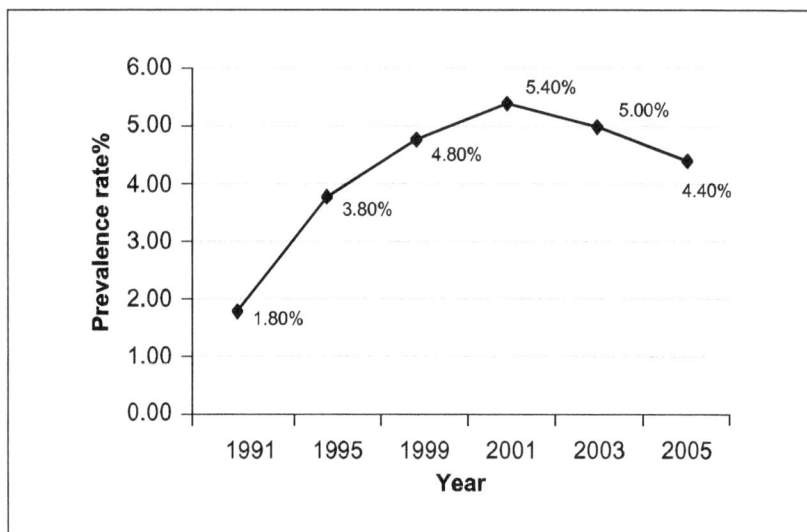

Although several women's rights NGOs were now part of the partnership, in the first three years they had little meaningful engagement, due among other things to limited understanding of how women's rights interacted with the issue of HIV and AIDS. In addition, there was often pressure from funding agencies to 'technicalise' their work to fit with NACA expectations. A review of the first multi-sectoral strategic plan[2] showed a low prioritisation of gender issues.

Partnerships in HIV and AIDS education in Nigeria

From the early 1990s NGOs had been able to source small grants from donors and foundations, and they implemented a diverse array of HIV and AIDS education programmes in schools. Gender issues were not a serious concern, and educational materials focused more on biological differences. These programmes had limited funding and in many parts of the country faced significant resistance to 'sexuality education', as it was then known. This resistance by teachers as well as parents and education departments was based on a fear that explicit discussions about sex and sexuality would lead young people to experiment sexually. Many of these fears were based on social and cultural beliefs about the importance of a girl's chastity, while encouraging male sexual experimentation.

Box 1: The Association for Reproductive and Family Health (ARFH)

ARFH, based in Ibadan, responded to the dilemma of controversial terminology by coming up with the concept of 'Life Planning Education'. This term was acceptable in that it suggested a broad process of educating young children to cope with life and its different ramifications, including growing up, getting married, and the reality of engaging in sex in the era of HIV and AIDS. (Unfortunately no evidence exists to suggest that this focused in any particular way on the unique needs of girls.) This concept has now been broadened to 'Family Life Education' (FLE), which enjoys wider acceptance in Nigeria.

The result was that many NGOs operated small pilot projects in schools where the leadership was more receptive, and experimented with terminology which would be acceptable (see Box 1). They often operated outside of the traditional school curriculum and school hours, for example in after-school clubs. Many NGOs used a peer-to-peer approach, training young people to reach out to their friends and classmates, often in one-to-one sessions (ActionAid International Nigeria and Society for Family Health 2002a). However, many of these approaches were poorly structured and lacked a rigorous analysis of gender relations and possibilities for negotiation of safer sex. Towards the end of the 1990s, a few of these programmes evolved to incorporate activities around 'youth-friendly health services', such as providing treatment facilities for sexually transmitted infections. They also began to work with the government on how to incorporate HIV and AIDS education into the curriculum (Action Health Incorporated 2002).

These early partnerships between NGOs, schools, and donors helped to begin to locate debates on HIV in the context of the practical realities of schools and the lives of young people (*ibid.*). The expansion of HIV and AIDS education in schools started in 2000, based on a broader partnership between civil society and government. This process was helped by the emergence of democracy during the same period. The Oyo State Expanded Family Life Planning Education project, supported by the UK Department for International Development (DFID), was instrumental in triggering this expansion (see Box 2). A major milestone was the National Family Life and HIV Education (FLE) Policy and Curriculum, although power, gender, and vulnerability are poorly captured in the policy, curriculum, and operational guidelines. The policy remained focused on the biology and psychology of girls and boys, with no recognition of the evidence indicating that a girl's first sexual experience will be often forced (Garcia Moreno 2003).

Box 2: The Expanded Life Planning Education Partnership

The Expanded Life Planning Education (ELPE) project took place in Oyo State public secondary schools. The project, which was supported by the UK Department for International Development, brought government and NGOs together in a unique partnership that was later to shape the integration of HIV into the education sector. This partnership included the Ministry of Health, the Ministry of Education, Science and Technology, the Teaching Service Commission (TESCOM), and the Association for Reproductive and Family Health. The project provided the first example of a truly multi-sectoral partnership between various units of governments as well as between government and civil society. A variety of interventions was used, including advocacy with the religious and traditional institutions on the new societal challenges posed by HIV and the consequent need to respond; capacity-building at managerial and operational levels for education ministries, departments, and agencies; promoting community participation to ensure the social support needed to deal with the sensitivity of having AIDS education in schools; and building effective partnerships with relevant government agencies and between government agencies. In all these components, the importance of gender had limited recognition in the construction and programmatic elements of the partnership, with the exception of the peer-education component. Lessons from the partnership included the importance of including faith organisations and community leaders.

To understand the challenges faced in scaling up gendered HIV and AIDS education within schools, it is important to understand the context of the epidemic in Nigeria. As in most of sub-Saharan Africa, in Nigeria the bulk of HIV infections are primarily transmitted through heterosexual sex. In Nigeria, vulnerability to HIV occurs within marriage either through serial relationships (multiple divorces) or concurrent (polygamous marriages) sexual networks. Though women are vulnerable as a result of these multiple relationships, this aspect of HIV prevention has rarely been discussed. Women's vulnerability to HIV infection was beginning to be understood as linked to their inadequate access to information, education, and sexual and reproductive health services; their experience of sexual violence and harmful practices (such as early and forced marriage); and a lack of legal capacity and equality in areas such as marriage and divorce (United Nations 2004).

However, a gendered approach to HIV-prevention programmes was controversial because it raised questions about sexuality. Faith-based organisations upheld values and expectations that girls and women should be submissive sexually, and they believed that discussion of sexuality in relation to HIV and AIDS could threaten the fabric of the community. But for successful HIV and AIDS education programmes there needed to be debate about collective cultural identity and individual rights. With growing realisation of the need to enter into this political and gendered arena, members of the partnership leading the national response began to actively involve religious leaders and traditional institutions. With this broader partnership, the first national conference on Adolescent Reproductive Health took place, which provided an important arena for debate and led to the creation of a national strategic framework (Action Health Incorporated 2002). Although gender was an important issue at the conference, there was a stark absence of feminist organisations. Nevertheless, it cemented the partnership between civil society and faith leaders, and led to the 2003 Comprehensive Sexuality Policy and curriculum for children from primary to tertiary levels of education (Action Health Incorporated 2003).

Box 3: The Civil Society Network on HIV and AIDS in Nigeria (CiSNAN) and Civil Society Action Coalition on Education for All (CSACEFA)

These two coalitions, facilitated by ActionAid Nigeria, emerged in 2000. The education coalition emerged as a direct response to the need to achieve a coherent civil-society engagement with the Dakar 2000 Education for All conference. Conversely, the HIV and AIDS coalition emerged in response to the need for an organised civil-society platform to maximise the gains for poor and excluded people in the emerging multi-sectoral response to the epidemic.

The two coalitions were unique in that they had a broad range of stakeholders that were connected to the two sectors. These included NGOs, traditional faith-based organisations, and professional organisations. Some of the members had interests across the two sectors and were active in both coalitions. While women's-rights organisations formed part of the initial membership, they were however not fully integrated into the day-to-day functioning of the coalitions. They have not managed to fuse their interest strongly with that of the wider coalition. Extensive internal dialogue in the two coalitions led to the development of a core position on a wide range of issues.

This process of dialogue was important in managing the varying levels of motivation across the group. It ensured that gatekeepers such as parent–teacher associations and religious and professional organisations had space to debate their fears and issues, as well as enabling the needed consensus which propelled some of the later success of the partnership. A key element of these core positions was HIV education in schools, including emphasis on a gendered perspective in building the education response to the epidemic. While the statements were clear, it is debatable how well they were operationalised, for example in the various strategic plans that the coalitions later shaped.

During this period, two separate national coalitions were set up in Nigeria: the Civil Society Network on HIV and AIDS in Nigeria (CiSNAN) and the Civil Society Action Coalition on Education for All (CSACEFA) (see Box 3). They drew membership from a wide range of interest groups across the country. ActionAid supported these two coalitions to link up and become a coherent platform for articulating policy options for HIV and AIDS education. This work demonstrated that civil society was a formidable force. Both CiSNAN and CSACEFA recognise gender as central to HIV and AIDS education and school-based programmes, and bring different comparative technical advantages in HIV and education. However, only a limited number of women's organisations and members of the women's rights movement joined this partnership or brought their particular expertise to bear on the work. Moreover, differences in approaches – from public-health 'whole community' approaches to gender-justice and women's-rights approaches – limited the benefits of partnership.

Moving from policy to practice

Despite differences and tensions, the creativity and energy of the partnership approach in Nigeria was highly successful in developing policies and curricula with support from a wide range of stakeholders. However, when it came to scaling-up and implementation, a new set of challenges arose. There was no nationally resourced implementation plan, and each state was expected to finance and deliver not only on the new curriculum but also in terms of teacher training. This limited the extent to which the policy was accepted and prioritised. In many states, the already limited gendered aspect of the policy and its related curriculum were watered down. New partnerships were thus needed at the state level to leverage financial resources and to help overcome the fear and resistance of parents and religious and traditional institutions.

This process of consensus-building was helped by the massive mobilisation of the faith-based response to the AIDS epidemic post-2001. This mobilisation process was led by ActionAid Nigeria in the Promoting Sexual Reproductive Health and HIV Reduction Programme (PSRHH), which was aimed at increasing the capacity for HIV and AIDS institutional and programming among some critical Islamic and Christian groups. The work focused on increasing the understanding of the faith-group leaders about young women's vulnerability, power, and patriarchy, and about how to promote enabling environments for tackling HIV and AIDS. While it was understood that faith-based organisations would have reservations, for example on condom use, it was important that they were part of the process and supported the elimination of practices such as violence against girls in schools, polygamy, and male infidelity in marriage. Faith groups also worked on reducing HIV stigma and accelerating the process of being openly HIV-positive (ActionAid International and Society for Family Health 2002b). This strategy served to reduce the silence surrounding HIV, sex, and sexuality, increasing wider understanding of the HIV epidemic and bolstering the commitment to provide gendered HIV and AIDS education through the school curriculum, especially at state level.

Many of the faith groups worked within civil society–government partnerships to support the roll-out of the policy and curriculum at state level. In order to increase scale-up at the state level, the Capacity for Universal Basic Education Project (CUBE) was funded by DFID and implemented by the British Council and ActionAid Nigeria. Implementation in each state involved a level of curriculum adaptation and collaboration between partners, but there remained a common process, including integration of the sexuality-education curriculum and gender awareness into 'carrier subjects';[3] development of the delivery scheme; training of teachers incorporating some basic sensitisation on gender and gender mainstreaming; production of resource materials (teacher-training manual and teaching aids); and the delivery and routine monitoring of the programme. While many of these materials highlight the gendered aspect of the epidemic, they also continue to foster negative gender stereotypes.

Issues and challenges

Complex partnerships are needed to support gendered HIV and AIDS education in schools, but this gives rise to many challenges, not least the ongoing dynamics and change involved in partnerships themselves over time and place (from short-term relationships in individual schools to formal alliances between coalitions for issue-based advocacy).

Raising recognition of women's vulnerability was a core issue, because of the complex socio-cultural context of Nigeria as well as the limited gender understanding and skills of the AIDS-in- school champions. Sustained effort and pressure from both civil society and the public sector is required. The gendered approach that the partnerships have managed to incorporate into their work has been the result of learning by doing. There has been an ongoing challenge of incorporating explicit statements on gender and HIV into practice on the ground, and into advocacy and campaign tasks. Lobbying around these has been less than systematic and co-ordinated.

Getting the women's movement involved in AIDS-in-school partnerships has not been as easy as expected, because of complex ideological and practical differences in ways of working. Partnerships, as noted at the beginning of this chapter, are about groups and institutions working together and negotiating knowledge, ideas, and approaches. Building a common vision, let alone a common strategy, across different networks is not easy, and feminist and women's-rights groups struggled to see how their agenda fitted into what they perceived as the more technical approach of the HIV and education coalitions. It was important to invest in discussions and debates about what constitutes gendered HIV education in school, in order to be open to different approaches from different members and understand their perspectives.

Time was needed for good communication between partners, and building consensus. It is also needed for taking learning from pilot school projects to the policy level and influencing policy directives. Moving from small pilots to national programmes demands a wide range of skills and knowledge. The skills needed for programme development and implementation in the pilot phase, and at the school and local education-system level, are different from those needed for influencing, advocacy, and network building.

Views on sex, sexuality, and HIV and AIDS are shaped by culture, tradition, and patriarchy. Many teachers and policy makers in the education sector need to deal with their own attitudes and beliefs about these sensitive areas before they can confidently and effectively incorporate sexuality education and women's rights into their teaching. Similarly, the attitudes and behaviours of the teacher trainers need to reinforce the learning and behaviour change of the teachers. The curriculum both at college level and school level still needs to incorporate a gender-based analysis, and for this to be done well the Ministry of Women's Affairs needs to be closely involved.

A key factor in taking forward this partnership agenda for gendered HIV and AIDS education in schools is secure funding. In the earlier stages, donor agencies funded small-scale civil-society projects which allowed experimentation and innovation with gender-sensitive school programmes. However, real success can be achieved only when the public-sector budgetary processes earmark monies for a gendered AIDS response in schools. This has started with support from some donors (such as DFID), but more can be done.

Conclusion

In conclusion, the experience in Nigeria has illustrated how partnerships for gendered HIV and AIDS education in schools have developed over time and gone through various phases. This has been important and necessary, as the fears and resistance of critical stakeholders such as parents, faith groups, and traditional leaders are understood and managed. Partnerships are dynamic collectives of diverse organisations which continually evolve and change in shape, composition, and nature. The HIV and AIDS epidemic and the need for a coherent and strong gendered response in and through schools demands partnership of multiple and diverse stakeholders, themselves often part of complex networks and coalitions. Different partners bring different skills sets and competencies, and at different stages in the partnership different leaders may emerge.

Civil-society organisations have been shown to be well placed to drive the initial phase of this partnership, and to confront and challenge the social and cultural practices concerning gender, sex, sexuality, and HIV and AIDS that make young people, especially girls, vulnerable to infection. They have been more able than government to take risks, and have the flexibility and independent funding to carry out labour-intensive work in pilot schools. But the impact at this level is often limited, the learning specific to the location, and the organisations themselves unable to challenge broader social and cultural beliefs and practices affecting women's vulnerability. Evidence-based advocacy and campaigning for broader awareness and policy change demands an alliance with other organisations and actors who can successfully influence political and financial agendas.

The education and HIV and AIDS NGO sectors need to come together and be willing to share space and build a partnership and common agenda based on their comparative competences. Critical to the success of a civil-society partnership with broad consensus is the inclusion of faith-based organisations, traditional institutions, and collectives of parents. Partnerships also need to be learning organisations where capacity on issues of gender and women's rights is built together. Gendered HIV education in schools will always be a controversial and contested space where debate and dialogue is needed for long-term success. The government and the public sector are vital members of any partnership for HIV education in schools. The government must recognise too that it cannot deliver such a challenging programme alone, and that it needs civil society and its organisations to broker dialogue in such a sensitive and controversial area as gender, HIV, and sexuality education in classrooms.

The next important move is for these partnerships to embrace the women's-rights movement and ensure that the members of the partnership for gendered HIV education in schools have all put women's rights and gender equality at the heart not only of their work but also of the *way* they work themselves. A strong multi-sectoral partnership, with a clear message about the changes needed to combat the HIV and AIDS epidemic, and strong monitoring and learning from good practice in schools, is critical for attracting secure funding and forging ahead to achieve long-term sustainable change in young people's lives.

Notes

1   Report from the Seminar 'Women and HIV/AIDS in CEE', 'Bringing Different Communities Together to Advance Common Goals', available online at www.astra.org.pl/hiv_aids-report2.rtf

2   UNAIDS 2004a; 2004b.

3   See Joint Programme Review of the Plan in 2006.

4   'Carrier subject' is used in this context to mean integrating various elements of sexuality education into existing related subject areas, for example integrated science, physical and health education, or biology.

References

Action Health Incorporated (2002) 'A Unique Partnership For Adolescents' Well Being In Nigeria: A Documentation of the Process of Convening the First National Conference on Adolescent Reproductive Health', Abuja.

Action Health Incorporated (2003) 'Enabling Access', Report of the Sexuality Education/Family Life Education Implementation Forum, 13 November 2003, Abuja.

ActionAid International (2007) 'Partnership Principles and Guidelines for Staff', London: ActionAid International.

ActionAid International Nigeria (2002) 'Memorandum of Understanding between FBO and PSRHH', ActionAid International Nigeria.

ActionAid International Nigeria and Society for Family Health (2002a) 'Situation Analysis of HIV Prevention Among Young People in Nigeria', ActionAid International Nigeria and Society for Family Health.

ActionAid International Nigeria and Society for Family Health (2002b) 'Policy and Advocacy Strategy', ActionAid International Nigeria and Society for Family Health.

ActionAid Uganda (2000) 'HIV&AIDS Review Notes', (internal unpublished document).

Adams, B., B. Bell, K. Crawford, D. Elias-Henry, C. Hansen, A. Kytwayhat, S. Penner, J. Reid, and T. Woods (1995) 'The Provincial Partnership Committee on Family Violence: Final Report', Regina, Saskatchewan: Family Violence Prevention Division, Health Canada, cited in www.swc-cfc.gc.ca/pubs/researchpartnerships/researchpartnerships_1_e.html (last accessed May 2008).

Allen, T. and S. Heald (2004) 'HIV&AIDS policy in Africa: what has worked in Uganda and what has failed in Botswana?', *Journal of International Development* 16(8): 1141–54.

Garcia Moreno, C. (2003) 'Sexual violence', *IPPF Medical Bulletin*.

Green, E. C., D. T. Halperin, V. Nantulya, and J. A. Hogle (2006) 'Uganda's HIV Prevention Success: The Role of Sexual Behavior Change and the National Response', *AIDS and Behaviour* 10(4): 335–46.

Msimang, S. (2003) 'HIV&AIDS, globalisation and the international women's movement', in C. Sweetman and J. Kerr (eds.) *Women Reinventing Globalisation*, Oxford: Oxfam GB.

National Action Committee on AIDS (2000) 'HIV&AIDS Emergency Action Plan-HEAP', National Action Committee on AIDS.

Nigeria Federal Ministry of Health (1999) 'HIV Situational and Response Analysis', Abuja: Federal Ministry of Health.

UNAIDS (2004a) '"Three Ones" Key Principles: Coordination of National Responses to HIV/AIDS Guiding Principles for National Authorities and their Partners', Geneva: UNAIDS.

UNAIDS (2004b) 'Landmark Agreement Reached in Fight against AIDS', UNAIDS Press Release.

UNIFEM (2001) 'Turning the Tide: CEDAW and the Gender Dimension of the HIV&AIDS Pandemic', available at: www.unifem.org/index

United Nations (2004) UN Special Rapporteur on the Right of Everyone to Highest Attainable Standard of Health, 'Report to the UN Commission of Human Rights', United Nations.

Conclusion:
HIV and AIDS and gender – the challenges for empowerment and change

Sheila Aikman, Elaine Unterhalter, and Tania Boler

At the beginning of this book we looked at different expectations of what schooling or other educational settings can do in response to two pressing and inter-connected problems. How can schools help transform unequal gender relations and thereby protect young people against HIV and AIDS, and how can they also contribute to caring for those who are infected and affected? Expectations of what education can do have changed with time, as understandings of the nature, dimensions, and language associated with the epidemic have developed. An initial concern that education programmes and school curricula should teach the bio-medical facts about the disease has shifted towards developing pedagogies that understand young people's sexual behaviour and how this influences their vulnerabilities to contracting HIV, and build strategies for reducing risk, appreciating different points of view, and negotiation. But these shifts have not been easy to effect. Sexual behaviour is influenced by complex social and cultural identities and values, and this book has drawn some very stark pictures of how unequal and sometimes violent relationships enmesh men and women in disempowering and abusive situations which schools do little to change. How can education not only teach new knowledge about HIV but also support young people to act on that information and change their behaviour, appreciate some of the values associated with gender equality, and overcome the prejudice and stigma that so often attaches to people associated with the epidemic?

In framing the argument for the book, we looked at different expectations of HIV-education programmes attempting to change sexual behaviour and knowledge about HIV and gender and help young people avoid risk. We looked at what we termed the 'optimistic view' – that behaviour change can be taught in schools or other education settings and that learning and teaching can be implemented as intended by those who develop curricula and train teachers. We also examined the view – a more pessimistic one – that unequal gender relations are deeply entrenched within educational settings themselves, which constrain the ability of students and teachers to change and bring about change. The chapters in this book urge us to lean towards optimism, by demonstrating that educational settings and institutions – adult learning centres, schools, community education centres – can be empowering, and the people who work in them, despite the existence of sometimes extreme hierarchies of gender in their society, can bring about change. The authors illustrate ways in which policy and programme interventions that serve to promote gender equality at school and in other educational contexts can contribute to reducing the vulnerability of all people to HIV infection. Schools can be places where, despite complex histories of discrimination, inequality, and poverty, children and adults can question gendered power relations and violence and develop new understandings and expressions of sexuality and social relations. Individuals have complex histories which influence and shape their identities and their actions, and acknowledging these may be one way to reflect on how to change those behaviours that put people at risk. Thus we argue against reducing issues of vulnerability to HIV to bald notions of all women as 'at risk' and all men as predators (essentialism). We also suggest that too thin a reading of gender equality as 'sameness', with no regard for taken-for-granted power relations that structure what is possible and what is not, is not likely to take educational work on HIV and gender far enough. Another way of viewing gender equality – as empowerment – provides a direction that we believe needs to underpin all HIV education (Chapter 1). Empowerment here means a concern with confidence and self-expression, the development of emancipatory knowledge, access to resources, actions for transformation, and participation in relations of power.

What do the chapters in this book tell us about how transformation and empowerment happen? Under what circumstances and conditions can young people become self-confident, use new knowledge, and take decisions about their relationships and sexual behaviour? While there is evidence that, broadly speaking, HIV is less prevalent among more educated populations than was the case in the early stages of the epidemic, suggesting that education does offer some protection (Chapter 2), an uncritical acceptance that education is a 'social vaccine' acting to protect young people from HIV infection can be misleading. The evidence in this book leads us to ask, rather, what is the nature of the knowledge, the learning environment, and the relationships between students and teachers? In other words, what kind of education and what conditions promote attitudes and behaviour which minimise risk?

The first part of the book set the scene; it mapped the challenges and the terrain. The second part of the book provided the insights and recommendations for taking forward an empowering agenda for HIV education for gender equality. These are summarised below.

Context and participation

To be effective, HIV and AIDS education must be based on an understanding of the broader social and cultural environment in which gender differentiation and hierarchies, power in sexual relationships, and the effects of stigma and discrimination operate. It must address the complexities of young people's lives, taking on board shifting forms of the family, and large numbers of children orphaned by the disease (Chapters 3 and 5). It requires developing an in-depth understanding of how the school, the teachers, and the students are located in this wider context, and what this means in terms of their vulnerability and risk to HIV, as well as opportunities for change.

Education for behaviour change in the context of HIV and AIDS means challenging deeply held values and religious beliefs and practices regarding women's sexuality and sexual behaviour. The authors in Part 2 illustrate how, through working not only with teachers and students but also with key members of the community and its leadership (both religious and secular), these values and beliefs can change. Through participatory and inclusive approaches to programme design and collaborative decision-making, adult education and school-focused programmes can engender ownership across the community. Chewa elders in eastern Zambia, whose instruction at puberty put boys and girls at risk of HIV, themselves became active proponents of new ways of teaching (Chapter 7).

We now have more evidence than ever before of schools as places of unequal gender relations and taken-for-granted assumptions about sexuality and gender violence, as researchers probe the culture and environment of the school from a gendered perspective (Chapters 3, 4, and 8). Violent or aggressive behaviour in the school mirrors similar behaviours in the wider society, and here too there is a need for carefully designed education programmes to transform masculinities which perpetuate violence against women, and coercive sex. In the slums of Mumbai, the changes which occurred through the *Yari Dosti* programme were the result of meticulous support which built ownership of the programme by young men themselves (Chapter 10).

Poverty is the backdrop for much of the discussion of gender inequalities in this book. Economic poverty constrains the educational opportunities and life choices of the young people in the pages of this book. Despite the abolition of school fees in many countries in sub-Saharan Africa and Asia, we still have instances of young girls engaged in transactional sex for commodities like shoes, for status, and for access to secondary school and higher grades. The unequal gender relations that have exacerbated the epidemic are themselves intensified by the injustices of global inequality and lack of income for the poorest people. Poverty also puts severe constraints on the quality of the education provision, reducing the time that poorly paid teachers are prepared to spend on complex subjects relating to HIV and gender, limiting the number of books available for children, and forcing governments to choose between the often competing demands for inclusion and equity. Addressing HIV and AIDS may, therefore, be in a queue for policy attention and resources along with programmes to redress regional inequalities, provide for the education of children with disabilities, or address the needs of refugees or internally displaced people.

Schools as democratic spaces

The second part of this book has expanded our understandings of what good teaching and learning about HIV and AIDS looks like in classrooms and schools. In Chapter 8, Unterhalter *et al.* illustrate the importance of teachers' creative and proactive engagement with the epidemic. The extent to which teachers are able to recognise and change their own normalised gendered identities and behaviours is important for the way in which they teach and model safe behaviour. The research in schools in South Africa presents a perspective on the development of new caring relationships between teachers and students which makes way for new visions of masculinity and femininity. This kind of change is not instant, and needs ongoing support as teachers and facilitators themselves challenge their own beliefs and behaviours and bring their own learning and understanding to support their students. Peer groups, not only for students but for teachers too, are important for providing mutual support and mentoring (Chapters 7 and 10). Teacher training, both pre-service and in-service, must engage with issues of gender equality, HIV, and interactive, facilitative teaching and learning styles. The authoritarian culture that still dominates schools in much of the world needs to be transformed, and standards and codes of professional and ethical conduct implemented. Only then will students and learners feel confident to discuss and debate issues of sexuality and sexual behaviour on equal terms with teachers and facilitators and in open and democratic spaces (Chapters 4 and 10).

Leadership and co-ordination

As the chapters in this book have illustrated, there is a huge diversity of educational responses to HIV in terms of programme and project aims, design and implementation. Across the globe many education programmes have been developed outside of the formal education system and operate on the margins of the official curriculum and practice. Many programmes continue to treat HIV and AIDS as a health issue, and those that are more focused on improving the quality of education have only sporadically incorporated a gendered approach (Chapter 6). As Idogho (Chapter 11) documents in the Nigerian context, HIV and AIDS education programmes often develop in a piecemeal fashion with small-scale donor-funded programmes. In many countries this has produced a plethora of small-scale un-co-ordinated interventions developed and implemented by a range of different NGOs and by formal and non-formal education departments of Ministries of Education. But this has also created space for the development of innovative programmes that have flourished through strong and effective partnerships between civil-society organisations and local and national education authorities. In eastern Zambia, project schools and District Education Officers considered the work of the NGO as crucial for mobilising the community, maintaining motivation and, not least, providing additional funding (Chapter 7). Working with existing government structures – such as parent–teacher associations, in-service training mechanisms, and the education inspectorate – and ministry strategic objectives was important for ensuring not only ownership but also sustainability.

In the non-formal adult-education sector, described by Duongsaa in the Thai context (Chapter 9), small-scale programmes, however successful and supportive at the local level, need to be complemented by similar approaches in the formal school system and through vocational and skills training to develop a critical mass of people who, through their awareness and new knowledge, are changing their sexual behaviour and questioning the nature of their gendered relationships.

Multi-sectoral partnerships

The discussion of the development of partnerships and government response in Nigeria (Chapter 11) raises the question of how governments are responding to the diversity and lack of coherence across the sector. The Nigerian case indicates the complexities of building a strong national response; time needed for dialogue and building common ground; and negotiation of differences and developing consensus – or not – with civil society, donors, and government, often working together in a state of creative tension. The diversity of international donors with their own interests and strategies suggests that at times 'partnership' may be no more than an aspiration. While there are a number of different initiatives for developing school HIV and AIDS curricula, learning materials, and teacher-training approaches that engage in a different way with NGOs, donors, and publishing houses (as described in Zambia in Chapter 7), collaboration and partnership may be overwhelmed by competition and turf protection.

The bringing together of coalitions and NGO networks from across sectors, as well as linking across ministries, is important for good HIV education. The Nigeria case illustrates a trajectory of partnership development from within the health sector to include also the education sector. Now, Idogho (Chapter 11) raises the challenge to women's organisations to add their voice and experience to the campaigning and advocacy for HIV education which has gender equality at its core. Government too must secure the link through engaging Ministries of Women or Departments for Women's Affairs, where they exist.

Ministries of Education have, with support from donors, adopted different strategies for mainstreaming gender equality through policies and workplace practices, often through establishing gender units within national and line ministries. However, the work of these units is not being seen or felt in education-sector responses to HIV. The capacity of ministry staff, teacher educators, and teachers in gender analysis, gender planning (and budgeting), and action for gender equality is low. Until it is improved across the education sector there is little hope of strong gender-equitable policies or transformatory practices for HIV and AIDS education. Putting gender at the heart of education-sector HIV responses will take time and money, which will be dependent in turn on political will and commitment as well as leadership. Leadership is needed from the top – central government and heads of ministries – as well as in the school through motivated and capable head teachers and religious leaders. Expertise in gender analysis is needed too, but should not just be tucked away in gender units with no resources and no status.

Evidence-based policy making: from rhetoric to reality

As Clarke reminds us in Chapter 6, without a specific policy in place it is very difficult to achieve a coherent, comprehensive, and scaled-up response to HIV and AIDS through education. Currently very few governments have developed specific detailed policies on HIV for the education sector, and those that have done so included limited coverage of gender-related issues and specific interventions. Developing a policy is an opportunity for discussion with and engagement of civil society in the development process. Having a policy is a means of demanding greater accountability from civil society and the myriad of small-scale projects that often do not prioritise the time or have the resources to document their learning or share their experiences. A policy should provide the framework needed for scaling up NGO and government collaborative programmes which have proved their effectiveness and quality through extensive monitoring and evaluation over time (such as described in Zambia). A policy is also important to guide curriculum development, teacher training, and workplace HIV policies at all levels of the system. Civil-society organisations and their national coalitions can use the statements of intent in policy documents to hold government accountable for their implementation. Idogho (Chapter 11) shows how slow progress has been, how limited the current resources and capacity are both for delivery and for monitoring and evaluation, and how much remains to be put in place. In Chapter 6 Clarke outlines some very concrete steps that governments can take, stressing, like Idogho, the importance of alliances with civil society and multi-sectoral approaches.

Good policies are built on good knowledge and learning about what works well. There is an urgent need for well-documented and evaluated fine-grained studies of local initiatives that are built with the ownership and support of community, students, and teachers for policy making and planning at national and international levels. Funding needs to be earmarked for evaluation studies to develop an evidence base on what works in gender and HIV education (Chapter 6). Longitudinal studies are needed to monitor and track changes in attitudes and behaviours, which takes time.

This book set out to show that while gender inequalities in society generally, and particularly within the education sector, are driving aspects of the epidemic and contribute to limitations in the work of prevention and care, in every sector – be it government, community, or school initiatives – there are actions that have been taken to confront and transform gender inequalities. This will enhance work on prevention and support care for people who are infected and affected. We have not provided a blueprint to follow, as this book demonstrates that there is not one approach. But we do highlight some of the creativity, connection, and self-criticism that we think are key dimensions of the challenge for the education sector working on gender inequality in education in the context of the epidemic. We see this volume as a beginning: an acknowledgement that education is not a simple social vaccine, but it is an important social space for working towards gender equality and empowerment.

www.ingramcontent.com/pod-product-compliance
Lightning Source LLC
Chambersburg PA
CBHW052011030426
42334CB00029BA/3167